FRENCH IMPERIALISM
in the MIDDLE EAST

The Failure of Policy in Syria
and Lebanon, 1900-1914

FRENCH IMPERIALISM in the MIDDLE EAST

The Failure of Policy
in Syria and Lebanon
1900-1914

William I. Shorrock

THE UNIVERSITY OF WISCONSIN PRESS

Published 1976
The University of Wisconsin Press
Box 1379, Madison, Wisconsin 53701

The University of Wisconsin Press, Ltd.
70 Great Russell Street, London

First printing

Printed in the United States of America

Publication of this book was made
possible in part by a grant
from the Andrew W. Mellon Foundation

Library of Congress Cataloging in Publication Data
Shorrock, William I 1941—
French imperialism in the Middle East.
Based on the author's thesis, University of Wis-
consin, Madison.
Bibliography: p. 197-208
Includes index.
1. France—Foreign relations—Syria. 2. Syria—
Foreign relations—France. 3. France—Foreign re-
lations—Lebanon. 4. Lebanon—Foreign relations—
France. I. Title.
DC59.8.S95S56   956.91'03   75-32078
ISBN 0-299-07030-1

TO MARJORIE

CONTENTS

ACKNOWLEDGMENTS

It is a pleasure for an author to acknowledge assistance and encouragement received during the lengthy process of researching, writing, and completing the final preparation for a book manuscript. An initial note of gratitude must go the History Department at the University of Wisconsin-Madison for generously providing a grant helping me to undertake the initial research in Paris. I am especially grateful for the kindly and helpfull assistance rendered by the staff at the Archives du Ministère des Affaires Etrangères in Paris, who made innumerable volumes of unpublished materials available to me with a minimum of delays. I would be remiss were I not also to mention the cooperation of the librarians and archivists at the Bibliothèque Nationale, the Archives Nationales, the Memorial Library at the University of Wisconsin-Madison, and the Cleveland State University Library. Gratitude is also expressed to the Instructional Media Services of the Cleveland State University.

Many individuals have had a hand in the preparation of this volume, but one deserves special mention here. Professor Theodore S. Hamerow of the University of Wisconsin-Madison saw the manuscript through its initial form as a dissertation some years ago and has been a constant source of advice and encouragement ever since. Although the book owes many of whatever merits it may have to these individuals and institutions, needless to say any errors of fact or judgment are mine alone.

An early version of chapter 10, dealing with the creation of a French economic sphere of influence in Syria and Lebanon, appeared in article form in *The International Journal of Middle East Studies* in 1970.

A final note of appreciation goes first to my parents, whose devotion has long been a source of strength to me, and finally to my wife, Marjorie, to whom this book is dedicated. It owes more than I can express to her enthusiasm and encouragement.

W.I.S.

October 1975
Cleveland, Ohio

FRENCH IMPERIALISM
in the MIDDLE EAST

The Failure of Policy in Syria
and Lebanon, 1900-1914

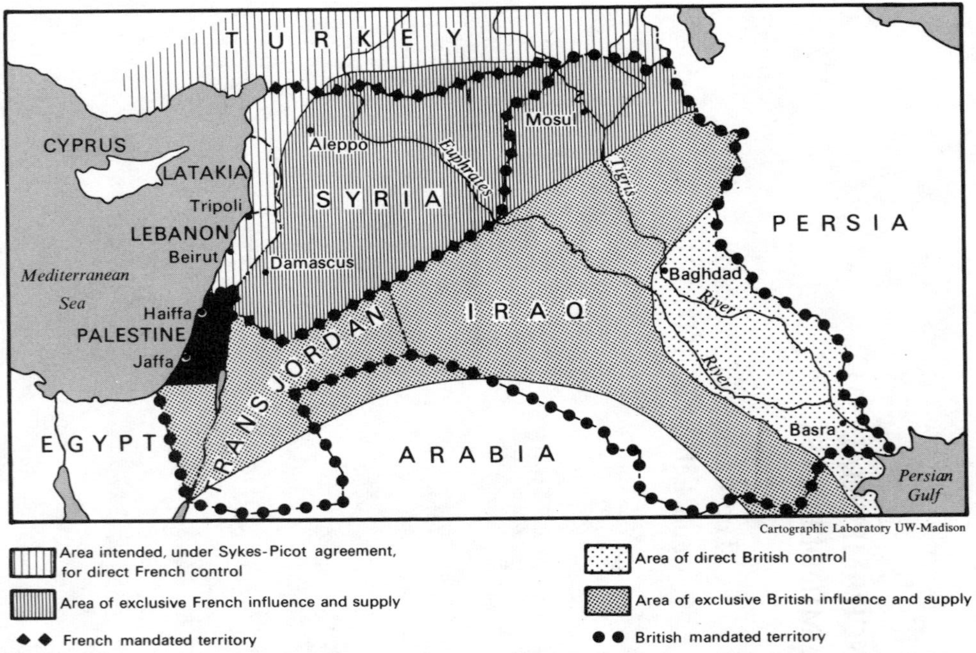
TURKEY
CYPRUS
LATAKIA
Tripoli
LEBANON
Beirut
Mediterranean Sea
Haiffa
PALESTINE
Jaffa
EGYPT
Aleppo
SYRIA
Damascus
Euphrates
Mosul
Tigris
TRANSJORDAN
IRAQ
ARABIA
PERSIA
Baghdad
River
River
Basra
Persian Gulf
Cartographic Laboratory UW-Madison
Area intended, under Sykes-Picot agreement, for direct French control
Area of exclusive French influence and supply
French mandated territory
Area of direct British control
Area of exclusive British influence and supply
British mandated territory

Sykes-Picot Partition of Asiatic Turkey and Ultimate Mandate Boundaries. Source: Stephen H. Longrigg, *Syria and Lebanon Under French Mandate* (London, 1958), p. 57.

1 INTRODUCTION

The Middle Eastern area handed over to France as mandated territory after the First World War contained some 57,900 square miles. Bounded by the Mediterranean on the west, Asiatic Turkey on the north, Mesopotamia to the east, and Transjordania and Palestine to the south, this area was inhabited by a vast mixture of peoples. The population of scarcely more than two million included some twenty-nine or thirty races or religions. The Muslims embraced approximately 1,200,000 Sunnites or Orthodox, with some scattered unorthodox Shiites and various dissident groups like the Druzes and the Alaouites. The 500,000 Christians included the Maronites of the Lebanon and some Greek Orthodox, Greek Catholics, Armenians, Syrians, and Chaldeans. Also located in this area were Protestants of various denominations and about 16,000 Jews.[1]

The story of the wartime agreements and how France actually came into possession of this mandate is one of undeniable drama and has been told many times before from various points of view. Its main features, therefore, can be summarized briefly. Although subsequent controversy arose over what was and what was not promised to the Arabs and to the French in the McMahon-Hussein correspondence of 1915-1916 and the Sykes-Picot Agreement of 1916,[2] it is sufficient to state that the British, in order to gain the sharif of Mecca's intervention against the Turks, offered, through Sir Henry McMahon, to support the establishment of native governments in parts of Syria and Mesopotamia, apart from the interests of their French ally. At the same time, however, the Sykes-Picot Agreement of 1916 between Britain and France stated that the two powers were prepared "to recognize and protect an independent Arab State or a Confederation of Arab States" in two areas marked on a map of the Middle East, one to be reserved for French protection and the other for British. The French area included the principal towns and cities of Syria, Damascus, Homs, Hama, and Aleppo. France also received a "Blue Area," comprising the coast of Syria (Alexandretta, Latakia, Tripoli, Beirut, Sidon, and Tyre) and the province of the Lebanon, in which she was "allowed to establish such direct or indirect administration or control" as she wished. Southern Syria, or Palestine, was set aside for international administration. During and after the war, therefore, many believed that Syria had indeed become a twice-promised land, partly to Hussein and wholly to France. The vaguenesses of these two agreements were to be a source of confusion and misunderstanding in the postwar period.[3]

The First World War ended in the Middle East with the British army entrenched in Syria. But on 13 September 1919, after months of intransigence by French Premier Georges Clemenceau, an agreement was concluded between the latter and British Prime Minister David Lloyd George, by which the British army in Syria was to be evacuated on 1 November. Damascus, Homs, Hama, and Aleppo were to be given over to the Emir Faisal, a son of the sharif, while the garrisons west of the Sykes-Picot line were handed over to France.

The Arabs regarded this solution as a British betrayal, a violation of the McMahon-Hussein commitments. On 7 March 1920, therefore, a General Syrian Congress proclaimed the full independence of Syria within her "natural boundaries," including the Lebanon and Palestine (thereby rejecting a national home for the Jews), an action which alienated both the French and the British. The congress named Faisal king. But the predominantly Christian Lebanese opposed the Muslim Syrian proclamation attaching the Lebanon to Syria. The sanjak of Lebanon had, since 1861, been an autonomous province of the old Ottoman Empire. On 22 March 1920, with the knowledge and support of French authorities, a meeting composed of the Administrative Council of the Lebanon, Lebanese notables, and representatives of the Christian communities gathered and called for the independence of the Lebanon.

A complicated web of national, religious, and Great Power aspirations was being spun. The situation became even further muddled a month later when the Mandate Commission of the Paris Peace Conference assigned Syria, including the Lebanon, to France as an "A" mandate, a designation indicating the most advanced of the areas falling to European administration. Palestine and Mesopotamia went to Britain. Syrians opposed this solution out of hand and demonstrated against the French mandate, while French forces were massed on the Syrian borders during the summer of 1920. In mid-July General Henri Joseph Gouraud presented an ultimatum to Faisal, calling for the restoration of order in Syria and acceptance of the mandate, or the French would take the necessary measures entrusted to them by the Mandate Commission. Gouraud emphasized that acceptance of the mandate would not impair Syrian independence; it called only for French advice and assistance.

Six days later, on 20 July, Faisal capitulated and accepted French demands. But the people of Damascus erupted against this "treason" in violent demonstrations against Faisal and France. In any case, the emir's acceptance arrived too late to stop French troops, whose movement into Syria had already begun. On 25 July 1920, French forces fought their way into Damascus and occupied the city. Military occupation also proceeded in the cities of Homs, Hama, and Aleppo. Faisal abandoned the project shortly thereafter, his independent Arab kingdom at an end.

Such in brief were the main outlines of France's assumption of the mandate for Syria and the Lebanon after World War I. But from this point on, the issue of French claims to this Levantine portion of the old Ottoman Empire became obscured in a new debate, one which erupted between contemporary polemicists and carried over into more scholarly analyses. For the issue of Syria and the Lebanon formed a classic example of the clash between Wilsonian idealism (the relatively new concept of national self-determination) and the "old diplomacy" of secret bargains and territorial arrangements among the Great Powers. It is not my purpose to try to resolve this dispute but merely to illustrate how its inception clouded the issue of France's original claim to Syria and the Lebanon. The debate emerged after 1917 and carried on into the immediate postwar era. It involved attempts by Frenchmen to justify their assumption of the mandate by proving their popularity among the Syrians and Lebanese. French opponents, of course, tried to prove exactly the opposite. It is quite interesting and instructive to contrast the French views of their own popularity in Syria and the Lebanon with the estimates of others. During the latter stages of the war, when it became evident that the Ottoman Empire would disappear, polemical literature poured from the pens of Frenchmen seeking to establish their country's claim to Syria and Lebanon in terms of the popular new doctrines of the American president. A typical example is a work by C. and Paul Roederer, who took great pains to emphasize that the long tradition of French scholarly and charitable activity in Syria entitled France to an "unchallenged" and "sovereign" position there. The authors proceeded to belittle the Arab national movement as an "unreasonable idea," propagated by "a very small party." The Roederers explained that France did not desire the annexation of Syria, but merely a liberal protectorate based upon the imperial principle of association. And all Syrians were agreed that this solution was best. "The Muslims," the authors said, "subscribe to this solution. . . . The Muslim knows quite well that France respects freedom of conscience in her African colonies and professes great respect for Islam. . . . No serious obstacle to a French protectorate resides in the Muslim question."[4]

This sort of unsubstantiated assertion and oversimplification might well be expected of patriotic Frenchmen in the heat of war. Maurice Barrès, well-known nationalist author, deputy, and member of the French Academy, was guilty of similar chauvinism in articles published after the war.[5] The French view was substantiated by the appearance in 1917 in Paris of a group called the *Comité central syrien.* In one of its first publications, President

Chekri Ganem, claiming to speak for all Syrians and Lebanese, wrote: "The program of the committee, which all of you have approved, is thus beginning to be achieved: the deliverance of our country, and its accession to independence under the aegis of France."[6] Several months later, Chekri Ganem, in the name of the committee, published an open letter to Clemenceau in his capacity as president of the Paris Peace Conference. It protested Faisal's demands to include Syria in an Arab kingdom and asserted that Syrians desired "the independence of Syria within her natural frontiers and organized into federative provinces with a democratic government under the aegis of France, a condition to which Lebanon subordinated her participation in the Syrian union."[7]

All these examples, particularly the latter, would appear to support the view that France was universally popular among the majority of Syrians and Lebanese. But can these statements be taken at face value? For one thing all the statements fail to differentiate between Christian and Muslim Syrian opinion. Uniate Christians (those recognizing the Roman papacy) naturally would be more amenable to France, because of the latter's long missionary tradition in the Levant. But this very tradition would tend to make France suspect among the Muslims, who formed a numerical majority, particularly in eastern Syria where Faisal's kingdom had been proclaimed. And if one reads carefully, there is much evidence in the 14 June letter from Chekri Ganem to Clemenceau to suggest that the *Comité central syrien* represented almost completely Christian opinion. The letter constantly refers to "our Syrian Muslim brothers," who have been coerced by Faisal into opposition to France. Much of the *Comité*'s support came from émigré Syrian clubs all over the world, which were composed primarily of refugee Christians, who had left their homeland either for economic reasons or because of the Christian massacres of the prewar and wartime periods. All this, added to the fact that Chekri Ganem himself was a Christian who had not set foot in Syria for some thirty years,[8] places some doubt upon the committee's authority to speak for *all* Syrians. Nevertheless, Chekri Ganem was a valuable man as far as French ambitions in Syria were concerned, and his committee fit the national self-determination argument very well indeed. Foreign Minister Stéphen Pichon even produced him before the Council of Ten to substantiate France's claim to a mandate.

On the other side of the ledger, non-French views of France's popularity in the Levant were less affirmative. For example, during the war, British Brigadier General Sir Wyndham Deedes wrote in his personal notes that the Syrian Arabs in Cairo felt strongly that "the French should not be allowed to go to Syria, that they should have no more at the very outside than economic and financial concessions. So great is their dislike of the French that it is very questionable that if the French were to reign today in Syria that they would not drive the Moslems straight away into the hands of the Turks. . . . The Christians too are by no means yearning for the French; in fact, with the exception of the Maronites, the Christians of Syria are as opposed to the French . . . as are the Moslems."[9]

Deedes' view was corroborated by the report of the King-Crane Commission, a task force assigned by the Mandate Commission of the Peace Conference at the instigation of President Woodrow Wilson to ascertain national sentiment in Syria. Ostensibly designed to clear up confusion on what parts of Syria ought to be mandated to whom, the commission was, in effect, an American venture, since both England and France found pretexts for not joining it. After several months' sojourn in Syria, King and Crane reported unexpectedly strong expressions of Syrian national feeling and general repulsion at the idea of a French mandate, except among parties in the Lebanon, who desired a separate state with French collaboration. Based upon the sentiment they observed, the Americans recommended that the United States be asked to assume the mandate for Syria or, failing her, Great Britain. They found themselves unable to recommend a French mandate.[10]

That the King-Crane report did not influence the Mandate Commission is clear, but there is still some confusion as to how well informed the two Americans were. One Arab scholar, George Antonius, admittedly a spokesman for the Arab national movement, regarded the King-Crane report as "a wholly objective analysis" of the state of feeling in Arab political circles immediately after the war.[11] On the other hand, a more recent work maintains that the two commissioners were influenced by a vast propaganda program set up by Faisal to demonstrate against any French participation in Syria. The author dismissed the report as being "as ill-informed as its influence on policy was negligible."[12]

What emerges from the contradictory nature of the debate is that the French thought themselves and their country popular among the great mass of the Syrian population. Yet the history of the French mandatory period in Syria, a period of hatred, mal-administration, violence, and bloodshed, proved that the anti-French feeling there was genuine enough. As Stephen H. Long-rigg has stated: "There was error, perhaps self-deception, in the French estimate of two things. One of these was the degree of popular support they enjoyed or would enjoy in Syria, which . . . they seriously overestimated; the other was the strength of the nationalist movement, which for all its faults and weaknesses, they gravely undervalued."[13]

But this debate, for all its sound and fury and undeniable drama, ignores and obscures the fact that based upon the old diplomacy France had solid claims to Syria and the Lebanon. What reasons did France have for desiring involvement in that area? What concrete economic, political, and cultural claims could the French advance to justify their acquisition of this portion of the defunct Ottoman Empire? Questions like these have been swamped by the debate outlined above. In dealing with them, I will delve no further into the story of the wartime agreements, documents which have often been cited to explain the confusion and misunderstanding surrounding Syria during and after the peace conferences. These wartime agreements do not explain France's claim to Syria and the Lebanon; they merely illustrate that she had one. The answers to the questions raised above lie in the more remote and relatively ignored prewar era. This work will, therefore, discuss the origins of the French involvement in Syria and the Lebanon, focusing attention on the period from the turn of the century to the outbreak of hostilities in 1914.

The problems will be attacked from three angles. First, from the religious point of view, the essay will discuss how France's traditional Catholic protectorate, theoretically extending throughout the Ottoman Empire, was systematically narrowed to Syria and the Lebanon in the years from 1901 to 1914. Second, it will examine France's political and diplomatic relations with the Christian and Muslim populations of Syria and the Lebanon. This section will involve France's role in what has come to be called the Arab Awakening. The focus of this problem will be from 1911 to 1914, since it was not really until the Italo-Turkish War that Arab separatist ideas began to attract substantial following. The seeds of misunderstanding between Syrians and Frenchmen, which were harvested after 1919, were planted deeply in the prewar era. A third focus of concentration will be on the economic sphere. Of primary consideration will be the railroad question, illustrating how France was forced out of the all-encompassing Baghdad enterprise (or rather how she withdrew voluntarily despite the anguished cries of heavily committed financiers) and instead concentrated on railroad development in Syria, where she already had a rather extensive network. This evolution culminated in the wide-ranging economic partition of Ottoman Asian territory in the agreements with Germany and Turkey in 1914. It is my contention that the period from 1901 to 1914, rather than the wartime era, was the crucial one in the solidification of France's claim to a special position in Syria and the Lebanon, a title the Mandate Commission recognized in 1920.

2 BACKGROUND

Official French contact with the areas now known as Syria and
the Lebanon can be traced as far back as the great Christian
crusades of the eleventh and twelfth centuries. Most Maronite
Christians came into communion with Rome during the crusades,
and one of the first indications of what in a later era was to
become the French protectorate of Christians in the Ottoman
Empire can be found in a letter from Saint-Louis to the Maronite
patriarch, dated 21 May 1250. "We are convinced that this
nation [the Lebanon] . . . is a part of the French nation, for its
friendship for the French resembles the friendship which the
French have among themselves. . . . We promise to give you and
your people protection . . . and to do whatever will be necessary
for your well-being."[1] In the thirteenth century French merchants, especially from Marseille, established themselves along
the coast of the Lebanon. But with the end of the crusades, most
soldiers and missionaries withdrew from the Levant, and this first
period of French influence became little more than a memory.

With the expansion of trade that attended the era of discovery
and the consolidation of national states in Europe in the following
centuries, however, the Levant once more became a desirable
area for French commercial expansion. After the conquest of
Constantinople by Muhammed II in 1453, the sultan, following
past custom, established the principle of religious autonomy for

the non-Muslim subjects of the empire. He also granted commercial privileges to large foreign trading companies established there. These privileges and immunities were known as capitulations and were granted unilaterally by the sublime Porte.

These first capitulatory arrangements were informal in nature. It was not until 1535 that the first more or less binding agreement was reached between Sulieman the Magnificent and the French king Francis I. According to this capitulation, France obtained the privilege of maintaining commercial relations in all ports of the Ottoman Empire. This privilege became a veritable right over the years, since other rival powers often had to borrow the French colors to gain entrance to Ottoman ports. But even more important for purposes of this study, the treaty also assured France that her nationals (pilgrims, traders, and travelers) would enjoy full religious liberty in the empire: "it has been expressly promised, concluded and accorded that the said [French] merchants and their agents and servants, and all other subjects of the [French] king can never be molested nor judged by the *cadi, sandjac-bey, soubachi* [local officials] nor other but by the Sublime Porte alone, and that they be neither imprisoned nor tried as Turks if they themselves do not freely request it by word of mouth, and that they be allowed to observe their religion."[2] This famous agreement of 1535 initiated the development of the French Catholic protectorate in the Middle East.

Successive renewals of the capitulations in 1569, 1604, and 1673 confirmed and clarified French prerogatives. The latter clearly specified that French subjects would be able freely to visit Jerusalem and the Holy Places and that French churches and other religious establishments in the empire would not be subject to local taxation.[3] Perhaps the most significant of all these capitulatory agreements was that accorded to France on 28 May 1740. This treaty recognized the exclusive right of France to protect those foreign nationals whose countries were without representatives at the Porte. The capitulation of 1740 gave permission to all members of "Christian and hostile nations" to continue to visit Jerusalem "under the flag of the emperor of France, with no permission to do so under any other flag." The final article bound future sultans to observe these obligations.[4] In this manner France acquired the right to protect all missionaries in the Ottoman Empire, regardless of nationality. The protectorate became one of the main pillars of French influence in the Levant.

It must be emphasized, however, that nothing in the capitulations conferred upon France the prerogative to protect native and foreign lay Christians. The capitulations covered only French Christians and foreign clerics. Nevertheless, over a period of time, by a gradual extension of the rights of the protectorate, France came equally to exercise it in favor of indigenous Catholics as well. An indication of the French attitude in this matter can be inferred from a letter written by Louis XIV and the queen regent to the patriarch of Antioch and the Maronite nation on 28 April 1649, in which the former took under their "protection and special safe-guard the very reverend patriarch and all the prelates and clerical and secular Maronite Christians who inhabit the Lebanon."[5] This policy was restated by Napoleon Bonaparte on 18 October 1802. The first consul maintained that the French ambassador to Constantinople "ought to take under his protection all the *hospices* and all the Christians of Syria, Armenia, and especially all the caravans which visit the Holy Places."[6]

Slowly the small body of native Catholic clergy escaped the control of local rulers and enrolled themselves under the special privileges of the French, and this protection gradually extended from them to their "flocks." And so long as the other Great Powers maintained only minimal diplomatic representation in the Levant, they accepted the French position, which was even championed by the papacy. Without ever recognizing this right formally, the Porte admitted it in fact by rarely disputing it. It passed into normal usage gradually by tradition. Thus France came to view herself as the representative throughout the Levant, not only of Catholicism, but of Christianity in all its forms.[7]

The capitulations, commercial, juridicial, and religious, had originally been granted by the Turkish sultans in an era when there was no difference between Muslim and civil law in the Ottoman Empire. Non-Muslim traders, travelers, pilgrims, and missionaries had to be protected. It also must be emphasized that over the centuries the Porte had signed similar capitulatory agreements with other major Western powers.[8] By the nineteenth century France no longer exercised the same monopoly she had enjoyed in the early modern period, although her protectorate over Christians remained fairly well intact. It was during this century, particularly during the great Tanzimat period of reform in the Ottoman Empire, that the Turks separated Muslim law from civil law and maintained that everyone of any religion would be subject equally to the latter.[9] One important thrust in this direction occurred with the law of 16 January 1867, by which the Great Powers obtained the right for their nationals to own real estate in the Ottoman Empire. But as a quid pro quo, these same powers had to agree that local tribunals could thereafter try certain cases involving this real estate without the presence and assistance of consular representatives, which had previously been required under the capitulations.[10] Agreements such as this constituted a serious weakening of the whole fabric of the capitulations, and Ottoman jurists and statesmen subsequently argued that they were now superfluous and ought to be abolished. But any such across-the-board abolition would have to be accomplished by agreement with the other European powers, which were reluctant to surrender their privileges in the empire and possibly cut themselves off from the patrimony of a ramshackle nation commonly referred to in European councils as the "Sick Man of Europe." The capitulations remained a thorn in Turkey's side until the First World War.

France's Christian protectorate assured her of being regarded by the Uniate Christians of the Levant, particularly in Syria, as their champion. Events in the Lebanon in 1860 solidified this position even further, and France's influence in this area reached its zenith. The period from 1840 to 1860 in the Lebanon was characterized by continual warfare and religious intolerance between the dissident Muslim Druzes and the Maronite Christians. The source of the trouble lay in the fact that the Maronites had supported the Egyptians during their invasion and rule from 1831 to 1840. When the Egyptian military leader, Ibrahim Pasha, was forced to withdraw from Syria and the sultan restored order, the Ottoman government began systematically to weaken the position of the Maronites, cultural protégés of France, by encouraging the Druzes to use violence against them. The Maronites began to seek support and advice exclusively with the French consuls, while the Druzes looked with hostility upon everything French and turned more toward Britain.[11] Finally, in 1860 massive Druze attacks on groups of Christians broke out in the southern part of the Lebanon. Violence spread, and the loss of life was estimated at 11,000, among the sufferers being Catholic missions and Jesuits.

Indignation prompted the European powers to act. Their justification for intervention on behalf of the Christians lay in the Treaty of Paris of 1856, a document which forbade interference in internal Ottoman affairs, but which also stipulated the Great Powers' determination to protect the rights of Christian minorities. In addition to humanitarian concerns, however, French Emperor Napoleon III was motivated in favor of the Maronites by domestic political factors. He had alienated Catholic support by his intervention in Italy in 1859, which led to a dismemberment of the papal states. By championing the cause of Catholics in the Middle East, he could hope to recover at least a part of Catholic support at home.[12] On 3 April 1860, acting as a representative of the powers, an expeditionary corps of 6,000 Frenchmen arrived in Syria under the command of General Beaufort d'Hautpoul to establish order. Christians in Beirut greeted the French troops enthusiastically, and the force remained until 6 June 1861 to help the Maronites restore their rights.

Meanwhile, representatives of the five European powers and the Porte met and hammered out an administrative document for the Lebanon known as the *Règlement organique,* signed on 9 June 1861. According to this document, the Lebanon became an autonomous sanjak. It was to have its own system of local government administered by a Christian governor with the advice of a representative council composed of a fixed number of delegates from each of the major religious sects situated in the Mountain.[13] The *Règlement,* slightly altered in 1864, remained the basis of administrative organization in the Lebanon until the institution of the French mandate in 1922.

These events are of importance for several reasons. First of all, the expeditionary force that actually landed in Syria was French.

This fact led Christians to assume, rightly so, that France had been the moving force behind the intervention on behalf of the Maronites. French prestige, as a result, was enormously enhanced among Levantine Christians in general. Second, one can observe a further development of Anglo-French competition in this area, since England had often championed the Druzes in the period from 1840 to 1860. But perhaps most important of all, one must realize that the French expeditionary force acted, not in the name of France alone, but as an agent of the five European powers, and that the *Règlement organique* was achieved only under the guarantee of these same powers. This meant simply that in the critical period from 1901 to 1914, when French diplomats were working to enhance the prestige of their country even further by seeking additional modifications of the *Règlement* in favor of the Maronites, such changes could only be achieved by agreement of all the powers involved. This agreement proved very difficult to attain, and the eventual French success in this matter in 1912 is a tribute to the skill of her diplomacy. This issue will be discussed fully in a later chapter.

French influence among Christians in the Levant, then, was at its peak after 1860. Using the events of that year as a springboard, French Catholic missionaries flocked to Asiatic Turkey, above all to Syria and Palestine, to set up numerous hospitals, orphanages, asylums, and schools. Jesuits, Lazarists, the Sisters of St. Joseph, the Dames of Nazareth, the Daughters of Charity, and the Sisters of the Holy Family were some of the main orders which established charitable works in the Orient. The French government and private societies of French propaganda openly subsidized these groups.[14]

Missionary work, including the French governmental subventions, continued even after 1871, when the new anticlerical regime systematically persecuted such groups as the Jesuits. Paradoxically, the expulsion of the Jesuits from their houses in France by the government of the Third Republic had the effect of encouraging their progress in the Turkish Empire. These missionaries, forced to expand their activities beyond French borders, remained one of the most useful aspects of French influence abroad. One Jesuit official remarked in 1880 that, "were we not such good Frenchmen, the British flag would presently be flying over all our oriental establishments."[15]

The focus of missionary activity in the Levant was on education, and the religious schools leaned heavily toward instruction in the French language and culture, as well as Catholic history. On the eve of the First World War there were some 500 French ecclesiastical schools in the Ottoman Empire, the great majority of which were concentrated in Syria, the Lebanon, and Palestine, counting between 50,000 and 60,000 students.[16] The French missionary establishment far outnumbered that of any other nationality. It was estimated in the first decade of the twentieth century that there were some 750,000 Catholics loyal to France in Asiatic Turkey. These included five patriarchs, thirty-seven bishops, and three archbishops of the Maronite, Melkite, Syrian, and Chaldean sects.[17] One French writer remarked that "without this protectorate, our consuls in the Levant would have no reason for being there. The French colony in Syria is insignificant; with the exception of the missionaries our country is represented there by a few cooks and restaurateurs, whose presence in the Orient could not justify the 25,000 franc salary given to each of our consuls."[18]

But did all this mean that France enjoyed an exclusive position among Levantine Catholics and other Christians? Not at all. It merely shows that France had a rather extensive religious investment in that area. Russian influence among Orthodox Christians was substantial, and by the turn of the century German establishments were regarded as a major threat to French influence in the Middle East. German penetration during the 1880s and 1890s directed itself toward the establishment of agricultural colonies, an area in which she held a great superiority over her rivals. Important German agricultural colonies sprang up at Haifa, Jaffa, and Jerusalem, while the German government launched a program aimed at directing emigration toward the Levant.[19] Later chapters will show how Germany and other European powers, particularly Italy after 1905, began to challenge the French protectorate and force the Third Republic to narrow its range of concentration to more manageable proportions; that is, to Syria and the Lebanon.

Ironically, the great missionary movement to the Middle East in the last half of the nineteenth century coincided with a marked decline in French diplomatic and political influence in the Ottoman Empire. France's defeat in the Franco-Prussian War of 1870-1871 was responsible for this. Russia, Austria, Italy, and Greece all sought to take over positions previously occupied by France. The French army mission to reform the Turkish military, which had been in Constantinople since 1850, was replaced by Prussian officers, and military functions were reserved for Germany. One of the few places of sympathy left for France in the empire lay in Syria and the Lebanon, where Christians had not forgotten the intervention of 1860. But if France's diplomatic and political influence was on the wane after 1870, this period was more fertile in the economic sphere. Granted, France suffered a serious check in 1888, when the Porte accorded Germany the right to build the Anatolian railway. But France obtained concessions too—notably the right to administer the ports and quays of Izmir, Constantinople, and Beirut; various railroad companies in Syria; and the *Tramways libanais* and the *métropolitain* at Constantinople.

It has been shown that, politically, France's main pillar of influence in the Ottoman Empire lay among the Christian populations of Syria. It would appear, therefore, to be in her interest to maintain this high level of prestige. But in the last decade of the nineteenth century, the tragic events in Armenia and France's reaction to them gravely threatened her prestige and reduced her influence among Ottoman Christians to its prewar nadir.

Article 61 of the 1878 Treaty of Berlin affirmed that "the Sublime Porte undertakes to carry out, without further delay, the improvements and reforms demanded by local requirements in the provinces inhabited by the Armenians and to guarantee their security against the Circassians and Kurds." In a key phrase, the same article required that the Porte "periodically make known the steps taken to this effect to the Powers, who will superintend their application."[20] Despite this assurance that a reform program for the Armenian Christians would be instituted, Sultan Abdul Hamid II chose to ignore it, and the Turks consequently maintained a corrupt, repressive regime. Massacres by Turkish-inspired Kurds resulted when the Armenians began openly to state their grievances and solicit foreign intervention on their behalf. The first major incident took place at Sassun in August 1894. The result was a great outcry in Europe, particularly in England. In November Ambassador Paul Cambon notified Foreign Minister Gabriel Hanotaux of a committee appointed by the sultan to investigate the Sassun massacres and to make recommendations for reform. But Cambon cautioned that the committee's mission "will not be serious." The sultan had instructed the committee to inquire into the subject " 'of the criminal acts committed by the Armenian brigands who have pillaged and devastated the villages.' " The sultan's purpose, Cambon maintained, was simply to confirm the Ottoman government's version of the events.[21]

The establishment of an Anglo-Franco-Russian commission of inquiry followed the Sassun events. Cambon was certainly one of the guiding lights of this "Armenian triplice" and the most outspoken proponent of positive French initiative in the Armenian matter. In April 1895 he submitted a program to ameliorate the plight of the Armenians. It was a comprehensive plan for administrative, financial, and judicial reforms with a specific blueprint for putting these measures into practice and assuring their exact execution.[22] The tripartite commission and the respective governments approved Cambon's proposals, and they were submitted to the Porte on 11 May 1895. Abdul Hamid, however, rejected the plan in favor of a reform program of his own. The sultan's program, submitted to the powers on 3 June 1895, ignored the specific Armenian situation and instead envisioned a generalized system of reforms to be applied in all the *vilayets* of the Ottoman Empire. Cambon's reaction, upon communicating the Turkish plan to Hanotaux, was to denounce it as "an informal work, containing no serious disposition and offering no guarantee."[23]

It was clear that the sultan was playing for time, knowing that the powers would not back up their insistence on reform with force. Britain would not act alone, although she was in favor of a reform program. Russia, with an Armenian minority of her own, was reluctant to do much to "overimprove" the lot of Armenians in the Ottoman Empire. That left France. And although Cambon vociferously and repeatedly urged French action, he could not budge the Quai d'Orsay. His correspondence with Hanotaux is especially revealing. In the fall of 1896 Cambon reported two audiences with Abdul Hamid in which he vaguely threatened European military intervention unless the sultan used his authority to ameliorate the conditions in the six Armenian *vilayets.* [24] On 30 September 1896 he notified Hanotaux that the Armenian affair was being prolonged precisely because the sultan considered himself immune from intervention. He urged the importance of declaring "that each of the six governments intend to send a battleship to Constantinople in case of further trouble. This would give the Sultan the true impression of a European concert." [25]

It was apparently Cambon's conviction that France could successfully mediate between the British and Russian views, thus reconstituting the "Armenian triplice" of 1894-1895. But there was little sympathy for such an aggressive policy in Paris. Hanotaux stood squarely for the defense and territorial integrity of the Ottoman Empire and in addition was loath to do anything which might prejudice the alliance with Russia. The foreign minister revealed his attitude plainly in a dispatch to Cambon on 15 December 1896:

> You shall not lose sight of what we continue to consider, in accord with the Russian Government, as the necessary condition for a concerted action of the powers: their previous agreement on the following three points:
>
> Maintenance of the integrity of the Ottoman Empire; no isolated action on any point; no condominium.
>
> I do not need to remind you that, in our thinking, the reforms ought to be applied to all the populations of the Empire without racial or religious distinction.
>
> As for the question of measures of coercion, we shall not refuse to examine it at the proper moment, if the powers were unanimous in recognizing its absolute necessity. [26]

Hanotaux was, in effect, telling Cambon to soft-pedal the issue discreetly at Constantinople, since Russia was not keen on any Anglo-French military power being exerted there. The Franco-

Russian alliance was, after all, only two years old. Conversations among the ambassadors continued at Constantinople, but little was actually achieved. They did produce a new reform program in 1897 which was never submitted to the Porte, since the Armenian question was engulfed by a new crisis concerning Crete. William L. Langer has observed that France followed Russia in this matter "in order to be of service to a new ally and in order to prevent the English from monopolizing the protection of Christians in the Levant. . . . The revolutionaries had succeeded in provoking the intervention of the European powers, but the intervention was such that it was doomed to failure. . . . The net result of this phase of the movement was that thousands of innocent Armenians lost their lives, and there was no real gain to be shown."[27]

In short, the Quai d'Orsay refused to take a strong initiative in the Armenian matter from 1893 to 1897 in order to avoid antagonizing Russia. Ambassador Cambon's contempt for this policy is clearly evident in his correspondence. As early as 1 July 1891, one month before he became ambassador to the Porte, Cambon wrote to Maurice Bompard noting the recent French move toward Russia and away from England in matters relating to Ottoman policy. He observed ironically that "the diplomat who would sacrifice the true principles of our eastern policy and the true interests of France in Syria to the Russian illusion would be disgraced in the near future; the one who would attempt to keep himself independent of Russia would be accused by the thickheads in Paris of lacking patriotism and of selling his country to England. . . . You are no longer French if you are not first a good Russian."[28] Cambon's position on this matter did not change fundamentally after five years on the job. He wrote to his mother on 23 December 1895: "At Paris there is no idea, no direction; it is as if we have confided our portfolio of foreign affairs to Baron de Morenheim [Russian ambassador at Paris]. I struggle as much as I can against this tendency of effacement before Russia. . . ."[29] But Cambon's efforts to galvanize French initiative were to no avail. The only alternative was to fall back on the "concert of Europe," an unwieldy instrument that could take action only insofar as the most unwilling and reluctant member would approve.

The judgment of France's role in the Armenian affair by a contemporary French historian was quite accurate, especially in light of Cambon's pregnant reference in 1891 to "the true interests of France in Syria." He wrote that France had indeed paid dearly for her alliance to Russia by a "diminution of our influence in the East, where our prestige is based above all on our traditional protectorate of the Christians."[30]

3 THE LORANDO-TUBINI AFFAIR

With her prestige among the Christians of Asia Minor at low ebb as a result of her conduct in the Armenian problem, France seized upon a seemingly trivial incident to attempt to bolster her sagging influence. The Lorando-Tubini affair of 1901 seemed tailor-made, since it involved only French nationals, thereby permitting France to intervene alone on their behalf and not as a member of the cumbersome instrument which the "concert of Europe" inevitably was.

The dispute between France and the Ottoman Empire at first seemed innocuous enough, involving little more than rival pecuniary claims. But it led eventually to a three-month rupture of diplomatic relations, further claims by France concerning her whole position in Asiatic Turkey, a French naval demonstration, and finally a capitulation by the Sublime Porte. This period from August to November 1901 was followed with much interest by the foreign offices of the various European powers and was given substantial coverage by the French press.

The initial issues were clear enough. First, in 1890 a society of French businessmen and financiers, the *Société des Quais, Docks et Entrepôts de Constantinople,* was constituted. It received a *firman* of concession from the sultan granting it the construction and operation of the quays of Constantinople, as well as the right to establish and operate customs warehouses and exploit tugboat

and tramway services.[1] But the society had never been abl
take possession of these concessions due to subsequent oppositio
from the Porte. When the sultan offered to repurchase the quays
on terms unfavorable to the Frenchmen, the latter appealed to
the French Embassy for support. The other two issues were both
of a purely pecuniary nature, concerning loans made to the
sultan, which were never repaid, by two Levantine financiers of
French citizenship, Lorando and Tubini.

The French foreign office did not become involved in these
matters until its aid was solicited in 1901. But it then entered the
controversy with enthusiasm. The Quai d'Orsay wished the concession of the Constantinople quays to remain in French hands in
order to offset the development of the port of Haidar-Pasha by
German investors. Thus, Foreign Minister Théophile Delcassé
took the position that the whole matter involved not only
pecuniary interests, but raised questions "of a wholly different
character, touching the position of France on the Bosporus."[2]

The French therefore took an uncompromising and intractable
position. Negotiations between French Ambassador Jean E.
Constans and the Turkish authorities dragged on throughout the
spring and summer of 1901 with seemingly no progress being
made. Several times Constans notified Delcassé that further conversations were useless. On 29 July the ambassador went so far as
to recommend his own recall and some further "energetic act."
Constans believed, probably thinking of the Armenian affair,
that "our inaction would be considered an avowal of impotence,
the consequences of which would be a real disaster for our
influence and interests in the Orient."[3] Delcassé took his ambassador's advice a month later when the Turks began to vacillate
after a seemingly satisfactory verbal agreement had been reached
on all questions. Observing on 21 August 1901 that "our dignity
does not permit us to continue discussions in the presence of the
bad faith of the Ottoman Government," Delcassé ordered his
ambassador to return to Paris.[4] Constans left the Porte on 25
August, beginning a period of ruptured diplomatic relations that
was to last until mid-November.

The months of September and October witnessed the settlement of the Tubini claims and the question of the *Société des*

Quais. But Turkey continued to demur on the Lorando claims, whose principal and interest had mounted since 1875 to the total of 344,488 Turkish pounds. France continued to press the Porte to meet the entire amount before normal diplomatic relations could be restored. France's firm stand throughout this period received plaudits from the French press, with the exception of that of the far Left. The general feeling was that France had to assert herself, especially after her role of effacement in the Armenian controversy, in order to make Turkey live up to her agreements.[5]

Perhaps the single most influential voice of dissent against French policy came from the eminent economist, Paul Leroy-Beaulieu. In an article in *L'Economiste français,* Leroy-Beaulieu applauded Delcassé's desire to have the rights and interests of French nationals in the Ottoman Empire respected. What he objected to was that Lorando and Tubini were claiming payment of debts at a 9 percent rate of interest, the maximum allowed in Turkey, whereas the normal rate of interest was 4 to 6 percent. He maintained that "it is no longer a question here . . . of guaranteeing a French citizen against spoliation by a foreign Government, but rather of procuring a considerable gain for him at the expense of this foreign Government . . . which is in [financial] distress." Leroy-Beaulieu went on to urge France not to abuse the use of force by setting a precedent for the 9 percent interest rate. This attitude would be self-defeating to France's policy of preserving Ottoman integrity.[6] The Turks themselves even used this article to attempt to force down the demands of the French government in the Lorando matter.[7]

Just how long this condition of reciprocal intransigence would have continued will never be known. During the late summer and early fall of 1901, Turkey committed a diplomatic blunder of the first order, one that stiffened French determination and led finally to the "energetic act" of which Constans had spoken in July. As a reprisal for the recall of the French ambassador, the Sublime Porte announced that religious and charitable establishments in the empire which had been opened without official authorization from the Porte would be subjected to regular customs duties and to the normal 5 percent property tax. In addition, no new schools could be opened without official authorization. This was a direct slap at French influence in the Levant, particularly in Syria and the Lebanon, since most of the religious schools and charitable establishments there belonged to French Catholic missionaries and were officially protected against discrimination by the French government. The French consul general in Syria notified Delcassé on 11 September of the dangers posed by the new Ottoman regulations to Catholic institutions in his area of jurisdiction and urged the necessity of acquiring the *firmans* necessary to protect these institutions from customs imposts.[8]

The French response to this thrust was immediate. Edmond Bapst, the French chargé d'affaires in Constantinople, pronounced the move contrary to the customs immunities guaranteed to the religious orders by the Porte in an 1864 treaty.[9] *Le Temps* denounced the new regulations as in violation of the Turkish capitulations to France of 1673 and 1740.[10] The conservative *Gaulois* articulated the feelings of many Frenchmen when it called the Turkish move an "odious act," indicating "that our foreign policy, previously so powerful, has lost all its prestige and tends more and more to disappear. We are leaving ourselves to be supplanted in the Orient by foreign powers. . . ."[11] Many Frenchmen justifiably regarded the increased construction of German and Russian missions in the Levant as a threat to the traditional prestige and influence of France in that area. The Porte clearly had antagonized France, thus forcing a change in the complexion of what had originally been a financial dispute.

The dispatches from the French chargé at Constantinople became more and more insistent as time passed. On 24 September Bapst notified Delcassé of discrimination against French missionary schools, saying that "the inauguration of a stable regime for the academic establishments which we protect has become an absolute necessity."[12] On 8 October Bapst reported further harrassment and concluded that the Turkish government "is profiting by the rupture of relations in order vigorously to push the execution of this program. . . . It is important to our interests that the existence [of our schools] be safeguarded; this question, it seems to me is . . . the most important of those whose regulation imposes itself on us at this moment."[13] The Lorando-Tubini claims had been virtually forgotten. Turkey had succeeded in creating a new issue, a much more serious one so far as France was concerned.

Using Turkish tergiversation on the Lorando claims as an excuse, the Quai d'Orsay formed a new set of demands, all relating to the position of France in the Orient, which Turkey would have to meet before diplomatic relations could be re-established. First, France demanded the recognition of the legal existence of French and French-protected schools. The customs immunities accorded to religious orders by treaty would be maintained concerning the schools. Second, she requested similar treatment for churches, hospitals, dispensaries, orphanages, asylums, and other French or French-protected establishments. Complete lists were annexed to these first two points. Third, France asked for the immediate deliverance of the *firmans* necessary for the construction or repair of a specified number of these establishments damaged during the Armenian troubles of 1894-1896. And fourth, France required the delivery of *bèrat* of recognition for the Chaldean patriarch, in terms acceptable to the Holy See.[14] These new demands were presented to the Turkish foreign minister, Tewfik Pasha, on 2 November 1901, along with the devastating piece of information that a French naval expedition would seize the customs on the large Turkish island of Mitylene and administer them for as long as it took the Sublime Porte to agree to French terms. There is some evidence to suggest that Delcassé required some prodding before actually committing the French fleet to action. Paul Cambon, the French ambassador in London, indicated, in a letter to his son on 2 November, that his advice "in conjunction with that of everyone who has any common sense has finally shaken up the Minister. At this moment a naval division is leaving for . . . Mitylene. We shall see what the Sultan will do. . . . Better late than never. A simple little thing is becoming a great event and we give the impression of going to war over it. The smallest demonstration two months ago would have settled the matter without any fracas." Cambon again expressed dissatisfaction at the dilatoriness of the Quai d'Orsay in the Mitylene affair in another letter to his son on 7 November.[15]

The French occupation of this large island off the western coast of Asia Minor, located half-way between the Dardanelles and the Gulf of Izmir, began on 6 November, and it shattered the Turkish will to resist. The precarious Turkish treasury could not afford the loss of valuable customs receipts. In a last desperate attempt to circumvent the new French demands, the Porte quickly agreed to a settlement of the outstanding Lorando claims, and the sultan issued an *iradé* to that effect. But this was clearly a case of too little too late. The Porte had unwittingly presented France with an excellent opportunity to recoup her prestige among the Christian populations of the Orient, and Delcassé was not disposed to relinquish it for the settlement of what now was a petty financial matter.

Reverence for the alliance with Russia had discouraged France from any energetic action in the Armenian controversy of the previous decade, since any great amelioration of conditions among the Armenians in the Ottoman Empire might well have created an uncomfortable position for Russia vis-à-vis her own Armenian communities. But the Franco-Turkish confrontation of 1901 offered no directly prejudicial repercussions to Russia. The French ambassador in St. Petersburg notified Delcassé on 5 November 1901 that "the Russian press approves the measures taken by the French Government to put an end to the Franco-Turkish conflict."[16] The enthusiasm of the Russian press was muted, however, after 8 November, with the ironic result that France's own ally was alone among the Great Powers in expressing disapproval of French action. Sir Charles Hardinge, British ambassador to St. Petersburg, notified Sir Francis Bertie, British ambassador to Paris, that "Lamsdorff [the Russian foreign minister] is evidently displeased at the proceedings of the French fleet. . . . The Russian press no longer applauds Delcassé's action, owing, I gather, to a hint from Lamsdorff. He complains that the peace of Europe is endangered for the sake of a parliamentary success, and he says that he daily thanks Heaven that there is no Russian Parliament."[17] Aside from St. Petersburg, however, even in Berlin and Rome, French action at Mitylene won approval, although Camille Barrère reported from the Italian capital that the Quirinal would become disturbed if the occupation became permanent.[18] The Vatican as well expressed

vigorous approval at France's decision to affirm the religious protectorate so enthusiastically.[19] The impression was unmistakable.
If Turkey could get away with cavalier treatment of French establishments in the Orient, she might well be able to do the same
thing against German, Italian, or Russian establishments if she
so desired. All the foreign offices were quite familiar with
Turkey's time-honored policy of playing the Great Powers off one
against the other. This was why the "concert of Europe" could
never function effectively there. This was also the reason why the
powers were willing to permit France to intervene alone, so long
as the intervention did not last too long, to teach the Porte a
lesson and to recoup some of the battered European prestige in
the Ottoman Empire.

In spite of the almost unanimous approval France seemed to be
enjoying, there was a domestic faction on the Left which refused
to be seduced. The opposition emerged at the Chamber of
Deputies session of 4 November 1901. A formal interpellation on
the Lorando-Tubini matter had originally been scheduled for 15
November, but in light of the departure of the French fleet from
Toulon, the session was held immediately. Leftist representative
Marcel Sembat requested knowledge of the destination of the
fleet, indicating that the government in this instance was under-
cutting the prerogatives of the Chamber by undertaking actions
which might well result in war. He also wanted full information
on the goals of the French fleet, indicating that there must be
more at stake than the satisfaction of the Lorando and Tubini
claims. "They [the government] did not put us in the ridiculous
situation of a nation which mobilizes part of its naval forces for
such a paltry result." The main thrust of Sembat's interpellation
proved to be a denunciation of French foreign policy, which had
become so intractable over the Lorando-Tubini claims but which
had silently accepted such atrocities as the Armenian massacres.
He quoted several documents illustrating recent Turkish brutali-
ties against Armenians and concluded with an appeal for uni-
lateral French action in behalf of that oppressed minority group.

In the debate which ensued, rightist deputy Denys Cochin
defended Delcassé's actions vis-à-vis the Armenians by citing the
importance of the Russian alliance. But he indicated as well that
France should not permit her alliance with St. Petersburg to

hinder her from defending her best interests in the Levant. Cochin said: "In the Levant, I see the Sultan's *iradés* threaten our establishments and schools. . . . Customs privileges are abolished. *Firmans* are accorded to Russian schools more willingly than to ours, and I dare say that they do more for French influence than the private bank accounts of Tubini and Lorando and the *Sociètè des Quais.*" Cochin requested firm assurances from Delcassé that France was taking firm action in the Levant, going well beyond the claims of Lorando and Tubini.

Delcassé was quite anxious to avoid any connection between the Armenian question and the present Turkish-French conflict. The foreign minister, therefore, answered Sembat in rather general terms, saying that any solution to the Armenian question could only be achieved in concert with the other Great Powers. Regarding Lorando and Tubini, he emphasized France's "exemplary patience" in the face of "the persistent denials of justice" on the part of Turkey. Nor did Delcassé satisfy Cochin in the latter's appeals for strong action in regard to the protectorate of charitable establishments and schools. The foreign minister did not yet inform the Chamber of the new demands concerning the official recognition of French-protected schools and charitable establishments, but simply requested a vote of confidence. After a rather lengthy debate, Sembat's Order of the Day[20] calling for French action in favor of the Armenians was voted down in favor of another expressing "confidence in the Government to have the honor and rights of France respected" in the Orient.[21]

The reason Delcassé did not inform the Chamber of the new French demands on the Porte during the interpellation of 4 November became clear after the public was notified a couple of days later. In a devastating article, socialist leader Jean Jaurès strongly criticized French policy. He felt that the demands for official recognition of clerical schools in the Orient as French protégés were a contradiction, since France now offered no protection to them at home. He castigated Delcassé for separating this issue from the Armenian problem, asking how France could be concerned about Catholic schools and not about the Christians of Armenia. Jaurès indicated that France was truckling to Russia, agreeing to leave the Armenian problem in Russian hands in exchange for a Russian approval of the present French action at the

Porte.[22] Jaurès' outspoken critique of French policy in the press shows clearly that Delcassé wanted to avoid a full-scale debate on these matters in the Chamber of Deputies at the same moment that Franco-Turkish negotiations were entering their critical stage. Hence his refusal to inform the deputies on 4 November.

Franco-Turkish negotiations did not last long. The seizure of the customs at Mitylene was a catastrophic blow to the fragile Turkish financial system. The Porte now realized that France meant business and that she had the support of most of the rest of Europe. No time was wasted in acceding to French demands. On 6 November 1901 Tewfik Pasha notified Bapst that the Turkish Council of Ministers had approved all the points demanded by France concerning the recognition of schools, hospitals, and asylums. The French list of 245 schools and 360 additional establishments received Turkish concurrence.[23] An imperial *iradê* to this effect was issued on 10 November, and French forces evacuated the Mitylene customs on the following day. The crisis was over, and France had won a diplomatic victory.

Judging from the dispatches of the French representatives in Asiatic Turkey, the Franco-Turkish imbroglio of 1901 had achieved the desired effect. The consul general in Izmir notified Delcassé that members of the Catholic community there had expressed great satisfaction at the results of French action.[24] Similar news concerning the "recrudescence of sympathy and confidence" arrived from Beirut.[25] From the French consul general in Cairo came the prediction that "the affair, so happily regulated by Your Excellency, can be the point of departure for a new and energetic policy the consequences of which will soon be felt to the advantage of our material and moral interests in the Ottoman Empire."[26] And from Constantinople itself, Bapst reported a year after the event: "Without doubt, the occupation of Mitylene by our navy has reawakened our prestige, which our great gentleness, taken by the Turks for weakness, had seriously compromised; the Sultan and the Porte can no longer deceive themselves into thinking that our threats will not be followed by consequences."[27]

Ironically, the reaction of France's domestic press was not nearly so favorable as that abroad. Enthusiastic plaudits came from *Le Temps, Le Petit Parisien,* and *Le Gaulois.* On the other hand influential newspapers such as *Le Matin* felt that the whole affair was unworthy of France and that she had made a mountain out of a molehill, while the nationalist *Liberté* editorialized that the sultan's *firmans* concerning the schools and religious establishments were not sufficient. France ought to remain at Mitylene until the promises were actually carried out.[28] Such reactions prompted *Le Temps* to point out that "the European press . . . accords more good faith to France than the French press, which expresses a lack of enthusiasm for the incontestible success of our diplomacy. Once more we shall demonstrate our extreme severity in regard to ourselves. It seems that we have ignored until now our true situation in the Orient and that we want at all cost to deprecate or to undervalue our recent success."[29] Paul Cambon noted Delcassé's poor press in a letter to his son on 13 November 1901 and blamed it upon the foreign minister's own initial uncertainty. But all in all, Cambon felt, "the Turkish affair is not badly settled, and considering everything . . . we are obtaining satisfactions of a general order which we would never have been able to attain as a result of the sultan's good will. . . . It is an unhoped for piece of luck to have obtained the sending of the fleet and thus to become extricated from an impasse which we thrust upon ourselves."[30]

The outcome of the 1901 crisis was clearly a French victory. Delcassé had acted to prevent France's "general interests" from being "disputed today, denied tomorrow, violated day after tomorrow."[31] A blow had been struck to leave an impression throughout the Middle East that France was determined to maintain her place there and was powerful enough to do so. But, intoxicating as the victory may have been, especially so to France at that particular time, it is necessary to keep the matter in perspective. Despite the bravado of language about the display of French force and determination at Mitylene, it must be obvious that diplomatic victories were fairly easily achieved when one's opponent was the "Sick Man of Europe" and when one enjoyed the support or at least the tolerance of all the Great Powers. France was to learn in subsequent years that the maintenance of this victory was to be vastly more difficult.

4 THE PROTECTORATE: PART 1

The Franco-Turk confrontation of 1901 raised French prestige among Ottoman Christians enormously. France's influence in the Levant climbed once again to the preponderant level it had enjoyed immediately after the 1860 intervention in Syria. The rights to the protectorate had been asserted, and it appeared to extend throughout Asiatic Turkey. Ernest Lavisse, one of France's most eminent historians, expressed the importance of the protectorate to the nation in the following manner: "In the Orient, where the authority of men is measured by the number of their clients, the development of our Catholic clientele is a national interest for us."[1] This attitude was prevalent in the diplomatic service as well. Paul Cambon's brother Jules noted that, "in the East, religion and nationality are indistinguishable; the religious protectorate was accordingly a factor which contributed largely to the moral influence, and hence to the political authority of France."[2] Delcassé himself, although an outspoken anticlerical in the years before coming to the Quai d'Orsay, proved himself to be a disciple of Léon Gambetta's dictum that anticlericalism was not an article for export. He took the protectorate much more seriously than had his predecessor, Gabriel Hanotaux. Upon becoming foreign minister in 1898, Delcassé wrote to Paul Cambon in Constantinople proposing that pressure be applied at the Porte to secure reparations for French subjects whose property had been damaged during the Armenian massacres. Cambon replied on 12 July 1898 to the effect that "your attitude does . . . have the advantage of forcing the Porte to open a discussion. Up to the present she has made no reply to our demands and has not even accepted the principle of an indemnity. It is important to rouse her from her torpor, and the present moment is all the more opportune because our Catholic protectorate is assailed from all sides and by our inexplicable inertia towards it we have provided excellent arguments for our adversaries in Rome and Berlin."[3] This question of reparations was, of course, settled by the Mitylene occupation of 1901.

Cambon's reference to Rome and Berlin implies that France's protectorate was indeed challenged by other European powers even before 1901. In the late 1880's Italy had sought to gain recognition of the right to protect her own nationals, lay and ecclesiastical, in the Ottoman Empire. But such was the extent of French involvement among Christians there that on 22 May 1888 Pope Leo XIII responded to the Italian requests with the encyclical *Aspera rerum conditio.* It informed all Catholic missionaries in the Levant that "the protectorate of the French Nation has been established . . . and confirmed by treaties concluded among governments. One ought, therefore, not to make any innovations in this matter: the protection of this Nation, wherever it is in force, ought to be religiously maintained, and the missionaries ought to be informed that, if they need aid, they have recourse to the consuls and agents of the French Nation. . . ."[4]

Nor was Italy the only threat to France's position in the Middle East in the pre-1901 period. German missionaries, schools, and charitable establishments had penetrated Palestine, Syria, and Anatolia during the 1880s and 1890s. German schools were generally felt to be inferior, but important German agricultural colonies were being developed at Haifa, Jaffa, and Jerusalem. During the final two decades of the nineteenth century, Berlin placed some emphasis on trying to direct emigration toward the Middle East. The French regarded the German agricultural colonies as a major threat to their influence.[5] These fears crystallized when Kaiser William II made his spectacular visit to the Holy Land in 1898. The ostensible purpose of the trip was to consecrate the Protestant Church of the Redeemer. The real purpose, however, was to demonstrate German-Turkish solidarity, and the Kaiser made several well-publicized assurances of friendship and good will to the Muslim community. But at the same time, the German emperor had declared himself a protector of Protestantism in the Holy Land. This role was certainly reaverred by the consecration of the Church of the Redeemer. But, in order to divide French influence in this area and perhaps to split the protectorate up according to nationalities, William II did not neglect any opportunity to pose as protector of the German Catholics as well. He repeatedly promised his support to all German nationals, regardless of their confession.

Such open thrusts against the sacrosanctity of the French protectorate engendered an almost hysterical response from Germany's western neighbor. The following example appeared in the influential *Revue des deux mondes:*

> Germany has military power, she has economic power, but she needs the support of moral forces: on the world's stage, she is ambitious to represent a principle. To base its universal preeminence on the protection of Protestant and Catholic Christianity, to link the main shafts of German influence to a double religious protectorate, to have in that part of the world a clientele which is both religious and economic who will spread German ideas, buy German products and who, while confessing the gospel of Christ, will extol "the gospel of the sacred person of the Emperor," such are the maxims which presently direct the policy of William II.[6]

But once again the papacy stood in the breach. On the eve of the Kaiser's visit to the Holy Land, the Vatican was on the verge of accepting diplomatic representation from the Porte, a move which would have implied that France was no longer competent to defend the church's interests in the empire. Delcassé, in his first foreign policy success, moved to avert this development. He consulted with Cardinal Langénieux at Reims, who in turn wrote to Leo XIII assuring the latter of France's continued interest in and zeal for the protectorate. The pope replied favorably on 20 August 1898 to the effect that "France has a mission in the Orient which has been confided to her by Providence: a noble mission which has been consecrated not only by secular practice but also by international treaties as well as being recognized by Our Congregation of Propaganda by its declaration of 22 May 1888."[7] The papal pronouncement occurred three months before the Kaiser's visit to the Holy Land, but it was clearly a statement in favor of the French protectorate and consequently against the German ambition to split the protectorate according to nationalities. Three years later a French diplomat in Constantinople, Edmond Bapst, acknowledged that "Germany is the country which today possesses the greatest influence on the Ottoman Government. She owes this advantage first of all to the belief . . . that she is the first military power in the world, but more to the considerable ascendancy which her sovereign has over the Sultan." But in spite of this position, Bapst continued, Germany's influence among the Catholics of Asia Minor was in its infancy.[8]

It was clear, therefore, that before 1901 France possessed a powerful ally in the papacy. And this ally had twice sided with France when other European powers had sought to break her monopoly on the protectorate. But how long could such an alliance continue in light of the anticlerical policies followed by the French government at home? How long could other ambitious powers be kept at bay? France had asserted her position successfully in the Lorando-Tubini affair of 1901, but she was destined not to emerge unscathed from the next Middle Eastern incident, which was not long in coming.

On 4 November 1901 an altercation took place between Orthodox and Latin monks at the Holy Sepulcher in Jerusalem. The dispute involved the question of which group had the right to sweep certain areas of a subsidiary chapel in the edifice. Latin monks claimed the right, while the Orthodox denied it; neither side had clear proof.[9] The sweeping incident itself was of little importance so far as the Great Powers were concerned. What mattered was that it involved Latin monks of various nationalities. According to French sources, the Greeks were the aggressors, and fifteen Latin monks of French, German, English, Spanish, Russian, Dutch, and Syrian nationality were wounded in the altercation.[10] The French consul general in Jerusalem set in motion the procedures of French protection.

The controversy dragged on in low key for some months until, on 8 March 1902, Ambassador Constans reported that the German and Italian ambassadors at Constantinople had sent a note to the Porte which recognized French rights in the religious protectorate, but demanded the right to intervene alone, without France, on behalf of their own nationals involved in the incident at the Holy Sepulcher. Constans reported that the Porte would probably agree to the demands and went on to say that "the Treaty of Berlin gives their consuls the rights which my German and Italian colleagues claim." France, therefore, ought to accede to this view, since "it would be better to adhere to my colleagues' demands, which seem well-founded, while reserving categorically our rights in all other instances, than to expose ourselves to a decision of Ottoman authority which will certainly be contrary to our interests."[11] The French ambassador further clarified his argument on 28 April 1902 by pointing out that the Porte was currently under considerable pressure from Baron Adolf Marschall von Bieberstein, the German ambassador at Constantinople, to recognize Germany's right to protect her own clerical nationals.[12]

Delcassé, however, was in no mood to sacrifice any of the predominance he had won in November 1901. He rejected the wise counsel of his ambassador, notifying the latter that French intervention on behalf of the Latin monks was in conformity with Article 62 of the Treaty of Berlin. Constans should, therefore, make it clear at the Porte that France would accept no procedure which allocated to the consul at Jerusalem a role inferior to that of his colleagues.[13]

The whole argument was based on the interpretation of Article 62 of the Treaty of Berlin. This article granted the same rights, advantages, and privileges to ecclesiastics, pilgrims, and monks of all nationalities in Turkey. But the controversy stemmed from an apparent contradiction between paragraphs 6 and 7 of Article 62. Paragraph 6 stated: "The right of official protection by the Diplomatic and Consular Agents of the Powers in Turkey is recognized both as regards the above-mentioned persons and their religious, charitable, and other establishments in the Holy Places and elsewhere." On the other hand, paragraph 7 maintained that "the rights possessed by France are expressly reserved, and it is well-understood that no alterations can be made in the *status quo* in the Holy Places."[14] Both France and Germany and Italy appeared to have a legal basis for their claims in the matter of protecting the Latin monks, depending upon which paragraph was emphasized.

The matter remained in abeyance until 17 April 1902, when the grand vizier, Tewfik Pasha, informed Constans that Turkey had acceded to German demands concerning her exclusive protection over German nationals in the dispute over privileges at the Holy Sepulcher. The inquest into the incident concerning the German monks would be heard only by the German consul in Jerusalem. No decision had yet been made concerning Italian monks, but Constans did not see how the Porte could act differently with them than it had done with the Germans.[15] Constans was right. Several days later the Turkish government made a similar decision in favor of the Italian monks injured in the scuffle at the Holy Sepulcher. In both instances France protested in formal terms, basing her action upon the Treaty of Berlin.[16]

Italy made her position in the matter quite clear in conversations between Foreign Minister Giulio Prinetti and French Ambassador Barrère. The latter reported on 9 May 1902 that Prinetti had assured him that "while he recognized the right of the French protectorate over religious collectivities, the Royal Government could not disinterest itself in the protection of Italian clerical subjects taken individually."[17] This was the first time that the difference between collectivities and individuals had been expressed, and the logic of the Italian position appeared impeccable. No government could survive if it refused aid to citizens soliciting it.

Delcassé, however, maintained his recalcitrant position, despite urgings from his ambassador at Constantinople to recognize the contradiction in Article 62 and give up French opposition in the matter. Even the *Direction politique* of the Quai d'Orsay, in a memorandum to Delcassé dated 5 June 1902, concluded realistically that "we cannot, in fact, normally protect foreign nationals against their will."[18] The foreign minister responded to such advice in October 1902 by saying: "Our right does not derive only from such and such an article—often very poorly defined—of

treaties with the Porte or with Europe; it has above all been forti-
fied by usage, developed by the interpretation which has been
conceded to us by Turkey, recognized as a kind of monopoly by
the Holy See."[19] Here indeed was an implied recognition by
Delcassé of the contradiction in Article 62. He was clearly grasp-
ing at straws in an attempt to preserve an exclusive French
position in the Holy Land by abandoning the firm ground of
treaties to tread the thin ice of "usage."

But by the time this statement was issued, six months had
elapsed since Turkey had accorded Germany and Italy the right
to intervene on behalf of their monks involved in the incident at
the Holy Sepulcher. There had been no *pronunciamento* from the
papacy upholding French rights as there had been in 1888 and
again in 1898. The price of an anticlerical policy at home had
been paid abroad. Nor were the other powers any longer willing to
see France intervene alone in Asiatic Turkey. France was in an
untenable position. She could clearly do nothing about the
German and Italian initiative in the Holy Land. She therefore
sought to extricate herself at the first face-saving opportunity.

That opportunity came in early November 1902, when Turkey
acknowledged that the custody of two places in the Holy Land,
the Grotto of the Agony and the Garden of Olives, belonged to
the Order of the Franciscan Fathers.[20] The Franciscans were
French protégés; therefore, the Grotto and the Garden were
annexed to the list of French-protected establishments agreed to
by the Porte as a result of the Mitylene intervention of 1901. This
victory could be but small consolation to Delcassé, who, on 10
November 1902, relinquished France's right to protect the
missions in Asiatic Turkey in the name of each of their members.
In a dispatch to Constantinople he wrote, "we recognize that our
official intervention in favor of non-French missionaries applies
only to the acts accomplished by them in their role as missionaries." There was thus a distinction made between the missionary
and the individual, the same distinction outlined by Prinetti six
months earlier. France would protect the foreigner as a missionary while the individual could be protected by his nation in whatever measure he wished his nation to intervene. Delcassé saw this
interpretation as "far from being a diminution of our preroga-

tives. . . ."[21] Actually, it was hard to see it as anything but a diminution of France's position in the Orient. Despite Delcassé's brave words, Italy and Germany had successfully challenged France, just one year after her impressive diplomatic victory at Mitylene.

One of the principal reasons France could afford such a surrender to Italy and Germany in the Holy Land was that her protectorate in Syria was not as yet being severely threatened. In the heat of the controversy concerning the Holy Sepulcher, Delcassé received the following dispatch from Consul General Sercey in Beirut: "I do not believe we have to worry too much about Italian actions in this area. . . ."[22] But in spite of such sanguine pronouncements from the major area of French missionary concentration, the years after 1902 show an increasing concern with Italian penetration. The record shows, however, that the German threat to French missionary preponderance was regarded as virtually a negligible factor. Throughout 1903 there were periodic warnings from French representatives in the Levant against the Italian menace. The Quai d'Orsay was informed from Jerusalem, Constantinople, Beirut, and even the Vatican that the best way to avoid jeopardizing the French missionary establishments was to grant increased subsidies and credit allocations to them. This, the diplomats argued, would mute the virulent effects of domestic anticlerical activities abroad.[23]

It was ironic that the French suspicion of Italian activity in the Levant should develop simultaneously with the important rapprochement between the two countries as a result of the accords of 1902, which pledged neutrality should either nation be the victim of aggression by a third power. But even more ironic is the fact that the development of this rapprochement led indirectly to France's severing diplomatic relations with the Holy See and the subsequent complete separation of church and state. The latter development opened the door even wider for Italian activity in Asiatic Turkey. In July 1904 the Vatican objected to a proposed official visit of French President Emile Loubet to the Italian king in Rome, viewing the trip as an affront to the church, which had never recognized Italian annexation of the city. When Paris refused to accede to the pope's request to cancel the Loubet visit, the Vatican began the harassment of two French bishops, threatening to suspend them if they did not appear in Rome to answer charges of freemasonry. The Quai d'Orsay retaliated by protesting to the Vatican that such action was in violation of the 1802 concordat which forbade any direct participation by the pope in affairs of the Gallican church.[24] On 29 July 1904 official relations were broken off between Paris and the Vatican.

It is important to note, however, that the only three ministers to oppose the rupture of diplomatic relations with the papacy were Delcassé, Finance Minister Maurice Rouvier, and the minister of public instruction.[25] It was precisely these three officials who were most concerned with the preservation of French influence in the Levant. Indeed it will become clear that the Quai d'Orsay consistently opposed anticlerical policies abroad and always supported increased allocations to missionary establishments in the Orient. Two days after the breaking off of relations with the Holy See, Delcassé notified his representatives in Constantinople and Cairo that "your instructions have not been changed, since our rights are based above all on our treaties with Turkey. . . ."[26] He was presumably referring primarily to the list of French-protected establishments outlined in the 1901 agreement with the Porte.

Delcassé was also concerned about the apparent attempt of Italian agents in the Middle East to use the French break with Rome as a lever for dislodging France from her position vis-à-vis the Catholics in the Levant. Such warnings arrived in Paris from French representatives at the Quirinal. They also included an extract from a French-language newspaper, *L'Italie,* dated 20 May 1902, which stated that "France has had, until recently, a powerful ally in the Vatican. By its hatred for Italy and the Triple Alliance, Papal diplomacy has been forced to continue France's secular privileges. But it is quite certain that the anti-clerical policy of the republican government has cooled the zeal of the Holy See in this matter. And that also proves to us that the French protectorate is fatally doomed."[27] Under the influence of such information. Delcassé ordered Barrère to persuade Italy "to dissipate these apprehensions by obtaining from the Italian Government the disavowal of all antagonism between our two Governments in the Orient and its adhesion to instructions limiting the zeal of her agents to respect for the *status quo.*"[28] In August 1904 the Quirinal sent such an instruction to Italian agents in the Levant, although no mention was made of French rights based on treaties.[29]

Despite the concern of the foreign ministry to preserve French influence among all Catholics in the Levant, there is some evidence in secondary literature of the time to suggest that French diplomats were not always careful in all areas of this policy. French consuls were accused of discriminating against Catholic missionaries from Italy and Germany. Whereas previously these missionaries would have sought sympathy and support from the French consuls, they now were turning more frequently to their own national consuls.[30]

That such accusations were well founded can be inferred from the fact that in the early months of 1905 two Catholic orders, predominantly Italian in membership but officially protégés of France according to the 1901 list, petitioned the Sublime Porte to transfer their allegiance to the Italian embassy. One of the orders, the *Frères Mineurs Conventuels,* was located in Constantinople, and its loss, therefore, was not regarded too seriously by the Quai d'Orsay. But the petition of the *Salésiens,* located in Palestine, struck more directly at French interests in Asia Minor. Italy had championed the requests of both orders, and in the summer of 1905 placed considerable pressure on the Porte to transfer the missionary groups in question to Italian protection. The Turkish government adopted the diplomatically correct attitude that it had no fundamental objection to seeing the establishments fall under Italian tutelege. Because of the 1901 Mitylene agreement with France, however, Turkey could not unilaterally assign a French protégé to the Italians. The grand vizier suggested that this was a matter which must be taken up directly between the Italian and French governments.[31] The Quai d'Orsay, however, took the position that France must resolutely refuse to modify the 1901 list of French-protected establishments. This decision was predicated upon three assumptions: (1) that modifying the list of 1901 would give the Porte the impression that French protection was revocable and temporary; (2) that among the Levantine populations, the transfer of the *Salésiens* would be viewed as weakness and the beginning of the abandonment of France's religious protectorate; and (3) that for Italy the *Salésiens* would be the first *international* establishment to be officially protected by her. Such precedents would be dangerous.[32]

In Constantinople, therefore, Ambassador Constans refused all modifications in the list of 1901. But in a dispatch to Delcassé on 16 May 1905, he hinted that, in light of the cordial relations then existing between Italy and France, the Italian foreign minister might be "well-disposed to resolve the difficulties amiably. . . ."[33] Exactly why the Quai d'Orsay decided to settle this matter in a friendly and rapid manner with Italy is not made clear in the French sources. Some guesses, however, can be made. For one thing the Moroccan crisis was in full swing, and Maurice Rouvier replaced Delcassé as foreign minister in mid-June 1905. Another factor may well have been the reports arriving in Paris affirming that in the Lebanon and Syria, the areas where French missionary activity was densest, the Maronites and Catholics had remained completely loyal to France, and the threat of Italian penetration remained minimal.[34]

In any case an agreement resolving the difficulty was hammered out between the Italian foreign minister and the French chargé d'affaires in Rome on 30-31 August 1905. In a *note verbale* Tommaso Tittoni wrote that Italy would look favorably upon all requests for protection made to her "spontaneously" by "Italian religious collectivities" in the Ottoman Empire, placed until then under the protection of France. But the transfer of protection would be made only after "previous notification" of the French government. In exchange for this guarantee France consigned the *Salésiens* of Palestine and the *Mineurs Conventuels* of Constantinople to Italian protection.[35] As previously suggested this agreement, in fact a concession to Italy, was probably dictated by international events as they existed in mid-1905. In later years this Franco-Italian accord received energetic criticism from private observers and from the Quai d'Orsay as well. A Foreign Office note dated 17 March 1913 maintained that the agreement of 30-31 August 1905 "is equivalent to the abandonment and to the sacrifice of our privileged situation," which if not remedied "will be sufficient to assure the hegemony of Italy in

Asiatic Turkey." Maurice Pernot, editor of the *Journal des débats*, after traveling through the Middle East in 1913, observed: "There was in the Levant, before 1905, only a single 'protectorate': the French protectorate. We ourselves have invented an 'Italian protectorate.'"[36]

But if France appeared willing to make concessions to Italy in Constantinople and Palestine, where the interests of her missionaries appeared marginal, she retained her intransigence in regard to Syria. In 1903 the Turkish sultan had questioned Constans on what the former regarded as a loss of French prestige in Syria. Constans reported to Paris that he did not take so somber a view of French influence in Syria but that it was indeed necessary "to give the Syrians material proof of our resources and of the interest which we have in their country."[37] This interest can be inferred from the fact that in 1905, while the three *Salésien* establishments at Jerusalem were transferred to Italian protection, the one at Nazareth, under the circumscription of the consul general at Beirut, remained under French jurisdiction. The loyalty of this orphanage was maintained as the result of diplomatic pressure and a 1000-franc allocation made by the French government.[38] A similar development took place in the midst of the *Salésien* controversy concerning the French Trappists of Cheikhle (in northern Syria). They had threatened to sell their agricultural establishments to German Trappists, but after vigorous urging by French diplomats, the general of the Trappist order "promised that the cession will not be made."[39] No greater contrast in attitude could be imagined than that between these last two examples and French policy regarding the non-Syrian-based *Conventuels* and *Salésiens*.

As long as the French-protected establishments in Syria and Lebanon were not seriously threatened, France took no measures to strengthen the protectorate over all the Uniate Christians of the empire or to repair the damage to French prestige among them as a result of the rupture of diplomatic relations with the papacy. Consular reports from Syria lulled Paris into a sense of security. From the consul general in Beirut came word in May 1906 that "the prosperity of our works is *not threatened* there. . . . Italy has made *no progress*."[40] A year later the consulate in Damascus replied in negative terms to a query about Italy's desire to create a protectorate there. "The different Christian communities [he reported] have always been very attached to us. . . . Their own interests order them to remain faithful to us. Italy inspires no confidence."[41]

The defection of religious orders like the *Conventuels* and *Salésiens* was not, however, ignored by the Quai d'Orsay. French statesmen realized that defections like these caused much inconvenience for French national influence, because these orders, it was felt, would lead the vanguard in opposing the opening of French schools or would create Italian schools right beside them.[42] The matter of ecclesiastical schools was of vital importance in spreading French language and culture in the Orient. In the latter part of the nineteenth century, the French government subsidized these schools more heavily than ever before, a portion of the yearly foreign affairs budget being allocated to ecclesiasitical subventions. French statistics show that in 1901, in Syria alone (that is the *vilayets* of Damascus, Aleppo, Beirut, and Lebanon), there were 473 French-subsidized congregational schools comprising 40,144 students.[43] This overwhelming concentration can be judged by the fact that according to 1904 figures, there were 526 French-subsidized clerical schools with 58,367 students in all of Asiatic Turkey.[44]

These totals represent numbers vastly superior to the educational penetration of any other European country in Asiatic Turkey. But missionaries from these other powers were making headway and founding numerous schools, particularly after the turn of the century. France's anticlericalism and her break with the Vatican spurred the creation of rival educational establishments in the Levant, as other powers, particularly Italy, began to urge their missionaries to fill whatever void might have been created in the minds of Middle Eastern Christians. France could also expect Turkey to use the anticlerical issue to balk at granting authorizations for new French missionary schools. Chargé d'affaires Edmond Bapst informed Delcassé in 1902 that "we must realize . . . that the Porte, in response to our . . . *démarches,* will answer by feigning astonishment at the fact that the Embassy accords its patronage to missionaries struck down by law in

France and seeks to reconstitute here what has been dissolved at home; and certainly it would not be without strong pressure and lengthy difficulties that we would succeed in obtaining the desired authorization."[45]

Opposition to French missionary education was manifested not only abroad but at home as well. A private group called the *Mission laïque* was founded to encourage the spread of French lay instruction abroad. The Chamber of Deputies became the focus of a "lay-clerical debate" concerning the schools in the Orient. Each year during the budget session dealing with Foreign Office allocations to French establishments, a debate between rival pro- and anticlerical factions ensued. The session of 26 November 1904 was fairly typical. Anticlerical speakers such as Fernand Dubief and M. Coulondre took the floor to deplore the whole proselytizing nature of religious schools and to demand that the entire 800,000 franc budget for schools in the Levant be set aside for the existing lay schools there and to encourage the founding of new ones. This policy, they argued, was the only one consistent with France's break with the Vatican. These arguments were rebutted at considerable length by proclerical spokesmen Jules Delafosse and Denys Cochin, after which Delcassé took the floor to explain the position of the Quai d'Orsay. In a short, impassioned speech he cited his support for the *principle* of lay education. But he said it would take time to create a sufficient number of lay schools to justify the allocation of the entire budget to them, and in the meantime France must conserve her religious influence. Delcassé argued that to deny subsidies to clerical schools would be equivalent to closing them. "Don't oblige me . . . to sacrifice these 300 schools which need our aid and which lead by the hand the 80,000 children [*sic*] who attend them, who are speaking French at this moment, who are impregnated with French ideas, who are growing up in the shadow of the French flag. . . ." Even Prime Minister Emile Combes, an anticlerical leader, agreed with his foreign minister, urging that the protectorate and the separation of church and state be regarded as separate issues. The protectorate, he argued, was not a question of domestic policy but rather "a question of foreign policy, which concerns the previous agreement of the French Government with foreign

Governments. Even after the Chamber will have voted the separation, the treaties concluded on the subject of the protectorate will remain in force."[46] It might well be pointed out that, compared to the figures cited by Delcassé for clerical schools, there were in 1901 only seven French lay schools in all of the Ottoman Empire, with a total enrollment of 718 students.[47]

The position of the Foreign Ministry was to change very little between 1904 and 1914. It always remained a staunch champion of the protectorate and the ecclesiastical schools. But the Quai d'Orsay did not want to antagonize the very influential anti-clerical forces at home; hence, its continued adhesion to the "principle" of the progressive transferral to lay education in the Orient. Even before the formal break with the Vatican, there is evidence to suggest that the Foreign Ministry was at least paying lip service to the expansion of lay education in the Levant. In a dispatch sent to Paris in 1902 by Bapst, the French chargé in Constantinople, and later submitted in a formal report to President Emile Loubet, the former praised highly the accomplishments of French missionary schools. But he concluded: "To develop these establishments, along with our lay schools equally worthy of being unreservedly praised, would be one of the best means of advancing our expansion in this country."[48]

As the figures show, however, the great concentration of French ecclesiastical educational activity was in Syria. So long as French preponderance in this area was unthreatened, the Foreign Ministry felt itself relatively safe in not muting the anticlerical criticism of the protectorate too much. Consular reports in 1906 concerning the schools told much the same story as those dealing with the other aspects of the missionary activity of foreign powers in Asiatic Turkey. They warned of the increasing Italian initiative but reported that Italian schools were making very little progress in Syria and were not a threat to French influence there.[49] But it cannot be denied that the lay-clerical debate prejudiced French influence and prestige among Catholics in the Levant. In subsequent years the disaffection was to spread even to Syria. This development, and the French reaction to it between 1906 and the outbreak of World War I, will form the basis of the next chapter.

5 THE PROTECTORATE: PART 2

The main issues in the "lay-clerical debate" concerning the missionary schools subsidized by France in the Levant are fairly clear. Those who favored continued governmental sponsorship cited facts and figures showing the extent of missionary educational activity among the Christians of Asiatic Turkey. To cut off subsidies, they argued, would be to imperil this whole aspect of French influence in the area. On the other hand, anticlerical leaders deplored the strictly religious nature of these schools and argued that subsidies should be devoted to the creation of lay schools in the Levant. The critics argued that clerical schools ignored the great masses of Muslims, while lay institutions would create Francophile sympathies among this majority element.

In an attempt to resolve the debate the foreign ministry commissioned Marcel Charlot, the French inspector general of primary education, to go the Middle East in the summer of 1906 to study French schools there. Since Foreign Minister Léon Bourgeois was an anticlerical figure disposed to cut subsidies to ecclesiastical schools in the Levant, one might expect Charlot's report to reflect the foreign minister's opinion. And to an extent it did; but not nearly so much as the opponents of all clerical subventions had hoped. Charlot's report, which appeared on 26 October 1906, did indeed note the important impact that French mission schools had had in the Levant, recognizing their service to French moral influence in that area. But he emphasized that the clerical contribution to French moral influence lay "in the past," implying that mission schools were out of date in 1906. He made several biting references to the "superannuated pedagogy" of the ecclesiastical schools and then raised the crucial question. Could France, in the twentieth century, when French predominance in the Levant was being questioned and challenged, continue to rely heavily on the missionary schools? He concluded that "the congregational school today can no longer completely fill the role [that it had filled in the past]." Charlot's main criticism of ecclesiastical schools was their tendency toward proselytism, which alienated the majority non-Catholics. But in spite of these allegations, Charlot's proposals for the future were not at all revolutionary. He recommended the suppression of state aid to clerical schools which persisted in proselytism but "to maintain the subvention to the others to the extent that they continue to serve French interests." He also called for the founding of new lay schools where no other French schools were then in existence and the orientation of their curriculum in such a manner as to emphasize not only French language but local history and geography as well. He also urged a more rigorous religious tolerance.[1]

Charlot's report is interesting because it resolved nothing. Proponents of both sides of the controversy were able to cite extracts of the report to support their respective positions. The debate continued. Support for the anticlerical accusations against missionary schools can be found in various document collections. In February 1904 Bapst informed Delcassé from Constantinople that of the 67,773 students enrolled in subsidized missionary schools in Asiatic Turkey, 50,462 were Catholic. In Syria, an area of prime concern for France, the figures were as follows:[2]

Main cities in Syria	Number of students	Number of Catholics
Aleppo (including Alexandretta)	2,153	1,873
Damascus	3,884	3,670
Beirut (including Lebanon and Tripoli-in-Syria)	32,000	27,000

These figures give a great deal of credence to the claims of the *Mission laïque* and its supporters that clerical schools had no appeal to Muslims, or that they discriminated against Muslims. The effect was the same in either case. French documents for 1913 also show a letter to the Quai d'Orsay from a Muslim citizen of Damascus urging the creation of lay schools in that predominantly Muslim section of the country.[3] British documents include a translation into French of certain passages from an Arabic book called *Irchad-ul-Hayara*. The Muslim author expressed his distaste for clerical schools in the following pungent manner: "Any Muslim who sends his son to the Christian schools exposes him to the most serious perils. . . . The sending by a Muslim of his son to the Christian schools, with the possibility of learning the Christian religion and sharing their cult, is such a serious action that it surpasses all commentary and is similar to the conduct of an individual who commits adultery with a woman in public."[4]

Spokesmen for lay schools in the Levant argued that the clerical schools alienated not only Muslims, but Christian schismatics as well. They cited figures illustrating that English, German, and American lay schools had been successful in attracting a diversified cross section of local populations. Their primary example of the direction in which they wished to orient French educational penetration was the College of Beirut, founded in 1909 by the *Mission laïque*. By 1911 the college enrolled 245 students, whose religious affiliations were as follows: fourteen Catholic Latins, eight Greek Catholics, twelve Maronites, two Protestants, five Armenian Catholics, one hundred Muslims, fifty-five Israelites, forty-three Greek Orthodox, three Druzes, and three Armenian Orthodox. This type of diversification could not be found among any of the French clerical schools.[5]

But the supporters of clerical schools were in no mood to submit. One hopeful sign for a compromise in the paralyzing debate, however, began to develop after 1907. Some French writers began to urge the simultaneous development of both lay and clerical schools. One author described as "well-founded" the criticism that Catholic schools failed completely to attract a Muslim clientele. But he dismissed as nonsense the idea that such conditions would change if all the confessional schools were to become purely *laïque*. Such a development might attract a few more Muslims, but France would certainly lose her whole Catholic clientele. He maintained that the error of the anticlericals "is to want to suppress the Catholic schools in order to benefit the others. The two types of institutions can very well coexist in the same cities."[6] These views were not isolated ones. As a matter of fact they became the "official" position of the proclerical forces in the lay-clerical debate over the schools. This really did not represent a weakening in the clerical ranks, since their proponents all tended to reserve the important field of primary and secondary education exclusively to the missionary schools. They urged the *Mission laïque* to concentrate on the development of higher education and technical instruction in the Levant.[7]

The proclerical school camp also had influential allies in the French consular representatives in the Levant. In May 1906 the consul general in Jerusalem reported that French religious schools and hospitals in Jaffa and Ramleh had had "fortunate effects from the point of view of our influence in this country where we have to struggle concurrently against similar foreign works. . . ."[8] On 10 June 1907 consul general Fouques-Duparc wrote to Paris in laudatory terms about the work of the clerical schools in Lebanon and Beirut. He said: "We must not hide from the fact that the creation of lay schools in the Lebanon will attract not only the hostility of the local clergy . . . but also the hostility of foreigners. . . ." The development of a purely lay instruction in the Mountain would provoke, among the foreigners, new [academic] foundations, which would thus increase our chances of failure." Fouques-Duparc recommended increased government allocations to ecclesiastical schools in his circumscription.[9] The consul general substantially repeated this evaluation in a dispatch to Paris on 21 September 1907.[10]

Ambassador Constans added a further dimension to the continued diplomatic support for clerical schools by linking the lay-clerical debate to the matter of the protectorate. On 21 November 1906, he notified Foreign Minister Stéphen Pichon that "it is necessary to realize the fact . . . that our projects of laicisation, which favor the religious propaganda of the Italians, are far from pleasing to Ottoman authorities." Constans explained that the latter feared the introduction of "modern ideas" in Oriental schools, and consequently could be expected to oppose the opening of new lay schools. The effect, therefore, of a continued French emphasis on lay education in the Levant would be to encourage the Turks to look favorably upon Italian designs to establish a sizable protectorate at French expense.[11]

It must be realized that Christians did form a majority of the population in Mount Lebanon. And with advice such as that cited above against the establishment of lay schools in areas vital to French interest, it is no wonder that the Quai d'Orsay hesitated to yield completely to the demands of the anticlerical faction at home. This attitude can be seen clearly in the Chamber of Deputies debates. On 12 December 1906 anticlerical deputy Fernand Dubief put forward a resolution to the effect that governmental subsidies to ecclesiastical schools in the Ottoman Empire be gradually discontinued over a six-year period. At the end of six years the entire budget would then be devoted to the expansion of lay education. Foreign Minister Pichon, just as Delcassé had done in 1904, proclaimed his support for the principle of lay education. But he urged the deputies to defeat Dubief's resolution on the grounds that such a time limit would deny the necessary flexibility to French policy and would result in the immediate closure of many Catholic schools, for which there simply were not enough lay schools to take their places. The consequences of such a development would be that Italian and German schools would rush in to fill the void. Dubief withdrew his resolution, but only after the Chamber voted another resolution counting on "the determination of the Government to favor the progressive and prompt substitution of lay instruction for confessional instruction in the Orient."[12] The sentiment in the Chamber was clear, but Pichon had circumvented the movement to deny subventions to missionary schools. In the years which followed, the Quai d'Orsay continued this practice, securing annual increases in the foreign affairs budget for subsidizing educational establishments, but with gradually increasing percentage amounts devoted to lay schools. But no time limit for the complete substitution of lay for clerical schools was ever adopted, and by far the largest part of the budget continued to be earmarked for clerical schools.[13]

The main issues in the lay-clerical debate concerning the

schools in the Levant were clear. So were the attitudes of the spokesmen for both sides. Very few were concerned about the native peoples. They spoke of the best methods of spreading French influence, language, and culture in the classic imperialist manner. As it turned out, the lay-clerical debate concerning the schools was never resolved before the outbreak of World War I. But it is understandable how such conflicting methods and general acrimony at home would alienate both Christians and non-Christians in Asiatic Turkey. This bitter fruit was harvested in the postwar era.

Perhaps France's activity in postwar Syria would have been less objectionable had her prewar statesmen, instead of engaging in a fruitless lay-clerical debate, heeded thoughtful observers such as Jules Harmand. Harmand, writing in 1910, was not concerned about the debate on colonial education, but with the effectiveness of the instruction itself. He denounced the emphasis placed upon spreading French language and culture in the primary schools. This could better be reserved for higher education, while local languages should be taught at the primary level. In any case Harmand maintained that emphasis on the French language should only be made in areas where extensive contact between Frenchmen and natives existed. In the hinterland such emphasis was useless, indeed harmful, since the populations became hostile and frustrated by losing deep contact with their own culture. Harmand also stressed the "responsibility" of the dominating power to learn the local languages, an excellent way to build up respect among native peoples. He also advanced the notion that professional, technical, and agricultural instruction was a good deal more important than literature and language.[14]

These were controversial suggestions, especially so in the charged atmosphere of 1910, but ones which made a great deal of sense. There is little evidence to suggest, however, that much of this advice was applied in the prewar period (except perhaps for a growing awareness of the need for technical schools). Much of what men like Harmand had to say was swallowed up in the lay-clerical debate and the competition in spreading language at the primary school level. Harmand, unfortunately for France, was a voice crying in the wilderness.

Anticlericalism at home was thus hurting French prestige in the Orient, as the defection from the French protectorate of the *Salésiens* and *Conventuels* had revealed. Perhaps more important, however, was the fact that Italy continued to use the rupture of relations between France and the Vatican as a lever to propel herself into a stronger moral position among Levantine Christians. On 4 September 1906 Ambassador Constans notified Paris from Constantinople that consular reports indicated that Italian agents were not adhering to the 1905 agreement to maintain the status quo regarding the French protectorate. Constans' somber view was reflected in this statement. "We are witnessing at the present time, in spite of all the assurances from Rome, the reconciliation between the Holy See and the Quirinal—at our expense. I believe it my duty to state that . . . the attitude of the agents of this power, since our rupture of relations with the Holy See, will lead, if we are not careful, to the ruin of our traditional and moral position in the Orient."[15] Paul Cambon's correspondence reveals a similar pessimism about the future of the French protectorate as well as a considerable bitterness toward the French government for its apparent lack of enthusiasm in this respect.[16]

Le Temps, often used as a mouthpiece for the Quai d'Orsay, observed editorially that France's religious policy was bound to have certain repercussions on her exterior policy. The transfer of the *Conventuels* and *Salésiens* to Italian protection was a good example. The article concluded thus: "The suppression of all intermediaries between France and the Holy See . . . has rendered the exercise of the protectorate in the Orient precarious. And without doubt unpleasant surprises in this matter have not reached an end."[17] An indication of the increasingly hazardous position of the protectorate occurred in April 1909. In that month the Hamidian counter-revolution made an attempt to recoup the powers of the sultan, usurped by the Young Turks during the previous year. It failed, however, and its defeat and the deposition of Sultan Abdul Hamid II were accompanied by a recrudescence of anti-Christian feeling among the Muslims of the Ottoman Empire. In early May a bloody massacre of Armenians took place in Cilicia, casualties being estimated at from 20,000 to 30,000. The question of protection for Christians was again to the fore, and the attitude of the Vatican was important. But Pichon notified Constans on 11 May 1909 that his sources indicated that the Vatican "regrets that the rupture with the Government of the Republic prevents the Holy See from soliciting the preponderant intervention of French protection and from ordering its missionaries to make appeal . . . to the exclusive action of French representatives."[18] Granted, the papacy did not endorse the exclusive protection of any other power, but the fact that the missionaries, with papal blessing, could direct their appeals to any nation could well lead to inconvenient problems among the various powers. France's position had indeed slipped from the place allocated to it by the papal encyclicals of 1888 and 1898.

But even more disturbing to the Quai d'Orsay must have been the fact that the years 1910 and 1911 were filled with reports from the various consulates and vice-consulates in Syria warning of the increased activity of Italian missionaries in their circumscriptions. Notes from Aleppo told of the increasingly unstable position of the French-protected Carmelite establishments of Alexandretta. Notices from Beirut alerted Paris to the possible transfer of the Syrian Capuchins from French to Italian protection.[19] The dispatch from Consul General Piat in Damascus to Pichon on 12 December 1910 was characteristic of the new, more somber appraisal of the protectorate in Syria vis-à-vis Italy. Speaking of Italy's intention to create a new hospital, chapel, and school at Damascus, Piat concluded: "I am convinced that Italy is presently seeking to play an important, if not preponderant, role in Syria."[20] In short, gone were the confident dispatches of the first half of the decade, which spoke of the security of the French protectorate and the lack of Italian progress in Syria, the area of major concern to France.

The real test of France's position there came in 1911, involving a Franco-Italian diplomatic imbroglio lasting from mid-April to mid-August. The spark was ignited on 10 April 1911, when the French vice-consul at Tripoli-in-Syria received a letter from the superior of the Carmelite missions in Syria announcing the decision of the order "to place its missionaries, its schools, its property, and all its works under the protection of the Italian Government. . . ."[21] This action did not affect all the Carmelites in Syria. Between 1906 and 1908 the order had split in half, and it was the predominantly Italian groups at Tripoli-in-Syria, Alexandretta, Kobbayet, Beylan, and Bicharra which in 1911 sought to escape the French protectorate. The rest of the Carmelites at Mount Carmel, Haiffa, and Saint-Jean d'Acre remained loyal to France. Nevertheless, the action of the Italian Carmelites was the first serious attempt of a Syrian-based religious order to escape the patronage of France.

Because no specific grievances were listed by the Carmelites as reasons for leaving the French protectorate, many observers, including the French consul general at Beirut, speculated that the Carmelites must have requested a subsidy from either the Italian government or a private patriotic group called the Italian National Association. Either source probably made any subsidy contingent upon the abandonment of the French protectorate. M. Couget in Beirut informed Foreign Minister Jean Cruppi on 21 April 1911 that the Carmelites' decision "seems more and more to have been provoked by the 'Italian National Association'. . . . It would thus appear that the 'Italian National Association' is presently conducting in Syria a rather extensive activity, the evident purpose of which is to smash [*battre en brèche*] our traditional influence."[22] Ambassador Barrère in Rome underlined the main point even more emphatically in a dispatch to the Quai d'Orsay on 30 July 1911. He referred to the Italian National Association and pointed out that while it was not being encouraged by the Holy See, the latter was at least tolerating its activities. And thus this society was "strongly attacking our protectorate where it was most important for us to maintain it, where it had never before been contested, in Syria and in the Lebanon."[23]

With her protectorate in Syria placed in peril for the first time, France moved into action. Cruppi wrote to Barrère in Rome deploring the action of the Italian National Association, contrasting it with France's effacement before Italian ambitions in Tripolitania (a statement which speaks volumes about France's ambitions in Syria). This contrast, he said, "can justify on our part a friendly remark [the word *démarche* had been stricken out and *remarque* inserted] to the Royal Government recalling to it our special position in Syria."[24] Four days later, on 12 May 1911,

Cruppi ordered his ambassador in Constantinople, Maurice Bompard, to instruct his consulates to treat the delegates of the Holy See well and "to give a really benevolent character to their actions in favor of the missions protected by us. . . ."[25] Bompard responded on 4 June that such instructions had been sent.[26]

France officially took the position that the transfer of the Carmelites of Syria from French to Italian protection was contrary to the Franco-Italian accord of 30-31 August 1905, which stipulated that transference could be made only with the previous consent of France.[27] In Rome on 19 May Barrère appealed to Italian Foreign Minister Marquis de San Giuliano concerning "our special situation in Syria" and France's "moral protectorate." San Giuliano in essence agreed that the Carmelite action was in violation of the 1905 agreement but pointed out that the matter had become one of honor and "face" for Italy as well. How could he confront public opinion if he denied protection to Italian missionaries? San Giuliano's suggestion was simply "to let the whole thing hang fire. I will not ask you to respond to our request for a transfer of the protectorate. We will thus gain time; and perhaps we can later find some accommodation."[28] The situation was complicated, however, because the Italian ambassador in Paris, Signor Tittoni, insisted that the Franco-Italian accord of 1905 be strictly applied to the Carmelites of Syria, since their establishments were predominantly of Italian nationality.[29]

Foreign Minister Cruppi was, however, well disposed to the San Giuliano proposal to leave the matter *en suspense.* Despite the Carmelite split of 1906-1908, France still regarded all eight establishments in Syria as one single mission with a mixture of nationalities. The Italian Carmelites, it seems, had applied directly to the Italian government for protection without notifying their superiors in Rome. A question of ecclesiastical discipline was thus involved, and France hoped that the superiors would somehow be able to force the recalcitrant Carmelites of Syria to conform to the French protectorate.[30] Otherwise a dangerous precedent would be set—that of allowing each individual religious establishment to decide whose protection it would prefer.

France was not even above putting financial pressure on the Italian government in the matter, indicating to an official of the

Banco di Roma that the Quai d'Orsay would withdraw its opposition to the quotation on the Paris Bourse of the bank's titles "on the day when the affair of the Carmelites of Syria will be regulated to our satisfaction."[31] It was hoped that the Bank of Rome would exert pressure on the Italian government. But it was all in vain, and France realized it. On 25 June 1911 Barrère informed San Giuliano that the transfer of the Carmelites of Syria could be made if "the Italian Government will engage itself for the future not to undertake any enterprise against our protectorate in Syria; and to this effect no longer to anticipate the arrangements of the 1905 accord in this region."[32] What Barrère was asking for in effect was a sphere-of-influence guarantee.

The Italians were not willing to go quite that far, but on 26 July 1911, Ambassador Tittoni wrote to the new French foreign minister, Justin de Selves, that "the international character of the convent of Mount Carmel and its dependencies [at Haiffa and Saint-Jean d'Acre] is an incontestable fact."[33] This statement clearly offered no guarantee, but it did offer France some security, since the accord of 1905 stipulated that missionary protection could not be transferred unless the nationality of a mission were predominantly Italian. De Selves was obviously satisfied, for on 27 July 1911, he ordered Bompard in Constantinople to carry out the transfer of the Syrian Carmelites with his Italian colleague. On 16 August the Porte was notified to strike the Carmelite missions at Alexandretta, Beylan, Kobayet, and Tripoli-in-Syria from the 1901 list of French protégés.

Another foot had been wedged into the doorway of the French protectorate in Asiatic Turkey, this time in the vitally important area of Syria. France's previously sacrosanct position there was no longer an uncontested fact. Barrère wrote from Rome: "It seems to me beyond doubt that the precedent of the Carmelites will be newly applied by other congregations unless we find the means to prevent it."[34] From Constantinople the chargé d'affaires notified the Quai d'Orsay on 9 September 1911 that twenty-four churches or convents and fourteen schools in the Ottoman Empire had cut their links with France in order to seek Italian protection. As a result, "our traditional patrimony in the Orient has thus suffered considerable losses. . . . We cannot hide the fact that what remains is severely threatened."[35]

The resolve of French diplomats to do something to retard the steady decay of France's religious protectorate was strengthened by another Middle Eastern crisis which dovetailed with the loss of the Carmelite missions. This was the outbreak, in the fall of 1911, of the Italo-Turkish War. For the duration Italy charged Germany with the protection of Italian missionaries in the Ottoman Empire, and French diplomats saw this development as a splendid opportunity to recoup France's losses in the missionary field. That the Italian victory in the war actually tended to increase her prestige among Ottoman Christians is not so important at this point as the fact that the war itself engendered some positive action from the Quai d'Orsay in the matter of the protectorate. The attitude of the diplomatic corps was best expressed by the French chargé d'affaires at Constantinople, who wrote to de Selves on 1 October 1911: "Would it be violating an impartial neutrality to try to recapture an academic clientele which the Italians did not hesitate to snatch from us under conditions which I do not have to recall to Your Excellency? Ought we not to make at this time, in the regions where the Italians would have liked to supplant us, a great effort to permit our directors of lay or congregational schools to assemble the students of the Italian schools. . . ?"[36] A similar attitude emerged in later communications from French representatives in the Ottoman capital as well as Rome and Damascus. The tone was always the same. The war was rendering an Italian religious position in the empire vulnerable; France, therefore, should seize the initiative to reassert the protectorate.[37]

That the outbreak of the Italo-Turkish War and the defection of the Syrian Carmelites increased the Quai d'Orsay's awareness of the problem of France's declining influence among Catholics in the Levant and stimulated a determination to do something about it, was reflected in a Foreign Ministry note of 4 November 1911. This note took cognizance of the fact that one of the main reasons for the defection of so many missionary groups from French to Italian protection was simply that the laws governing the separation of church and state did not permit missionary groups to recruit new members on French soil. The French missionary population in the Middle East was therefore declining by default, since only Italian or German missionaries were available to replace dead or retired Frenchmen. This was how the Carmelites of Syria, previously completely French, had become predominantly Italian. Under these circumstances the Foreign Ministry "is thus led to conceive of the organization on French territory of several centers of special recruitment for French missionaries destined for the different countries in question."[38] Two later notes dated 5 September 1912 and 17 March 1913 further indicate that the Quai d'Orsay came to support the recruitment of missionaries on French soil as a means of combating the Italian missionary influence in the Levant.[39]

The defection of the Syrian Carmelites and the outbreak of the Italo-Turk War also served as a catalyst for the action of private individuals in France interested in the preservation of the protectorate. In December 1911 the *Comité de défense des intérêts français en Orient* was founded in Paris in order "to maintain and develop our moral, political and economic situation in the Orient. . . . The Committee proposes to appeal to opinion and to assist French policy by employing its resources and its propaganda to support all the works which do honor to France in oriental countries and contribute to expanding her influence there."[40] Its membership included an impressive list of French statesmen and parliamentarians, such as M. A. Ribot, Léon Bourgeois, Paul Deschanel, Denys Cochin, Louis Barthou, Charles de Freycinet, Gabriel Hanotaux, Paul Leroy-Beaulieu, Stéphen Pichon, and Raymond Poincaré. The activity of the committee was to be based on the findings of Maurice Pernot, distinguished editor of the *Journal des débats,* who was commissioned to travel in the Levant from January to August 1912 and report on his findings. The results of Pernot's trip and his suggestions for action were embodied in his book, *Rapport sur un voyage d'étude à Constantinople, en Egypt et en Turquie d'Asie.*

Pernot found that the great appeal supposedly enjoyed by the French language in Syria was an illusion. English was more widespread, and Italian was making rapid progress. He reported that the Tripolitan War had increased Italian prestige among Ottoman Christians and that Italy was capitalizing on this development by moving vigorously to establish more schools and charitable works in Syria. He also believed that the lack of missionary recruitment facilities in France was hurting the effectiveness of the protectorate in Asiatic Turkey.

Pernot's suggestions to combat the dwindling of France's prestige in the orient were as follows:

1. He cited the necessity to establish novitiates on French soil to permit the religious orders to recruit and train new missionaries. He judged that lay personnel could not take over the place which the congregationalists occupied there.

2. In order to spread the French language, Pernot urged that private French societies, such as railroad companies and banks established in the Levant, be solicited to help finance new teaching establishments and to revitalize ones already in existence. These groups naturally benefited from a French-oriented society, and their contributions would augment governmental subsidies.

3. Pernot pointed out that the rupture of relations between Paris and the Vatican had created an ambivalent situation for French missionaries—that between their loyalty to Rome and their natural French patriotism. Italy had capitalized on this situation to secure the loyalty of several previously French-protected establishments. His most controversial proposal was to favor a reestablishment of purely diplomatic relations with the Holy See.[41]

The importance of these suggestions and of the work of the *Comité de défense des intérêts français en Orient* was evidenced by the fact that two top-ranking French ambassadors brought Pernot's book to the attention of the Quai d'Orsay in the spring of 1914. Both Jules Cambon in Berlin and Maurice Bompard in Constantinople enthusiastically endorsed all three of Pernot's proposals.[42]

This stand was not a new one for Cambon and Bompard. As early as 15 January 1912, the latter, basing his recommendation on reports from the consulate general in Beirut, informed Paris that "in my opinion it is indispensable that we establish the means to facilitate the recruitment of the congregations who devote themselves to the French cause in Turkey. The future of our schools depends on it."[43] Cambon had taken the same position in April 1913. A year later he went so far as to assert the following: "Without going to Canossa . . . one can imagine that between the policy of the Concordat and that of reciprocal ignorance, there is room for political relations [with the Vatican] which can regulate questions where both the State and the Church are involved."[44]

Such appeals from France's top diplomats and from the *Comité de défense des intérêts français* were not ignored at the Quai d'Orsay. Its attitude was strikingly evident in March 1912, when the Lazarists sought authorization to open a house of recruitment and missionary training at Angers. Raymond Poincaré, then president of the *Conseil* and minister of foreign affairs, transferred the request to the Interior Ministry, citing the very serious personnel crisis among French missionary establishments in the Orient. On 4 March 1912 Poincaré took a stand on the issue by supporting the founding of the Lazarist *maison* on French territory at Angers.[45] Despite Poincaré's request for urgent action, the Interior Ministry reached no decision on the matter until 21 August 1912, when it placed so many conditions upon granting the Lazarists the authorization for the Angers facility that it amounted, in reality, to a refusal.[46]

The matter was dropped for nearly a year, but in June 1913 the Lazarists resubmitted their request. By this time Stéphen Pichon had been reappointed foreign minister. He took the same position as his predecessor in supporting the Lazarists' application. He wrote to the Interior Ministry on 28 June: "Since that time [of the previous Lazarist application] the recruitment crisis has become even more severe, as much so for other French missionary congregations as for the Lazarists. This situation raises great apprehensions in my department concerning the development of our works in the Orient and in China. I can only ask you to take the greatest care in the new examination . . . of the request presented by the Congregation of Lazarists."[47] That both Pichon and Poincaré had championed the Lazarists' petition gives credence to the view that their position represented that of the Quai d'Orsay rather than the personal predilections of any single individual.

But the Ministry of Interior was unmoved, and no action had been taken on the Lazarists' application, or on those of any other missionary group, when World War I intervened in August 1914. Similar matters were treated with an analogous lack of concern in the Chamber of Deputies. When proclerical deputies François Deloncle and Denys Cochin spoke on 10 March 1914 in favor of reestablishing diplomatic relations with the Vatican, their speeches were interrupted frequently by laughter and derisive comments from the powerful anticlerical faction of the Left.[48] The next day, during the budget debate on the allocation for French works in the Orient, Georges Leygues, chairman of the Foreign Affairs Committee of the Chamber, spoke passionately about the Italian threat to the French missionary schools. He called for the establishment of novitiates which could recruit and train novices in France. Gaston Doumergue, president of the *Conseil* and minister of foreign affairs, followed Leygues with a brief statement of his intention to protect the religious influence of France in the Levant. And then Louis Marin, the *rapporteur* of the foreign affairs budget, took the floor to suggest that the Chamber support a motion permitting the religious congregations to establish novitiates on French soil.[49] Although the 1914 budget for French works in the Middle East, including the clerical schools, was increased slightly, the Chamber took no action on the matter of relations with the Holy See or the recruitment of French missionaries.

The sources thus show convincingly that France's traditional religious protectorate over Catholics in Asiatic Turkey was being eroded away. In 1901 it had extended throughout Asiatic Turkey. Italy and Germany successfully challenged the protectorate in the Holy Land in 1902, and the French rupture of diplomatic relations with the papacy in 1904 opened the sluice gates. Despite Léon Gambetta's old dictum that anticlericalism was not an article for export, that policy exercised at home was bound to have unfortunate repercussions among Christians abroad. The Laws of Association of 1901 prevented missionary groups from recruiting members in France. Dead or retired Frenchmen were thus replaced primarily by Italians, and between 1905 and 1914 a considerable number of clerical establishments, along with their Levantine Christian clientele, abandoned French in favor of Italian protection.

These desertions forced France to concentrate her protectorate more and more upon Syria and Lebanon, the area where her missionaries were most firmly entrenched. So long as the protectorate there was unthreatened, the Quai d'Orsay took little action to allay Italian successes elsewhere. But the transfer of the Syrian Carmelites to Italian protection in 1911 alerted the Quai d'Orsay and the diplomatic corps to the dangers inherent in France's anticlerical policy.

But two successive ministers of foreign affairs were unable to convince the rest of the government that a reevaluation was necessary. This can be explained in several ways. In the first place many thought that the changes secured by France in the Lebanese *Règlement organique* in 1912 had increased France's prestige among Christians in the Lebanon. Second, Britain had at the same time given France assurances concerning Syria which were interpreted by many to amount to a British endorsement of a *carte blanche* policy for France in that area.[50] And finally, the railroad agreements reached between France and Germany and France and Turkey in 1914 most definitely established Syria and the Lebanon as an economic sphere of influence for France.[51]

Under these circumstances it was not surprising that the strongly principled anticlerical forces would not yield to appeals from the Quai d'Orsay to preserve France's religious influence in Syria. They regarded France's title to it as secure. On the other hand it would not be astounding either if Syrian Christians regarded the French government's seeming lack of interest in them as a betrayal, a marked deemphasis of the religious protectorate once the economic sphere of influence seemed secure. If so, Frenchmen should not have been particularly astonished to find that their physical presence in Syria after the First World War engendered suspicion, bitterness, and occasional hostility on the part of the Christian populations. The Quai d'Orsay cannot be held wholly to blame for this development.

6 FRANCE AND THE ORIGINS OF THE SYRIAN NATIONAL MOVEMENT TO 1912

France's claim to a mandate in Syria and the Lebanon at the end of World War I rested upon the cultural and economic position that she occupied in these territories of the defunct Ottoman Empire. The religious position held by French missionaries has been outlined in the previous chapters. The extensive economic foothold gained in Syria and Lebanon by French businessmen and financiers before the First World War will be discussed fully in chapter 10. But the decade before the outbreak of the war was also a period in which French diplomats and statesmen attempted to gain political influence among the disparate populations of Syria and the Lebanon, both Christian and Muslim.

France's desire to establish herself politically in this area was understandable enough. By the turn of the century the Ottoman Empire was in a generally recognized state of decay. Despite the pledge of the European powers to preserve Ottoman territorial integrity, embodied in the Treaty of Paris of 1856 and again in the 1878 Treaty of Berlin, this dictum was losing much of its force in the early twentieth century. Statesmen no longer spoke hypothetically about the dissolution of the empire; they were saying "when" and not "if." The uncertainty led to a great deal of mutual suspicion among the Great Powers during the last decade of the nineteenth century concerning plans for the partition of the "Sick Man's" domain. The German Kaiser, for example, had proposed such a formula to Lord Salisbury, the British prime minister, in 1895—a proposal often erroneously attributed to Salisbury himself.[1] Although most European states officially maintained their adherence to the doctrine of Ottoman territorial integrity, it has frequently been maintained that the main factor hindering actual partition was the inability among the Great Powers to agree on an equitable distribution of the spoils. In any case, the prevalence of such thinking inevitably led imperialist-minded Frenchmen to look to their own interests in the strategically important eastern Mediterranean region, particularly since rivals such as Great Britain had a strong foothold in Egypt and at Suez, and Germany was rapidly gaining economic and political influence in northern Asia Minor as a result of concessions granted to German financiers in 1888 to build the Anatolian railway.

In the political domain France looked to Syria and the Lebanon, primarily because her missionaries had already established considerable religious influence among Christians there. But political penetration was a delicate operation. In the first decade of the twentieth century the whole Arab community was in ferment. The southern parts of the Arabian peninsula were in open revolt against Turkish authority and influence. Ideas of reform, decentralization, local autonomy, and even of complete separation from the Ottoman Empire were spreading among elements of the politically aware in Syria and the Lebanon. The situation was complicated by the tremendous religious differences and rivalries in the area. Both Christians and Muslims were thinking in terms of reform and separation. To insinuate herself politically into this kind of milieu, France had to tread lightly, for her desire to become politically involved with the disaffected elements in Syria implied in many ways a contradiction of her stated policy of maintaining Ottoman integrity.

In this sphere, therefore, French diplomacy worked covertly. No mention is made of French activity among Muslim and Christian reformist and separatist groups in the *Documents diplomatiques français,* the document collection published, for the most part, during the years when historians were turning away from the Versailles interpretation of the origins of the war and were distributing "war guilt" more equitably among all the Great

Powers. Most of the information concerning this aspect of French Middle Eastern policy has, therefore, been culled from unpublished documents found in the archives of the Quai d'Orsay in Paris.

France's attempt to become politically involved with Muslims and Christians in Syria and the Lebanon before the war brought her into contact with some of the more violent and reckless Syrian and Lebanese nationalists. The next chapter will deal more fully with France's extensive involvement with some of these groups and with Syrian reformist organizations after 1912. Her eventual abandonment even of the peaceful reformers in 1914 led Syrians, both Christians and Muslims, to regard France with a bitterness and recrimination which expressed itself dramatically after 1920. This chapter will offer some general observations about the development of the Syrian national consciousness and France's attitude toward it up to the decisive era opened by the Balkan wars of 1912 and 1913.

France's political involvement in Syria was especially significant because Syria formed the focal point of sophisticated Arab discontent with Ottoman administration.[2] A British observer, Patrick Seale, has pointed out that "Syria can claim to have been both the head and the heart of the Arab national movement since its beginnings at the turn of the century, both the generator of political ideas and the focus of countless dreams and patriotic fantasies."[3]

In 1908 Gabriel Hanotaux, a former French foreign minister, defined two kinds of reform movements within the Ottoman Empire. The first he called Christian reform, which was characterized by a desire for local autonomy and religious particularism. This he contrasted with Turkish reform, the object of which was to protect the health of the Ottoman Empire by calling for integration of Muslims and Christians. "The first argues for liberty by dissociation, and the other by organization; the first calls for foreign support, the latter is nationalist."[4] An example of positive "Turkish reform" would be the ill-fated constitution of 1876, which called for extensive reform and reorganization among the communities of the empire.

Hanotaux ignored a third area of reform agitation—that of the

Muslim Arabs. But his oversight is understandable, because manifestations of Muslim Arab desires for reform were barely discernible before 1908. Hanotaux had, however, pinpointed one of the main aspects of pre-1908 reform agitation. Recent scholarship has shown that during the reign of Abdul Hamid II, the nationalist and separatist movement was carried on primarily by Christians in Syria and the Lebanon.[5] The reason for this was found in the policy of Abdul Hamid, who, after 1876, turned away from the integrationist Turkish reformers of the Tanzimat period and began to seek support exclusively among his Muslim subjects. This pan-Islamic movement openly favored the Muslim Arabs. In Syria and elsewhere, therefore, they stood to gain little by opposing the sultan-caliph and working toward separation from an empire in which they enjoyed special privilege. It was the Christians who carried the brunt of reformist and separatist agitation before 1908, and they inevitably sought support from foreign powers, particularly from France.

This is not to imply that there were no Muslim Arab reformers in Syria before 1908. There were. The explanation is simply that their mild agitation for the restoration of the constitution of 1876 was very difficult to distinguish from the program of the Young Turks, since the main emphasis of both was opposition to the sultan. The Young Turks were exiles living in western Europe who wished to mitigate the severities of Abdul Hamid's regime through liberal reform, including implementation of the constitution of 1876. In December 1907 exiles in Paris established contact with dissident Turkish army officers, who rebelled in Macedonia in July 1908. The movement spread rapidly, leadership falling to a group of young officers called the Committee of Union and Progress. On 24 July Abdul Hamid bent to the committee's pressure and restored the constitution.

After the seizure of power by the Committee of Union and Progress, the Young Turks gradually abandoned the integrationist principles inherent in the constitution of 1876. Although they never completely discarded the Hamidian policy of pan-Islamism, the C.U.P. did embark upon a more nationalistic policy aimed at the "turkification" of the Ottoman Empire. Its adoption alienated the previously pacific and cooperative Syrian Muslims.[6]

By 1909 Muslims had taken over from the Christians as leaders of the reformist and even the separatist agitation. There were some Muslims who began to work for the creation of a huge Arab empire. Most Syrians, however, would have been satisfied to achieve a large measure of administrative decentralization and local autonomy, and those who did think in terms of complete independence envisaged a separate Syrian state, independent of both Turkey and the rest of the Arab community.

The Christian attitude naturally changed as Muslims assumed control of the Syrian national movement. In the interior minority Christians tended to go along with it. But in the Lebanon, where Christians formed a majority of the population, they became increasingly suspicious of the Muslims. They clearly did not want to become part of either an Arab empire or an independent Syrian state. A movement for Lebanese independence developed among the Christians of the Lebanon, particularly among the Maronites, whose links to France were close.

Apart from the Lebanon, however, there was evidence of substantial Christian-Muslim cooperation to achieve a more liberal regime in Syria. Many Syrian leaders saw in the spread of the ideal of national unity the only way to escape from the religious differences which had weakened their country for so long.[7] But there always remained an undercurrent of animosity and suspicion between Christians and Muslims. An anonymous author for the *Revue du monde musulman* wrote in 1912 that there existed a general feeling among Muslims that the Christian populations "would never be satisfied with the rights and guarrantees which would be accorded to them and would never participate loyally in the government of the country."[8]

Such, in outline form, were the main characteristics of the Arab national revival in Syria. It was a complicated development, filled with the imponderables of ethnic distrust and religious intolerance. It was in these troubled waters that France felt compelled to fish between 1901 and 1914 in order to gain political influence in Syria.

Any discussion of France's political involvement in prewar Syria must begin with a consideration of her ecclesiastical schools located there. The part played by French missionary schools in inculcating French cultural influence in Syria has already been considered. But what role, if any, did these schools have in the Arab national-political revival? Eugène Jung, an advocate of a huge, independent Arab empire, wrote in 1906 that, "thanks . . . to the action of foreign missionaries, especially the French missionaries, thanks also to the rapid communications established between the coasts of Syria, Egypt and Europe, the Arabs are at last civilized and becoming aware of their own nationality; they have forgotten former internal quarrels which divided them before the Turks."[9] A native of Beirut reported to Turkish authorities during the First World War that the principal task of French missionary schools and their teachers was to capture the minds of the students and inculcate in them ideas hostile to the Ottoman government.[10]

Recent scholarship, however, leaves an impression quite different from that of these early polemical works. The noted scholar of modern Middle East history Zeine N. Zeine points out that the role of missionary education in the national-political enlightenment of Arab youth has been greatly exaggerated. The curriculum of these schools was totally apolitical, emphasizing language and religion.[11] George Antonius, an Arab nationalist leader, goes even further, maintaining that French missionary schools helped in a negative way to transfer the leadership of the Arab national movement from Christian into predominantly Muslim hands. Since the schools' primary emphasis was on the French language and since their clientele was overwhelmingly Christian, the Muslims preferred to send their children to the religiously and linguistically orthodox community schools. They thus grew up in the traditional way of life and consequently were able to appeal more widely to Syrian loyalties after 1908.[12] The missionary schools may be regarded, therefore, as rather a negligible factor in assessing France's political influence among Muslim Syrian leaders, although they did give French diplomats a basis of contact with Christian elements of the population, especially in the Lebanon.

The first concrete expression of the developing Syrian national consciousness was embodied in the Beirut Society of 1875, a small, clandestine group which was composed largely of Christians. It made attempts, however, to include Muslims and Druzes within its program. The society fulminated largely against Turkish misrule and used the technique of placarding the cities of Beirut and Damascus at night. The movement collapsed after the consolidation of the Hamidian regime in the Ottoman Empire, but it was important because its program embodied many of the demands espoused by Syrian reformers and separatists of the immediate prewar period. It called for Arabic as the official language in Syria, the removal of censorship and other restrictions on free expression, and the employment of locally recruited militia units. It also demanded the independence of Syria in union with the Lebanon.[13] The disappearance of the Beirut Society under the thumb of Hamidian despotism did not mean the end of Syrian political activity. A Frenchman traveling in Syria in 1882 recorded the continuing spirit in the following manner:

A spirit of independence is abroad. During my stay in Beirut, young Muslims were busy organizing societies to promote the establishment of schools and hospitals and to work for the regeneration of the country. An interesting feature of this activity is its freedom from all taint of sectarianism. The societies which are being formed are designed to admit Christians and enlist their cooperation in the national task. The Turks are left out of account. . . .[14]

If covert resistence to the Turks emerged in Syria, some portions of the more remote sections of the Arabian peninsula were in open revolt. Although the Ottomans did not rule central Arabia, in 1904 Turkish troops intervened on behalf of the Rashidis' efforts to prevent the Saudi reconquest of the Nejd. Ibn-Saud defeated the Rashidi-Ottoman force, and the Turkish regulars were withdrawn. Shortly thereafter Ibn-Saud was recognized as master of the area, excluding the Turkish littoral provinces of Al Hasa, Hijaz, and Yemen. Even in the latter Turkish authority was under mounting pressure, a situation which was at least partially responsible for the sultan's decision to encourage the construction of the Hijaz railway, which could be employed for military purposes in addition to its principal function of transporting the Muslim faithful to the Holy places. This revolt of the Arabs against Turkish authority and intervention in the central and southern parts of the peninsula caught the imagination of Arabs in Syria. As early as 1901 the French consul in Aleppo notified Delcassé about growing unrest among Arab tribes in Syria and cited rumors that they might form a militant coalition against the Turks. The consul reported the situation to be "much more serious than the Turks themselves realize. . . . I believe . . . that the way things are going, in seven or eight years, perhaps sooner, the Arab question will be much more serious than the Macedonian question."[15] These were prophetic words indeed.

One of the first articles in French publications which departed from a strict reportage of events in the rebellious areas of Nejd appeared in January 1903. The author speculated about the effect on Great Power Middle East policy if this area succeeded in formally breaking away from the nominal suzerainty of Constantinople. English influence, he pointed out, was paramount in the Red Sea and the Persian Gulf, while the Baghdad railway would give Germany important areas of influence along its route. The point of the article was that France must be prepared to exert pressure for her share of influence in Syria.[16]

This was the background for the foundation in 1904 of the *Ligue de la patrie arabe.* The *Ligue,* with headquarters in Cairo and Paris, was organized by a man named Négib Azoury, who in 1905 outlined its program in his book, *Le Réveil de la nation arabe.* He called for the Arabs to rise up and proclaim their will to live independently, to substitute an administration of Arab leaders for the Turkish functionaries. Azoury, significantly enough, was a Maronite Christian, but his book spoke to Muslim and Christian Arabs alike, urging the abandonment of religious squabbles in order to recall their Arab heritage in a common movement against Turkish oppression.

Azoury called for the creation of a new Arab empire extending to the limits of its "natural frontiers, from the valley of the Tigres and Euphrates to the isthmus of Suez and from the Mediterranean to the Sea of Oman." From these boundary citations it was clear that Syria was to be included in this Arab empire, but Azoury's Christianity was evident in his assurances that the autonomy of the Lebanon would be respected, as well as the

Christian sanctuaries of Palestine. His program envisaged no sacrifices or armed intervention from the European powers but assured that all the interests and concessions granted to them in the Arab territories by the Turks would be respected.[17]

Despite the fact that the program of the *Ligue* requested no help from the European powers, Azoury, in his book, made laudatory references to French missionary activity in Asiatic Turkey and particularly in Syria. He felt that France had done more than any other country to civilize the Arab world and bring it to national consciousness. He said at one point, "We beg France to continue her generous traditions and to favor this movement. The rest of Europe will follow her beneficent example."[18] There are even in existence some letters from Azoury to a person he addressed simply as "Monsieur," but who must have been some sort of liaison between him and the French Ministry of Foreign Affairs. These letters, dated 8 January and 22 January 1905, are located in the French document collections at the Quai d'Orsay. In them he appealed for the "precious sympathy of France" for his movement and even requested a subsidy of 100,000 francs, the denial of which might well be followed by certain unspecified disasters for "the prestige of France and her patrimony in the Orient."[19]

The Quai d'Orsay, of course, followed Azoury's movement with interest. The publication of his book in 1905 and the appearance the next year of his cohort Eugène Jung's *Les Puissances devant la révolte arabe,* with their hints about the gains France could make by supporting the *Ligue,* attracted a rather wide flurry of interest and speculation in the Parisian press. But there is no evidence to suggest that the Quai d'Orsay ever actively supported or encouraged Azoury and Jung. Reports from Syria obviously did much to dissuade the Foreign Ministry from making any commitments to the *Ligue.* On 14 February 1905 the consul general in Beirut notified Delcassé that the publication of Azoury's program created a brief stir of interest in Syria but that it probably represented a "corrupt emotion" on the part of its author, "the most suspect and least recommendable of persons." He concluded his statement by assuring Delcassé that "an Arab national sentiment does not exist among the people of this country, who

are completely divided on questions of religion, rite and clan and
who, by nature, are destined to live, for a long time if not forever,
under the domination of a foreign element."[20] The consul general
was probably correct about the state of Arab national consciousness in Syria at this time, but his affirmation about the destiny of
Syria always to remain under foreign domination exemplifies a
naïveté typical of French diplomats in that area. This attitude was
to display itself again and again between 1906 and 1914. It
blinded France to the depth eventually achieved by Syrian
national awareness and contributed to the debacle of the postwar
mandatory period. But that a recognizable Syrian national consciousness had not developed by 1905 was corroborated by the
French chargé d'affaires in Constantinople in a dispatch to
Rouvier on 26 September 1905. Basing his views on information
from Beirut, Damascus, and Jerusalem, J. A. Boppe reported no
interest at all in Négib Azoury and concluded that the rumors
about a national movement in Syria "seem to exist only in the
imagination of certain Parisian journalists."[21] Even as late as
1911, there is evidence to suggest that Syrian separatist ideas were
not generally popular.[22]

Another factor in France's suspicion of the *Ligue de la patrie
arabe* was that some people viewed it as an Anglo-Arab scheme
designed to increase English influence in the Arab countries. The
influential French political commentator René Pinon noted that
"it is convenient . . . to remember that it is at Cairo, under the
eyes of English administration, that the 'Arab National Party' has
its committee, and that it is from there that it seeks to spread its
ideas and plant its agents in Asiatic Turkey."[23] The organ of the
Comité de l'Asie francaise, a committee dedicated to propa-
gating French influence, language, and culture in the Orient,
observed: "One knows that it is generally considered that the
Arab movement is encouraged by England, who would employ
Egyptian intermediaries in this purpose."[24] Even the French
consul general in Beirut noted that such a feeling was widespread
in the city.[25] Such sentiments underlined the distrust France had
for England in the Middle East, a development which will be discussed more fully in a later chapter. But there is no evidence to
suggest that the *Ligue de la patrie arabe* was an agent of English
influence.

As a matter of fact, although Négib Azoury himself worked in Cairo, the center of the *Ligue*'s activities was in Paris, where Eugène Jung published a monthly sheet called *L'Indépendence arabe*. This journal, however, discontinued operations in September 1908, after the success of the Young Turk revolution in Constantinople. The last issue noted a desire to cooperate with the Young Turks in reforming the empire. "Our program is now indistinguishable from theirs. . . . We shall abandon our present activities in order to work by constitutional means to establish administrative autonomy in our country."[26]

France wisely ignored Azoury and his movement. Consular reports proved it had little support in Syria. It was interesting as an example of the Christian leadership of the early expressions of Arab discontent with Turkish administration. But his movement was too radical for its time and could not rally great support from Syrian Muslims, who remained quite wary of any move that might disrupt the only great Muslim power in the world. Azoury's *Ligue* disintegrated in the general enthusiasm and optimism generated by the Young Turk revolution of 1908. Historians generally agree that so far as the total Arab movement itself was concerned, Azoury's effect was negligible.[27]

The *Ligue de la patrie arabe* may have been unrepresentative of Arab opinion, but its reaction to the Young Turk revolution and the restoration of the constitution of 1876 was symptomatic of the response throughout Syria. French consular reports for August 1908 indicated that both Christians and Muslims greeted the new regime enthusiastically in Beirut, Tripoli-in-Syria, and Latakia.[28] The French impression was corroborated by the British consul general in Beirut, who reported to his ambassador in Constantinople, Gerard Lowther, that signs of rejoicing were evident on all sides. "What the general public will most . . . appreciate is undoubtedly the abolition of the spy system to be speedily followed, it is to be hoped, by reforms in all Government Departments."[29]

France also took a stand wholly in support of the Young Turk program. French statesmen realized that the revolution had been one against continued outside pressure for reforms and against foreign intervention, and therefore France's best hope of maintaining a position at the Porte lay in supporting the new, apparently liberal regime.[30] Paul Deschanel echoed the sentiments of the Quai d'Orsay when he said in the Chamber of Deputies on 26 November 1908: "Our political, economic, and moral interests are bound up with those of Turkey. Consequently our primary duty is to guarantee her territorial integrity and her independence."[31]

The honeymoon stage of Arab-Turkish relations, however, was short-lived. The Young Turk policies of nationalism and "turkification" soon disillusioned Muslim and Christian Syrians and dampened the optimism that had been created by the restoration of the constitution of 1876. Hopes for reform and decentralization in Syria were abandoned first by the Christians, a process accelerated by the massacre of Armenians following the Young Turks' defeat of the Hamidian counter-revolution in April 1909. The first manifestation of this discontent occurred in December 1908, with the formation in Paris of a *Comité central syrien.* Headed by a Greek Catholic Melchite named Rechid Moutran, the *Comité*'s program accepted the Turkish constitution as the legal basis of Syria's national existence but maintained that "we intend to do everything possible for the development and prosperity of our dear fatherland." The proclamation concluded: "We await the decisions of [the Ottoman] Parliament with fear and trembling, firmly decided to conquer our self-government by all the means at our disposal. We owe it to our glorious past and to our great future."[32]

Moutran was speaking from Paris on behalf of all Syrians but, like the *Ligue de la patrie arabe* before him, had little actual support in Syria. A dispatch from Beirut to the Quai d'Orsay said that Moutran's proclamation, published in a number of Syrian newspapers, attracted little favorable response.[33] The British consul in Damascus notified London that the *Comité*'s program was received with disapproval and contempt throughout Syria, particularly from the Muslim community.[34] Moutran was of little practical importance but he illustrated the faltering grasp of Christian leadership on the reins of the Syrian national movement.

The attempt at counter-revolution in April 1909 frightened the Young Turks. From this time on, thoughts of reforming the empire took second place to the C.U.P.'s attempts to solidify their position by centralizing control in Constantinople. Disaffection among the Arab populations in Syria grew apace during 1909 and 1910. On 16 June 1910 British Consul General H. A. Cumberbatch wrote to Gerard Lowther from Beirut that "it is undeniable that the practical results, so far, of the reforms so loudly preached . . . have not come up to expectations."[35] The increasing impatience of Arab leaders with Turkish dilatoriness was evident to the French consul general at Damascus. He informed Paris that Syrian Arab representatives to the Ottoman Chamber of Deputies were returning home during vacations to undertake anti-Turk propaganda among their constituents. They accused the Turks of neglecting Arab needs and aspirations by not appointing Arabs to important administrative positions and conspiring against the Arab language in the educational system.[36]

The Turks combated such internal criticism by the time-honored dodge of calling attention to the dangers from without. They sponsored xenophobic and Islamist campaigns in the Syrian press against foreign encroachments in the Ottoman Empire. These programs were often directed against France in particular, focusing on the capitulations which gave Frenchmen and their Christian protégés a privileged position in Syria. These attacks also criticized French administration in her Muslim colonies of Algeria and Tunisia and encouraged Muslims dissatisfied with French control there to emigrate to Syria. These anti-French campaigns attracted some support in Syria, particularly among the Muslim notables. They were successful in delaying any overt anti-Turkish activity among the Syrian populations.[37] French diplomats and officials watched this anti-French outburst very closely and with a great deal of apprehension, the more so because it will be recalled that this anti-French activity occurred simultaneously with Italy's severe challenge to the French religious protectorate in Syria. French influence was under attack from two directions at the same time.

Turkish activities, therefore, had the effect of muting Syrian Arab dissatisfaction with the lack of genuine administrative reform throughout 1910 and 1911. What finally ended the patience of Syrian leaders with the Turks in the matter of reform was the outbreak of war with Italy in October 1911. This war ended a year later, but its culmination was overshadowed by the simultaneous outbreak of war in the Balkan Peninsula. These events convinced the Syrians that a meaningful reform program would never be granted from above while the Young Turks were preoccupied with warfare in other parts of the Ottoman Empire. Matters would clearly have to be taken into their own hands. The Syrian reaction to Turkish difficulties took varied forms. Reformist societies were organized to force the hard-pressed Turks to grant sweeping measures of decentralization and autonomy. Some out-and-out separatist societies appeared, working for the complete independence of Syria and the Lebanon. Differences between Muslims and Christians were evident, but there were also significant examples of cooperation between the religious groups. These developments and France's policy toward them will be examined more fully in the next chapter. What remains now is to survey France's reaction to the climate of opinion in Syria as it developed during the stormy years of 1911 and 1912. This was a period of formulation for France, as her diplomats groped for a policy which could deal effectively with the contradictory phenomena of her assurances to Turkey regarding Ottoman territorial integrity and the emerging aspirations of a Syria whose destiny France hoped to control.

The Young Turks were advised by one of their own ambassadors against engaging in a war with Italy over Tripolitania. Moukhtar Pasha in Berlin urged the Committee of Union and Progress simply to accede to Italian demands, since war would only agitate the ticklish situations in the Balkans and in Arab territory, thus weakening Turkish control in these vital areas.[38] Moukhtar was right. Arab leaders in Syria greeted the outbreak of war with Italy in October 1911 with consternation. The British consul general in Beirut reported that "the Arab Muslims of Beirut are not so keen upon sacrificing their lives and their fortunes on a war which they know must end disastrously for them and their country."[39]

The outbreak of war was attended by some anti-Christian activity among the Muslims of Syria. France's first reaction to this development was to send a warship into Syrian waters to protect her traditional clientele, an action which redounded to her prestige among this element of the population but which also led to numerous frigid confrontations between Foreign Minister Poincaré and Italian Ambassador Tittoni.[40] But France could not remain satisfied with the support merely of the minority Christian population. The magnitude of the problem posed to France by the outbreak of the war in Tripolitania and the Balkans, and the consequent determination of the Syrian peoples to secure a better life, was best expressed in a dispatch from France's consul general in Beirut to Poincaré on 12 November 1912. He noted that these events "have posed the Syrian question with enough clarity . . . that one can foresee eventual solutions and can consider that a crisis exists, which could lead, perhaps in the near future, to the detachment of Syria from the Ottoman Empire." The most important fact about the Syrian separatist sentiment was that it was divided between Christian and Muslim Arabs. But whereas the Christians looked to France for deliverance from Turkish servitude, the dispatch continued, sentiment among wealthy Muslims was turning more and more toward England. They compared the stability of the Egyptian regime to the chaotic conditions in Syria. Several Arab Muslim committees were formed to agitate for the joining of Syria to Egypt under British overlordship. Because of this situation, the consul general concluded, France must increase her activity in Syria to emphasize that she had not abandoned her interest there to England. "Syria is a ripe fruit ready to be plucked. If one is not careful it will detach itself from the Ottoman stem, perhaps in the near future, and fall in its neighbor's [Egypt's] yard."[41]

The pro-Anglo-Egyptian sentiment among Syrian Muslim notability was not peculiar to Beirut. Throughout 1912 its existence was reported by French diplomats in Constantinople, Damascus, Tripoli-in-Syria, and among the Syrian émigré community in Cairo.[42] But there were other reports during this same period which reflected a more optimistic view of the French position vis-à-vis Syrian Muslims. The French minister to Egypt, upon completion of a trip to Syria and the Lebanon in June 1912, reported to Paris that several Muslim groups had expressed to him their desire to rid themselves of Turkish domination with the aid and under the control of a foreign power—"to us if we so desire, to someone else if we disinterest ourselves in Syria. It seemed to me however that the most generally admitted preference was for us. . . ."[43] In November the minister in Cairo again reported to the Quai d'Orsay that the Syrian Muslims were divided among themselves, "in a proportion impossible to define, some favorable to France and others to England."[44] A similar report arrived in December 1912 from Tripoli-in-Syria, citing the general Muslim disaffection with the Turks. Many of them felt it impossible to escape domination by themselves, so they were openly seeking outside assistance. "They will welcome it with relief whether it be French, English or someone else."[45]

The general tone of these dispatches was that Syrian Muslims were unanimous in desiring some kind of amelioration of conditions in their territory, but that they were divided upon the means with which to achieve this end. Some groups were clearly separatist and desired foreign assistance to escape the Ottoman Empire. Other groups were merely reformist, wanting to put pressure on Young Turkey to grant sweeping measures of decentralization and local autonomy. The impression left in Paris by the dispatches from French diplomats in the Middle East was this: that whereas Uniate Christian Syrians were pretty solidly favorable toward French assistance or intervention, the Muslims were divided and generally indecisive. These groups would support whichever power first showed an inclination to assist them in their aims. The problem for French policy makers was succinctly outlined by the French minister in Cairo, who wrote to Poincaré on 28 November 1912:

If, in the more or less near future, we find it necessary to choose between intervention or abstention in Syria, it is certain that the decision taken at that time would irrevocably determine the whole future of France in the Orient: abstention would mean not only the abandonment of Syria to a foreign Power, but the definitive abandonment of French influence in all the countries washed by the eastern Mediterranean. . . . We must concentrate our efforts, not only to overcome adverse theories [attachment of Syria to Egypt], but to accustom [people's] minds to the eventual realization of resolutions which we will have adopted.[46]

The last sentence of this statement clearly shows the covetousness with which French diplomats viewed Syria, and this undoubtedly prejudiced their reporting of events. But the analysis of the problem confronting French policy makers at the Quai d'Orsay was quite accurate.

What then was the policy eventually worked out by the French? They chose in effect to burn the Ottoman candle at both ends. Publicly France continued to be an outspoken advocate of Ottoman integrity with regard to the Asiatic domains. But covertly her diplomats in Syria maintained close contact with Christian and Muslim reformist and even separatist groups. The next chapter will show that France's representatives in the Orient never completely discouraged the volatile separatist organizations or made them believe that French assistance or at least benevolence was impossible in the future.

In short, France evolved a policy that might possibly have served her well whether the Ottoman Empire in Asia endured or dissolved. It was of necessity a timorous policy, oscillating between the Young Turk movement, Syrian ambitions, and France's own traditions as protectress of Ottoman Christians. Publicly France maintained the diplomatically respectable doctrine of Ottoman integrity, evidenced when Poincaré ordered Paul Cambon to assure the British that France was holding "scrupulously" to that principle. "France has no intention of profiting from the collapse of Turkish power in Europe to deprive her of some scrap of territory in Asia."[47] Even in his memoirs, Poincaré left no indication that France followed any other course. He proclaimed piously of France's Turkish policy during the Italo-Turk and Balkan wars that "the integrity of the Ottoman Empire was for us not only a highly respectable diplomatic dogma, solemnly consecrated and proclaimed at the Congresses of Berlin and Paris and the London Conference, it was also the safeguard for French interests, moral and material, in the east. At the same time it was also the best guarantee for the tranquility of our Islamic possessions."[48]

But that these statements did not represent the sum and substance of French policy in Asiatic Turkey can be inferred from the following instructions, sent by Ambassador Bompard to the French consul general at Damascus on 27 January 1913:

At the moment when the Great Powers find themselves in the grip of such serious difficulties for the regulation of questions which concern European Turkey, it is important that the question of Asiatic Turkey does not come to the fore. It is your job, *while conserving the most cordial contact with the Muslim or Christian notables who address themselves to you,* to prevent the Syrians from taking any initiative which may be susceptible to opening a similar question, and at the same time engaging our policy . . . and even that of our allies.[49]

The italics are mine. But they show that France was determined to cultivate her influence among all levels of Syrian dissatisfaction with the Turks. The diplomats were to counsel prudence among the more volatile separatists and reformists. This document could be interpreted as an example of France's loyalty to her proclamations of Turkish integrity. But the next chapter will show convincingly that the French policy of encouraging prudential and moderate behavior in Syria had quite another purpose altogether.

7 FRANCE AND THE SYRIAN NATIONAL MOVEMENT, 1912-1914

The outbreak of war in the Balkans late in 1912 made it seem highly probable that the disaffection might well spread into Syria. Such speculation required France to define her attitude toward Syria and make her position public. Two events occurred in Syria and Lebanon in December 1912 which permitted Foreign Minister Poincaré to assert his government's attitude toward Syria and the Ottoman Empire. One of these events involved some changes, the first since 1864, in the Lebanese *Règlement organique*. These changes, achieved largely at the instigation of France after difficult and protracted negotiations among the six Great Powers and Turkey, granted increased authority to the Administrative Council of Lebanon in its relations with the Turkish-appointed governor general. These changes redounded to the prestige of France among the Christian population living in Lebanon.

At the same time the second event of importance for France's political position in Syria was a statement from British Foreign Minister Sir Edward Grey to the effect that Britain most certainly had no territorial ambitions in Syria. The revelation of this statement helped remove the wind from the sails of the Muslim Syrian movement to attach Syria to Egypt under English overlordship. Both of these events, then, tended to increase French prestige in Syria and the Lebanon. They prompted Poincaré to tell the French Senate on 21 December 1912: "in Lebanon and Syria we have

traditional interests and . . . we intend to see they are respected.
. . . The English Government has declared to us in a very friendly
manner that in these regions it has neither intentions, nor designs,
nor political aspirations of any sort. We ourselves are resolved to
maintain, in Asia, the integrity of the Ottoman Empire, but we
shall not abandon any of our traditions there . . . nor leave any of
our interests there in abeyance."[1]

Both Christian and Muslim leaders in Syria and the Lebanon
tended to misinterpret Poincaré's energetic statement to the
Senate. They overlooked his reassertion of Ottoman integrity and
appeared to regard his other words as laying the groundwork for
French intervention in Syria in the near future. Poincaré's intention was, however, merely to emphasize that France would not let
any other power occupy Syria and would work for reforms under
Ottoman sovereignty. Some Christians and Muslims, however,
misunderstood this point. On 26 December 1912 groups of
Lebanese living in exile approached French representatives in
Cairo and Alexandria to plead for the aid of the Quai d'Orsay in
restoring Beirut and the area of the Bekâa' to Lebanon. They
argued that "all annexation to Lebanon will be an annexation to
France."[2] Four days later the Syrian Catholic patriarch and the
Greek Orthodox bishop of Beirut paid a visit to the French consul
general in that city. They felt that the Balkan situation precluded
the possibility that the Turks would ever grant a meaningful Syrian
reform program. Fearing Muslim fanaticism, the two Christian
prelates urged the consul general to have France work toward the
incorporation of the *vilayet* of Beirut into the Lebanon, both to be
placed under the control and guarantee of the Great Powers.[3]
What these Christian leaders did not realize was that this kind of
internationalization of the Syrian question was precisely what
France was trying to avoid by advocating a Turkish-sponsored
reform program.

Christian separatist leaders were not the only ones to turn
toward France in late December 1912. An example of Muslim
separatist activity illustrated the growth of French prestige in the
area and also provided a telling indication of how the new French
diplomacy was prepared to deal with the separatists. The French
consul in Aleppo reported conversations he had had with a repre-

sentative for a group of Muslim separatists who had indicated connections and affiliates throughout Syria. The consul was told of their dissatisfaction with the Ottoman government and their desire to confide their future to a foreign power. The group had been rebuffed by the English, but now, they declared, " 'We offer Syria to France.' " The intermediary then outlined a plan for French-Muslim cooperation, a plan calling for a simultaneous revolution in all areas of Syria; the Turkish functionaries would be dispossessed and the entire country turned over to French forces which would have been waiting off-shore. The whole plan would be coordinated with the Christian populations in order to avoid any possibility of massacres. These proposals were blatantly separatist and revolutionary in character. But when the intermediary suggested that French Consul Laporte meet with official delegates of this group, Laporte "did not believe that he had to decline this proposition." He requested instructions from Paris.[4]

On 9 January 1913 Poincaré notified Bompard in Constantinople of his instructions to the consul at Aleppo. The dispatch clearly illustrated France's official attitude toward the separatists and spotlighted the contradiction between this attitude and the declared policy of respect for Ottoman integrity. Poincaré had informed the representative at Aleppo that "there was no need to discourage his petitioners while recommending the greatest prudence to them and that we are interested in his maintaining a contact with them which must be discreet enough not to awaken the sensitivity of the local authorities." Poincaré also requested his consul at Aleppo to keep him fully and promptly informed of "all manifestations of this new state of mind" among the Muslim population in his circumscription.[5] France clearly was determined not to discourage even the most extreme Syrian groups, indeed to maintain political and diplomatic contact with them.

The Turkish authorities were most certainly aware of the growing separatist sentiment among the Muslims and Christians of Syria and the Lebanon. In June 1912 the Committee of Union and Progress had been turned out of power in Constantinople by a group of Turks known as the Liberal Entente. This party was much more decentralist in outlook than the C.U.P. and was consequently more susceptible to the cries for reform in Asia Minor. It was the Liberal Entente which unfortunately inherited the Balkan crisis and the resulting confusion in Syria as well.

In December 1912 the Turkish governor general of Beirut telegraphed to Constantinople that "the country is being overrun by different influences. In order to ameliorate its increasingly intolerable situation, parts of the population are turning either toward England or toward France. If we do not take the initiative for reforms, the country will escape us."[6] The Liberal Entente in Constantinople thus authorized the governor general to invite the people of Beirut to formulate their grievances. The result was the formation in January 1913 of the *Comité des réformes de Beyrouth,* a committee of eighty-four members roughly proportioned according to the religious composition of the *vilayet* of Beirut.

The *Comité* published its program for reform and decentralization on 31 January 1913, the main points of which were as follows: (1) the Syrians wanted Arabic to be recognized as the official language in Syria; (2) all functionaries named to Syria must have a working knowledge of Arabic; (3) local authorities ought to be consulted on the nomination of all civil and judicial functionaries; (4) a local High Court of Appeals ought to be created (at that time all appeals went to Constantinople); (5) military service should be regional in peacetime; (6) provincial revenues should be divided into two parts: customs, postal, and military imposts could remain at the disposition of the central government, but all other revenue should be placed at the disposal of local government for local needs; and (7) the Syrians demanded some foreign advisers to help reorganize the police, the judiciary, and the finances.[7] The program of the *Comité des réformes* was clearly not separatist. It was one which France could support openly and enthusiastically, since the Turks themselves had solicited the grievances from the Syrians.

But the enthusiasm engendered by the formation of *Comité des réformes* was dampened by the coup d'état of 24 January 1913 which returned the Young Turks to power in Constantinople. According to Consul Laporte at Aleppo, the coup created increased anxiety among Arabs who had placed their faith in the Liberal Entente party's pledges of reform. They feared a renewal of the policy of turkification.[8] The British consul general in Beirut reported to Whitehall that the general feeling there was that all hope for a betterment of their position must be abandoned. He went on to say that the C.U.P.'s return to power might engender "a recrudescence of separatist ideas."[9] The fears of the Syrians were well founded. On 29 January 1913 French Consul General Couget in Beirut reported that the governor general had recently received a note from the Sublime Porte which, while admitting the need for reforms, stated that nothing could be done about them while the *patrie* was in danger in the Balkans. The Porte ordered the *vali* (governor general) "to make it understood that the time for reforms would come, but for the time being the health of the Empire must take precedence over all else."[10] Dr. Georges Samné, an influential Lebanese Christian man of letters, reported that the general Syrian attitude toward such vague promises of future reforms was one of profound skepticism. Syrian leaders viewed such Turkish statements as merely preludes to further tergiversation in order to prevent foreign intervention in the Levant.[11]

That separatist sentiment was again on the rise in Syria can be gauged by a letter written to French Consul General Couget by a group of Christian members of the *Comité des réformes de Beyrouth* on 12 March 1913. The letter cited the general dissatisfaction among Christians at the dilatory attitude of the Turks regarding reforms. They expected no action from the Porte and were therefore turning to France for help. The Christians of the *Comité* ended their letter in the following manner:

> The heart's desire of the Christians of Syria is the occupation of Syria by France.
> . . . the undersigned members of the Executive Committee, in the name of the Christians of Beirut . . . have put forward the following suggestions, the only suggestions they deem adequate to meet the political situation in Syria:
> 1. The occupation of Syria by France.
> 2. The complete independence of the *vilayet* of Beirut under the protection and supervision of France.
> 3. The incorporation of the *vilayet* of Beirut into the Lebanon, which is to be under the actual suzerainty of France.[12]

But if the Christians were in this way affirming their attachment to France, elsewhere in Syria the rise of Muslim separatist feeling was taking another direction altogether. Early in April the French consul in Damascus notified Foreign Minister Pichon that the old campaign to join Syria to Egypt was once more in full swing. He said that the Turkish loss of Adrianople to her Balkan adversaries made it appear that a general partition of the whole empire was at hand. Sentiment in Muslim *milieux* was again developing an anti-French hue, tending toward the creation of an Arab caliph, and the most likely candidate for that high religious post appeared to be the khedive of Egypt.[13] Other documents for the spring of 1913 suggest that Muslim separatist opinion resented the fact that French agents in Syria seemed to concentrate their attention too fully on the Christians. Muslim leaders feared that if France did eventually control Syria, she would rule to the exclusive benefit of the Christian populations. The Quai d'Orsay moved to counteract this impression by ordering a more even-handed attitude on the part of French diplomatic representatives.[14]

The Quai d'Orsay's reaction to this reappearance of Christian and Muslim separatist sentiment, with all that it implied for the future of French political influence in Syria, was immediate. An agency of the Foreign Ministry, the *Commission des affaires syriennes,* reported to Pichon on 3 March 1913 that France had "no interest in precipitating the disintegration of Asiatic Turkey. . . . However, if our Syrian policy is not one of political ambition, it must be a policy of precaution." The report warned that if the reformers became too rambunctious and precipitated a revolt, the result might be an intervention of the powers. With the Syrian question thus internationalized, France would surely lose her privileged situation there. French diplomats must placate the more volatile Syrian separatists and reformers. The commission re-iterated its position on 31 March, stating that "all action threaten-ing to provoke a sort of internationalization of the reform question in Syria must be carefully avoided. It thus seems to be in our best interests to delay as long as possible the moment when we will have to take a position on this subject."[15] The implication of these two documents makes it absolutely clear that France's policy of urging moderate behavior on the Syrian separatists had very little to do with her often repeated desire to preserve Ottoman territorial integrity. What France wanted was to prevent at all costs the precedent of any other foreign power or group of powers developing a political role in Syria and thus imperiling her own privileged situation there. France wanted to prevent the whole of Syria from falling under a system of international supervision such as existed in the Lebanon. The *Commission des affaires syriennes* was attempting to preserve isolated French interest in Syria for the future.

The event that really brought the question of reforms in Syria to a head was the forcible dissolution of the *Comité des réformes de Beyrouth* by the Committee of Union and Progress on 8 April 1913. The Young Turks regarded the *Comité* as superfluous after a series of ministerial decrees granting a restricted usage of the Arabic language in Syrian law courts, petitions, and schools had been issued. These reforms, although certainly welcome, were a far cry from the extensive autonomist demands of the *Comité des réformes,* and consequently Syrians greeted its forcible dissolution with alarm and consternation. Protests and demonstrations were reported in Beirut and Damascus and among Syrian émigré groups in Cairo and Alexandria.[16]

One of the important consequences of the precipitate action of the Young Turks was the development of an apparent solidarity between Christian and Muslim Syrians in the face of the common Turkish threat to their plans. Both the French and the British consuls general in Beirut observed and commented upon this phenomenon.[17] The dissolution of the *Comité des réformes* naturally led to an intensification of the separatist movement and also to the creation of independent Syrian reform societies, unsanctioned by the Turkish authorities. Ambassador Bompard defined French policy in these circumstances in his instructions to the French consul in Damascus, instructions which were approved by the Quai d'Orsay. Bompard said on 28 April 1913 that France had every interest in discreetly favoring the native Syrian movement for reform and progressive decentralization. Bompard urged his representative in Damascus to preach prudence and moderation among Syrian activists. "But at the same time it is necessary to avoid discouraging those who come to us for advice and to let them know the sympathy with which their efforts are watched in France."[18]

The dissolution of the Beirut committee of reforms thus placed

France in an awkward position. In order to maintain political influence in Syria, France was forced into closer cooperation with reformist groups whose activities were unsanctioned by the Turkish government. The out-and-out separatist societies, with which France also maintained a discreet contact, were obviously not approved by Turkish authorities. In spite of the fact that the published French documents make no mention of French diplomatic activity among these groups, Turkish authorities were nevertheless well aware of it during the First World War. When Turkey declared war on the allied powers late in 1914, the French consul general in Beirut, as he left his post, neglected to destroy or to take away with him a whole series of confidential documents in the consulate. These documents recorded the conversations and contacts of French diplomats in the Middle East with various Muslim and Christian separatist and reformist societies. The Turks captured these documents in 1915 and published them under the title *La Vérité sur la question syrienne*.[19] The Turks published the book first of all to prove that these societies were made up of a small group of extremist agitators who did not represent the true aspirations of the Syrian peoples. But it was obviously also an attempt to justify to the world the severe methods of repression followed in Syria by the Fourth Turkish Army. The documents cited in *La Vérité* are revealing enough. They prove that there was extensive contact between French diplomats and Syrian separatist and reformist groups. But the effect of this contact can be overestimated, as was done by Djemal Pasha, commander of the Turkish Fourth Army and viceroy of Syria during the war. He maintained in his memoirs that "there was not the slightest doubt that the Arab revolutionaries were working under French protection and, indeed, under the guidance and for the benefit of the French Government."[20] Djemal, undoubtedly for propaganda purposes, had exaggerated the amount of influence France really exercised over the separatists and reformers between the period from the dissolution of the *Comité des réformes de Beyrouth* and the outbreak of the war in 1914.

The Turkish book mentioned French contact with several different separatist or reformist groups in Syria. Two of the most interesting were *En Nahdat ul-Lubnanye* (the Lebanese Revival) and *Ella Merkézyé* (the Society for Decentralization). The former was secret and dedicated to achieving the independence of Lebanon under the aegis of France. On 15 January 1913, a representative of the Lebanese Revival visited the French consul general in Beirut and expressed the society's intention to obtain the annexation of Baalbek and the Syrian area of Bekâa' to the Lebanon, and "for this we need the support and protection of the French Government." The visitor went on to describe the pro-French sentiment of the people in these regions and tantalized the Frenchman by describing the whole area as "the major key to the center of Syria and the routes to the interior." In reporting this incident to Bompard in Constantinople, the consul general said that he greeted the Lebanese Revival's proposal with courteous reserve, making no definite commitments, but remaining very friendly and encouraging.[21]

The second organization under consideration, the Society of Decentralization, was founded at the end of 1912 and had its headquarters in Cairo but maintained branches in all parts of Syria. This society was not separatist, but it did desire a rather substantial amount of local self-government and autonomy for Syria and other parts of the Ottoman Empire. Its program was very similar to that of the defunct *Comité des réformes de Bey-routh*, but unlike that group its existence was unsanctioned by Turkish authority. French contact with this society was nevertheless intimate, since one of its members, a certain Michel Tuéni, worked as a dragoman in the French consulate general in Beirut. On 23 March 1913, Tuéni, who was a delegate to an important meeting of the Decentralization Society in Cairo, reported to the French representative in that city that all the delegates of the society, Muslims and Christians alike, had voted that the most desirable solution to the Syrian question was as follows: "A constitution for Syria as an autonomous principality, governed by a Muslim prince freely chosen by the population and placed under the protection of France."[22]

Tuéni's pronouncement must have caused some confusion to M. Defrance, the French minister in Cairo, since he notified the Quai d'Orsay on 28 March 1913 that a previous informer had told him that the Muslim delegates of the Decentralization Society had expressed strong preference for English protection. Defrance reached the conclusion that the truth of the matter lay somewhere between these two views, expressing the opinion that if Syria were one day to be placed under foreign protection, "the Syrian Christians would desire almost unanimously that this protection be French, and among the Muslims, of which a considerable part have preferences for England, some would accept French protection because they would be sincerely partisan to it, while others would accept a French or English protection indifferently, following whatever would be decided for them."[23]

These documents show that French officials were in contact with Syrian organizations and that they indeed made little effort to discourage even the most radical schemes. But Djemal Pasha, the real author of *La Vérité sur la question syrienne,* made the point, one which had a great deal of validity, that these societies were not large and that their influence in Syria was not particularly widespread.[24] That is why the conclusions drawn by men like Defrance concerning the sentiments of all Christians and Muslims in Syria, based as they were only upon his contact with the Society for Decentralization, were particularly dangerous for France. They led Frenchmen gravely to overestimate the extent of their appeal and support among the whole body of Syrians, Christian and Muslim.

An indication of this overestimation is the fact that the secret society *al-Fatat,* one which George Antonius maintained played a more important role than any other in the history of the Arab national movement, although its greatest significance occurred after 1918, was not mentioned in *La Vérité.* This society, mostly Muslim in membership, was founded by Arab students in Paris in 1911 with the purpose of working for the independence of the Arab countries. Its headquarters was shifted from Paris to Beirut in 1913. The fact that *al-Fatat* was not mentioned in *La Vérité,* or even in the unpublished French documents, indicates that this important group remained unknown to the Turks and had no contact with French diplomatic representatives.[25] From the French side a good example of the extent to which French citizens overvalued their country's appeal among Syrians can be found in a speech delivered by Count R. J. M. Cressaty to the *Alliance française* on 21 May 1913. Cressaty, a Syrian by birth, had spent most of his life in France. He made it clear that he favored some kind of French take-over in Syria in spite of treaties and declarations regarding the maintenance of Turkey's integrity. Cressaty went on to say that France "will never find a land better prepared or an atmosphere more propitious to her influence. . . . No people is nearer to you by its character and moral affinities than the Syrian people, none is more closely attached to you by links of affection and memory. . . . In Syria the national sentiment in favor of France is incredibly intense."[26] Such sweeping judgments, rendered by individuals far removed from the actual scene, secured the basis for much of the misunderstanding and recrimination of the mandatory period after the First World War.

To strengthen his case against France and against the Syrian separatists, the author of *La Vérité* asserted that the Lebanese Revival and the Society for Decentralization made a decision even before the war erupted to work together to precipitate a general conflagration in the Arab Ottoman areas. He said that aid was solicited from the French minister in Cairo to help them sustain a revolt in Syria. According to the author, Defrance promised to give the rebels 20,000 rifles, to protect them during the insurrection by sending three French battleships to guard the Syrian coasts, and finally to see that the two societies received all the financial aid they needed.[27] These allegations can probably be regarded as a matter of gilding the lily, since no documentary evidence exists to give them credence.

Despite these contacts with underground organizations, however, France continued her efforts on the public level to urge Turkey to grant a meaningful reform program in Syria. French sympathies in this matter were manifested in June 1913 when she permitted, much to the disgust of the Turkish ambassador, a Syrian Arab Congress to meet in Paris. The purpose of the congress was to gather Syrian leaders together, in a forum well exposed to world opinion, to devise a program of reform which would be submitted to the Young Turk regime. Delegates from several Syrian societies met in Paris from 18 to 23 June 1913. There were representatives from the Syrian Committee of Paris;

the *Comité des réformes de Beyrouth,* which had continued a
clandestine existence after its official dissolution; the Cairo-based
Society for Decentralization; and from several important Syrian
colonies in the United States and Mexico.[28] The congress remained unhindered by French authorities probably because the
delegates came from groups which were not separatist (although
al-Fatat had played a leading role in organizing the congress) and
were evenly divided between Christians and Muslims.

There is substantial evidence, however, to suggest that the
congress did not enjoy the support of the entire Syrian population. British officials reported to their superiors in Constantinople
and in London that the delegates to the Paris congress held no
written mandates and that influential members of the Muslim
communities in Aleppo and Damascus disclaimed any connection
with them.[29] The French consul in Damascus reported to Pichon
on 22 May 1913 that a group of Muslim notables in that city
distributed a communiqué saying that they had not sent a delegate to the congress and that those Syrians assembling in Paris
were "virtual unknowns" in Syria.[30] A month later a protest
appeared in *Le Temps* from a group of *uléma* (Muslim religious
leaders) from the area of Gebel-Amel, proclaiming themselves
opposed to the pretentions of the Syrian Congress to act on behalf
of all Syrians and requesting that "similar reforms be elaborated
by our Parliament and by our provincial councils."[31] These protests were, of course, well publicized by the C.U.P.[32] During the
same period, however, the French consul general in Beirut received a notice signed by the leaders of the major Christian sects in
Syria which affirmed that the congress delegation "has received
the express mandate to go to Europe to formulate the grievances of
the whole population of the *vilayet* without religious distinction
and to work for the realization of these claims."[33] The fact that
disapprobation came from Muslims whereas approval emanated
from Christian leaders may be regarded as significant.

The program adopted by the Syrian Congress in Paris between
18 and 23 June 1913 was virtually identical to that outlined by the
Comité des réformes de Beyrouth earlier in the year. It was a program not of separatism but of decentralization. The consensus of
the congress was that Syria and the rest of the Arab community

should remain within the Ottoman Empire. But one of the most striking things to emerge from the reform program developed by the congress was the clear desire of the Syrians not to be identified with the rest of the Arab community. Although the proposals called for reform and decentralization in all of Asiatic Turkey, each of the articles clearly separated Syria from the rest of the Arab *vilayets.* [34]

What also emerged from the Paris congress, a factor of over-riding significance, was that nowhere, either in the general reform program or in the delegates' speeches, was a word said in favor of eventual French or other foreign intervention or occupation to help achieve Syrian aspirations. To be sure, one plank in the congress program called for the nomination of foreign advisers to help implement the judicial and financial reforms on a local level, but the idea of foreign occupation was clearly rejected. [35] Djemal Pasha noted that a Muslim delegate told Foreign Minister Pichon that although the Syrian Congress was being held in Paris, "our only object is to obtain reforms for the Arab provinces from the Ottoman Government. We want neither a French occupation of Syria nor a French protectorate." [36] It has already been suggested that the congress perhaps did not enjoy the support of all Syrians, but that it was a vastly more representative body than any single one or even a group of the more violent separatist societies must be clear. In assessing France's serious miscalculation of her own unpopularity in Syria after the First World War, it must be concluded that perhaps Frenchmen took the clandestine declarations of a few radical separatist organizations more seriously than the open manifestations of the Syrian Congress.

In any case the publication of the reform program outlined by the Syrian Arab Congress gave French statesmen another chance to urge the Turkish authorities to reach some peaceful accommodation with the Syrians, and in that way avoid the possibility of violence, which might necessitate an international intervention there. France, then, became an enthusiastic supporter of the Syrian reform program. This policy was adopted at the recommendation of the French minister in Cairo, who reported on 19 June that the maintenance of calm in Syria was possible only if

serious and deep reforms were initiated. But as far as French
political influence was concerned, Defrance continued, these
reforms must be recommended and supported by France and
executed with her participation. He emphasized that the Syrians
must be made to realize that any reform program would come
only as a result of the influence and action of France. But at the
same time the Porte had to be persuaded that France's counsels
of reform emanated only from her desire to maintain Turkish
territorial integrity in the Asian provinces.[37]

France, therefore, continued to support the Syrian reform
program, and the Quai d'Orsay was pleased to learn on 6 July
1913 that the Committee of Union and Progress had "put an end
to the Arab question" by contacting the delegates to the Arab
Congress in Paris and reaching an accord with them.[38] News that
an accord had been reached was greeted with cautious optimism
in Syria, a sentiment which tended to wax more and more pessi-
mistic as time went by and no word about this reform program
was published. It can be assumed that the Turks agreed to a
reform project with the Syrian Congress in order to keep the
Syrian question on ice during the decisive stages of the campaign
in the Balkans which regained Adrianople for the Ottoman
Empire. With this victory to embolden them, the C.U.P. felt safe
in reneging on the promises made to the delegates of the Syrian
Congress in Paris. In August 1913 the Turkish government published a reform program which provided a good deal less than
what had been promised the Syrians nearly two months before.
The Turkish program called for local military service in peacetime, but emphasized that the central government had absolute
control over troop deployment. The use of the Arab language for
instruction was granted, but only in higher education. "Secondary instruction," according to the Turkish directive, "will
always be maintained in the Turkish language." Some control
was allocated to local authorities in the nomination of lesser
Ottoman functionaries, who "should" have knowledge of the
Arab language. The Turkish program did make provision for
European "inspectors" in the Arab *vilayets,* but only "where the
Government will deem their presence necessary."[39] The judgment
about this program from the British consul general in Beirut was

apt. He told his chargé d'affaires in Constantinople that the document "has come as a great blow for it is only too evident that nothing definite whatever has been granted but that each article is couched in the vaguest terms and may mean anything or nothing."[40]

Syrian discontent with the Turkish proposals was manifested in an open letter addressed to all the Great Powers in late August 1913 from a group called the Central Committee for Reform and Defense of Syrian Interests. The letter stated that the Syrians "are thus left without the slightest hope of obtaining the desired reforms from the hands of the Committee in power." This group appealed to all the powers to intervene collectively to secure the Syrians' desired reforms, which "if they are frustrated again, . . . might well lead to regretable excesses."[41] There was some indication that this group was composed to a large extent of Maronites and other Christians who were more prepared than the Muslims to accept the protectorate of a Christian power.[42] But the general unrest and impatience among all religious groups in Syria was confirmed by the correspondent for *Le Temps* on 11 September 1913[43] and by the French consul in Damascus, who reported early in October that unless meaningful reforms were enacted shortly, Syrian sentiment would gravitate more and more toward a completely separatist position.[44] Elie Kedourie has maintained that in the aftermath of the Syrian Arab Congress, the nationalists "were prepared to assert [their rights], if need be, by force and rebellion, and with the help of any foreign Power which might encourage their ambitions."[45]

The Quai d'Orsay was, of course, unalterably opposed to the kind of internationalization of the Syrian question envisioned by the Central Committee for Reform and Defense of Syrian Interests. This was especially true during the months of September and October 1913, when French diplomats were deeply engaged in negotiations with both the German and the Turkish governments concerning important railroad concessions to French financiers in Syria and Lebanon. The success of these negotiations would secure France's exclusive economic position in Syria, and she wanted no international disturbance in that area to disrupt them. Consequently, French diplomats continued to

mollify violent Syrian sentiment in the hopes of avoiding an
embarrassing situation there. In Damascus, the seedbed of the
discontent, French Consul Ottavi urged Arab leaders to avoid
intransigence by accepting posts offered to them in the Ottoman
government, even though wide-ranging reforms had not yet been
granted.[46]

French negotiations with Turkey involved the matter of a
French loan to the chronically destitute Ottoman treasury. But
the disappointed Arab leaders in Syria, remembering France's
championship of the reform programs of the *Comité des réformes
de Beyrouth* and the Syrian Arab Congress, urged French
officials to make the granting of a loan to Turkey contingent upon
the effectuation of reforms in Syria. From Damascus Ottavi
reported to Pichon on 19 September that many Arab leaders were
seeking him out to lobby precisely along those lines. Without
guarantees, they argued, a French loan would be sunk entirely
into military and naval equipment rather than being used to
finance a reform program.[47] Ottavi reported in a similar manner
once again on 10 December 1913, saying that the Arabs felt that
the end of the Balkan wars wrote *finis* to any Turkish inclination
to grant measures of administrative decentralization, unless
forced to do so by attaching the appropriate strings to the French
loan still in negotiation.[48] That the French consul in Damascus
had indicated to Syrian leaders that France indeed was acting in
accordance with their wishes in the matter of the loan to Turkey
may be inferred from the following document. On 19 February
1914 Ottavi informed the embassy in Constantinople that many
Young Turks in Syria wanted to continue a policy of turkification
à outrance. "But the most intelligent among them have understood that the moment for mending their ways can no longer be
deferred. The position taken in favor of reforms by the French
Government has contributed much to this change of attitude,
since the Unionists need the French loan."[49]

Ottavi had thus created the impression that France was
working toward the achievement of a reform program for Syria.
And that explains why the Syrian peoples, particularly the Muslims, were so disillusioned with the French once the loan negotiations with the Sublime Porte reached fruition on 9 April 1914. In

exchange for a French loan to Turkey, there was not one word about a reform program for Syria. Instead France settled for numerous railroad concessions to her financiers and a number of guarantees regarding her own clerical schools and missionary establishments, concessions which were important to France in Syria but which could hardly be expected to endear France to the great majority of Syrians. Christian Syrians and Lebanese profited to a certain extent, at least those who were associated with French missionary establishments. But some Syrian leaders regarded the outcome of the Franco-Turkish loan negotiations as a betrayal of their interests by France. Eugène Jung, who worked tirelessly, if perhaps unrealistically, to goad the Quai d'Orsay into a more energetic championship of Arab separatist ambitions, was not far off the mark when he condemned France's Syrian policy as being guided "not by political sense, but only by the satisfaction of certain [economic] interests."[50]

The magnitude of the French political eclipse in Syria can be gauged by the consular reports for 1914, which filtered into the Quai d'Orsay from all parts of Syria. They reported massive press campaigns, primarily from the Muslim press, directed against French influence in Syria. The bitterness was particularly strong in Aleppo and Damascus, although Muslim newspapers in Beirut also joined the attack.[51] British sources confirm the anti-French activity among Syrians prior to the outbreak of the First World War. The British Embassy in Constantinople received reports from Beirut and Damascus on the 25th and 29th of June 1914 attesting to the fact that Muslims in the two cities were becoming more and more separatist in sentiment, as all hope for a meaningful reform program had vanished. The consul general in Beirut added, "It is also probable that the declared French policy of 'hands off' [regarding other powers' ambitions in Syria] and the activity of French Agents in Syria, especially in the Lebanon, have helped to strengthen the move for Arab independence, as the idea of a French protectorate is not popular among the Moslems. . . ."[52]

The British sources indicate that even after the war erupted, distrust and hatred of France still remained in evidence among Muslim Syrians. Gertrude Bell, an influential British Middle East official, in a letter of 5 September 1914 which was passed on

to the War Office in London, wrote that "Syria, especially southern Syria . . . is exceedingly pro-British . . . dislike of growing
French influence is universal." Sir John Maxwell, general officer
commanding British troops in Egypt, corroborated this sentiment. In a telegram to Lord Hubert Horatio Kitchener, British
high commissioner, on 27 November, he referred to "considerable pro-English feeling" among the Syrian Muslims and added
that "all except the Maronites are anti-French." A telegram from
the acting head of the British Agency in Cairo dated 9 November
1914 quoted an Arab dignitary as saying that the Muslims of
Syria were anxious for an understanding with the British. "If
given a guarantee that France would not occupy Syria they would
side whole-heartedly with Great Britain."[53] The anti-French
opinion in the sources is clear, although the pro-British sentiment
is undoubtedly somewhat exaggerated. There is evidence to suggest that Syrian Muslims, although remaining fairly favorably
disposed toward England, were gravitating more and more
toward Germany, particularly in light of the German military
successes in the early stages of the war.[54] The change in military
fortunes eventually played an important role in persuading the
Arabs to cast their lot with the Entente powers. But the distrust
for France remained, firmly embedded in the Syrian mentality
before the war ever broke out. It was not to be eradicated by a
comradeship in arms which must have seemed rather distant to
the Syrians. French forces remained for the most part on the
European continent, and it was the British army under General
Edmund Allenby which eventually liberated Syria from the
Turks. The wartime agreements between the Arabs and the
English and the English and the French, with their apparent
contradictions and inconsistencies concerning what territory was
promised to whom, have often been cited as the source of the
Franco-Syrian misunderstanding after the war. That these agreements contributed to the mandatory fiasco in Syria cannot be
doubted. But the documents cited in this and the previous chapter demonstrate clearly that the roots of the Syrian distrust for
France lay deep in the prewar period. The documents also show
that French diplomats in Syria and in Cairo never took the Syrian
national movement wholly seriously. They felt that the Syrian

mentality would always be characterized by a desire to be guided by a larger foreign power, and that this power would certainly be France. But France's abandonment of Syrian desires for reform and decentralization early in 1914 ended this possibility once and for all. France's underestimation of the Syrian national movement and her overvaluation of her own popularity there[55] blinded her to the realities of the Syrian political situation. The Christian majority in the Lebanon indeed did remain loyal to France, but in 1914 France sacrificed her future political influence and attractiveness among the majority of the Syrian peoples in order to secure an economic sphere of influence and religious guarantees for her Christian protégés.

France's double-edged foreign policy had been designed to give lip service to the doctrine of Ottoman territorial integrity. But at the same time the Quai d'Orsay had wanted to create a basis of French popularity and political influence among the peoples of Syria. French diplomats thus worked rather closely with all varieties of Syrian reformers and separatists. Their counsels of moderation to the latter were not meant primarily as an adjunct to the policy of preserving Turkish integrity, but were given merely out of fear that any disturbance in Syria would result in an international intervention of all the powers. This, of course, would have imperiled exclusive French influence there. But the agreements with Germany and Turkey in early 1914 gave France an economic sphere of influence to go along with her religious protectorate. After this, it became clear that in the case of any outbreak of violence in Syria, France alone would most likely be called upon to restore order, or at the very least to administer order once it had been restored. In these conditions she could afford to abandon the complications of supporting a Syrian reform program against the wishes of a reluctant Turkish government, whose favor she also wished to curry. The abandonment of Syrian reform marked the end of France's political influence among the majority of the population in that country. The negative reaction of the Syrians to the French assumption of the mandate for that country after the war should have been foreseen.

8 FRENCH POLITICAL INFLUENCE IN LEBANON, 1901-1914

Whereas the people of Syria rejected the concept and the reality of a French mandate after the First World War, substantial segments of the Lebanese populations accepted and welcomed it. What was the basis for this difference in attitude? Certainly one explanation can be found in religious affiliation. The majority of the Lebanese were Christian, and Lebanon formed the fulcrum of the French missionary establishment in Asiatic Turkey. The missions had created numerous schools, hospitals, orphanages, and asylums in that territory, which naturally tended to create an affinity between the majority Christians and the French. And after the war these people reacted negatively to the prospect of becoming part of a Syrian state which would be predominantly Muslim.

But these religious considerations, although important, do not tell the whole story of why France was welcomed in Lebanon and yet rejected in Syria. After all, there were substantial numbers of Christians of various sects living in Syria, and they followed the Muslim majority's lead in vilifying France. France's role in the Lebanese political milieu in the prewar period is equally important in assessing the Lebanese attitude toward France after the war. No greater contrast could be imagined than that between the French abandonment of Syrian reform and the real achievements which she helped to bring about in Lebanon between 1902 and

1914. In short, while France lost her political influence in Syria, she maintained it in the Lebanon.

Lebanon's political existence emanated from the *Règlement organique* of 1864, by which she was governed as an autonomous province of the Ottoman Empire. The Great Powers guaranteed this special status, a situation which made exclusive French influence there especially difficult. It was precisely this kind of internationalization which France attempted to avoid in the Syrian question between 1911 and 1914. It is ironic that, in these circumstances, French political influence endured in the Lebanon and perished in Syria.

Even as late as the turn of the century, France's political prestige remained high among the Christians of the Lebanon as a result of her military intervention in 1860. On 28 February 1902 Foreign Minister Delcassé received a petition signed by more than 1500 Lebanese Christians which recalled this intervention in glowing terms. The petition urged France to continue this tradition by helping the Lebanese protest to Constantinople against the reappointment of the present governor general, Naoum Pasha. The petitioners accused Naoum Pasha of working in collusion with Turkish officials by helping to rig village elections, by creating new taxes unauthorized by the *Règlement organique,* and by pressuring local judges to make decisions according to the wishes of their entourages.[1]

Although Paul Cambon in London counseled against any French action concerning the petition,[2] on 7 May 1902 the French consul general in Beirut wrote to Delcassé to corroborate all the accusations of the Lebanese petitioners. He confirmed the fact that Naoum Pasha had been acting like an "absolute emperor," but he blamed weaknesses in the *Règlement organique* much more than the person of the governor general for this situation. The consul general urged the Quai d'Orsay to take the initiative at the Porte to secure the necessary constitutional changes to correct these abuses.[3] This position was shared by Ambassador Constans, who notified Delcassé on 15 June that he had come to the conclusion that "the regulation of a number of articles of the *Règlement* of 1864 is the only practical means of realizing the

desired amelioration." Constans thus ordered the consul general
in Beirut to draw up a number of constitutional changes which
would be submitted to the regular conference between the representatives of the Great Powers and the Ottoman foreign minister.
Such conferences took place every five years when the tenure of
the Lebanese governor general expired. Constans concluded by
saying that none of the European powers favored the renomina-
tion of Naoum Pasha.[4] This final remark indicated that perhaps
constitutional changes for the Lebanon could be wrung from the
Porte in exchange for Great Power approval of Naoum Pasha for
another term as governor general.

From Beirut Consul General Sercey outlined some desirable
changes in the *Règlement organique* on 4 July 1902. His suggestions were as follows: (1) that the *Medjliss* (Administrative
Council) must meet once a year for a determined length of time
(at that time the governor general did not have to call it at all); (2)
that the village elections of the local sheiks must be supervised by
a bureau composed of representatives of each religious sect living
in the village; (3) that a set procedure must be adopted for the
election of the Administrative Council of the Lebanon, the main
deliberative body, which was elected by the sheiks of each village;
(4) that judges henceforth must be paid an adequate wage in
order to forestall the time-honored Ottoman tradition of *back-
chich,* or bribery, and that all cases of venality would be inves-
tigated by the Administrative Council; and (5) that local taxes
must be approved by both the Porte and the six guaranteeing
powers, and that the governor general and the Administrative Council must establish and publish a regular budget each
year.[5]

These proposed changes, based upon the complaints of the
Lebanese, were indeed placed on the agenda of the Great Power
conference to determine the new governor general of the Lebanon. But the six ambassadors were unable to reach any agreement on the French proposals, fearing perhaps that the adoption
of the program would redound too much to French prestige in the
Lebanon. The incident illustrated for the Quai d'Orsay the
difficulty of developing political influence in an area where the
"concert of Europe" was involved; it was probably an important
consideration in the subsequent refinement of France's Syrian

policy. Unable to reach agreement on constitutional reform, therefore, the conference haggled endlessly over a suitable replacement for Naoum Pasha as governor general. The latter's term ran out in mid-August, but the dispute over his successor was not resolved until 27 September 1902. On that date a protocol was issued naming a certain Mouzaffer Pasha as the new governor general. In addition the protocol made three innocuous guarantees, intended more as palliatives than as substantial reform, concerning the Administrative Council elections, the organization of the juidiciary, and the conduct of local magistrates.[6]

Mouzaffer Pasha began his tenure auspiciously enough, promising a number of reforms. Among the most important were an improvement in the communications media, new roads, the creation of seaports, and the reorganization of the militia. But these problems never got beyond the paper stage and were never effected. Throughout 1903 and 1904 the French consul general in Beirut kept the Quai d'Orsay informed about the sporadic, inefficient, and often bumbling rule of Mouzaffer Pasha.[7] One incident which particularly annoyed Sercey occurred in July 1904, when Mouzaffer arbitrarily dismissed a provincial official of the Lebanon who had been particularly favorable to France in the past. The consul general regarded this action as a slap at French prestige, and urged the embassy at Constantinople to put pressure on the Porte to annul the dismissal. The embassy, however, declined to make an issue of the matter, since the *Règlement* gave the governor general full control to name and dismiss all administrative agents, but "it is one more complaint to add to our already bulging dossier against Mouzaffer Pasha."[8]

Exactly why Mouzaffer's regime was unsatisfactory is not completely clear. At least one source considered him a true reformer, quite serious in his promises to the Lebanese people at the time of his election. But his good intentions were undercut by his wife. It was "Madame la gouvernante," with her insatiable desire for personal luxury, who dominated her husband and was responsible for his regime's corruption.[9] Despite this assessment, the British consul general in Beirut tended to agree with his French colleague that "there is no prospect of any reform in Municipal affairs so long as they are under the complete control of the

Governor General." But, while he acknowledged the weakness and corruption of the Lebanese governor general, Sir R. Drummond-Hay also complained of his French colleague's propensity for interfering in the affairs of the Lebanon. He blamed this interference for much of the trouble there and especially for the ineffectiveness of Mouzaffer Pasha.[10]

Mouzaffer died in June 1907 while the representatives of the Great Powers were once again haggling over his successor. After some delay a certain Youssouf Pasha was chosen to succeed to the position of governor general, much to the disgust and apprehension of the citizens of the Lebanon. Youssouf was a relative of the hated Naoum Pasha, who had been ousted in 1902. But French reluctance to approve Youssouf's nomination was abandoned when Ambassador Constans indicated that he would probably prove amenable to French influence in the Lebanon.

During 1907 and 1908 one of the most important problems France had to face in the Lebanon was that of Christian emigration. In 1860 many Maronites had been driven by Druze fanaticism to take refuge in Beirut, which was not part of the Lebanon but rather a curious enclave within it. Beirut became virtually a Christian city. But by 1907 the reverse process was taking place. The threat of Muslim violence in Syria and Beirut reduced the security of life for Christians there and slowly drove them back into the Lebanon. Lebanon's rocky soil could not support this new influx of people, and the result was the emigration of these Christian peoples to Egypt, Europe, and South and North America. French figures, submitted by the consul general in Beirut to Delcassé as early as 1903, indicated that about 80,000 Lebanese Christians had emigrated during the previous fifteen years.[11] This trend not only reduced the French Christian population, thus calling the future of France's influence into question, it also fostered Lebanese Irredentist demands.

There are numerous indications that Lebanese Christians preferred that France, rather than any other power, take steps to help alleviate the emigration crisis. That Italy was attempting to insinuate her influence in the Mountain is made clear in the chapters on the religious protectorate. Even Germany was attempting to capitalize on the Lebanese problems to establish a base of influence there by extending her successful agricultural colonies north from Palestine.[12] But most Christians remained loyal to France. Mgr. Emmanuel Pharès, secretary to the Maronite archbishop of Sidon, urged in 1908 that France undertake the task of establishing factories and schools necessary to stem the tide of emigration before her influence was supplanted by others. Pharès wrote that "the Maronites, these "Frenchmen of the Orient', remain the intrepid champions of French influence in spite of the bitter rivalry and the prodigious efforts of all your rivals—and they are numerous—who seek to develop their zone of influence . . . in our regions."[13] The Maronite patriarch himself, Mgr. Hoyek, referring to the attempts of other European powers to undercut French influence in the Lebanon, maintained that the Catholics "desire only to remain under the French flag. . . . While awaiting better days, we shall preserve our old love and fidelity for France."[14]

But the emigration problem created cries for more than just factories and schools. In 1908 a thick book on the Lebanon was published by M. Jouplain, a *nom de plume* for Paul Nujaym, a well-known Maronite lawyer. In the book Jouplain called for sweeping territorial adjustments, including the annexation of the port city of Beirut to the Lebanon. He also urged the extension of Lebanese frontiers to the northeast, into the fertile areas which would ease the problem of food production. The author took cognizance of the international character of the Lebanese regime and advised the Porte to assist the Lebanese in their aspirations. But above all, he said, the people of Lebanon "appeal to France, their protectress over the centuries, to that French nation with which they have so much cultural affinity . . . to assure a normal, legitimate solution to the question of Lebanon and of Syria: liberty and autonomy."[15] A Lebanese Committee, chaired by Chekri Ganem, was formed in Paris to agitate for a Lebanese expansionist policy into the areas of Bekâa' and Baalbek, which would become an agricultural preserve capable of stopping emigration. Ganem's program also called for the inclusion of the city of Beirut into the Lebanon.[16]

The problems were exacerbated even further by the Young Turk revolution of July 1908, which resulted in an invitation to the Lebanese to send delegates to the Ottoman parliament in Constantinople. Previously the Lebanon had not been represented. This issue, according to the British consul general in Beirut, split Lebanon into three factions. The conservatives, composed primarily of Maronite clergy, wanted no change in the organic statute and declined all representation in the Ottoman parliament at Constantinople. The liberals were the largest faction and were made up mostly of small landowners and tradesmen. They were willing to be represented at Constantinople, but only if such representation would not prejudice the special privileges reserved in the *Règlement organique.* A small but noisy group of radicals on the Left desired parliamentary rights whether or not they would endanger Lebanese autonomy.[17] No assurances could be wrung from the Porte concerning the future of Lebanese autonomy. And since the great majority would consider parliamentary representation only if their autonomy were not threatened, the elections that took place in October 1908 were a flop. They died a natural death, and no representatives to the Ottoman legislature were elected.

The acting French consul general in Beirut notified Foreign Minister Pichon on 7 August 1908 that the revolution had led to an increased strength of the Committee of Union and Progress in Beirut and Lebanon. This group was beginning to exert the familiar pressure on the new governor general, the result of which was that Youssouf Pasha was acting "more and more like a Turkish functionary . . . and not like the agent placed by the powers in accord with the Porte to see that the privileges of the Mountain are respected." These developments, the French representative maintained, were hurting French influence. He recommended that the Quai d'Orsay "respond to the desire expressed by the Maronite Patriarch and indicate . . . that the French Government is ready to support the efforts of the great majority of Lebanese with regard to the conservation of their privileges."[18] But in regard to Lebanese Irredentist ambitions, this same French diplomat was much more reserved. He notified Pichon on 21 December 1909 of the existence of an annexationist group called the *Union libanaise* but warned that "its intemperate zeal could become dangerous. . . ." The foreign minister himself, in response to the news of the desire of the *Union libanaise* to increase Lebanon territorially in the northeast, penciled in the margin: "This is foolish and contrary to our eventual interests in Syria."[19] French policy in the Lebanon, therefore, did not differ from that in the rest of Syria. France was not inclined to tolerate any radical schemes which might stir up trouble and occasion an international intervention.[20]

The years 1910 and 1911 were characterized by a growing rift in the Lebanon between the governor general and the elected Administrative Council. The latter felt that the governor general was working too closely with Turkish authorities and indeed was conspiring with them to end the autonomous position of the Lebanon guaranteed by the *Règlement organique.* Several incidents were reported of Youssouf Pasha dismissing members of the Administrative Council who had expressed opposition to his policies.[21] These developments led to increasing impatience among some of the citizens of the Lebanon. On 15 March 1910 the acting French consul general in Beirut notified Pichon of an article written by a group of Maronites which was strongly critical of the Great Powers and their attitude toward Lebanese grievances. René Ristelhueber reported that "it is to my knowledge the first time that the control of the foreign powers over Lebanese administration has experienced such a lively attack and in such wounding fashion, particularly for France."[22] Another indication that French prestige and political influence were being called into question was a letter from the Lebanon addressed to the Quai d'Orsay on 6 June 1911. It urged France to defend the *Règlement organique* more energetically, since England and Germany, jealous of French influence in the Lebanon, were following a policy hostile to Lebanese autonomy. France's silence in the matter thus permitted the governor general, in actuality a pawn of the Turks, to exercise a "veritable dictatorship." The note concluded that England and Germany wanted "to annihilate, at the opportune moment, our privileges, our autonomy, and consequently the essential element of the prestige of France, of her policy and interests in the Orient."[23]

By 1911, therefore, French authorities had been presented with several Lebanese requests for assistance in achieving some guarantees against the arbitrary rule of the governor general as well as some lampoons for having taken no action. But the real problem, so far as French initiative in the matter was concerned, was that the only favorable moment to act on the Lebanese demands was when it came time for the renewal of the powers of the governor general. This was the only time that the Great Power representatives got together to discuss Lebanese affairs, and it was clear that any alterations in the *Règlement organique* would have to be approved by all of them.

On 5 June 1911 a list of Lebanese grievances and aspirations concerning the powers of the governor general, excessive taxation, and the desire of Lebanon to be permitted to open and operate port and customs facilities was presented to the French consul general at Beirut. The latter seized this opportunity to urge the Quai d'Orsay to take the initiative in interesting the other European cabinets in a discussion of the Lebanese situation.[24] Youssouf Pasha's term as governor general was to expire in July 1912, and France wanted the Lebanese to realize that she was taking the lead in sponsoring the reform measures which were sure to be discussed in conjunction with the selection of a new chief executive.

France indeed did take the initiative in proposing changes in the *Règlement organique.* Ambassador Bompard submitted proposals to the ambassadors' meeting on this matter in May 1912. The French consul general in Beirut had originally drawn up the suggestions, which included several changes in judicial procedure and in the electoral laws governing the Administrative Council and also recommended that the latter should participate in drawing up the yearly budget. Bompard further proposed a tax increase for the Lebanon, but in exchange the Porte would agree to permit Lebanon to open port facilities and operate customs bureaus to augment the local treasury.[25] The whole matter was attended with some skill by French diplomats, particularly Ambassador Bompard. Bompard's English counterpart, Gerard Lowther, conceded this point as early as 4 May 1912. In a dispatch to Sir Edward Grey, Lowther reported how he had in the past hoped that the British and French embassies could work together in the matter of Lebanese reform. But because of

France's special concern with the welfare of the majority Christians in the Lebanon, Lowther surrendered the initiative in the question of reforms exclusively to France. Lowther complained, however, that Bompard had taken so much time in making his proposals that only two months remained before the governor general's term expired. By waiting until the last minute Bompard hoped to prevent any objections from delaying the adoption by the powers of the full French reform scheme, since another five years would have to elapse before reforms again could be attempted. Bompard's motives, Lowther concluded, were not far to seek. "If his scheme were carried [which was in fact what happened], the knowledge that the improved conditions in the Lebanon were due to French initiative would considerably enhance French prestige and influence locally . . . and will more than ever earmark the Syrian provinces as a close French preserve."[26]

Discussions between the representatives of the six powers and the Ottoman foreign minister continued on beyond the July 1912 deadine which signaled the end of Youssouf Pasha's term as governor general of the Lebanon. One of the main obstacles to any agreement on Lebanon during the early summer of 1912 was the Young Turks' intransigence regarding such key items as the opening up of ports in Lebanon and the curtailment of the powers of the governor general. The Committee of Union and Progress wanted to get the consent of the powers for a new governor general first and only after that to discuss changes in the *Règlement*. France, however, argued that the two matters were inseparably linked and that Turkey, once the governor general was named, would resort to dilatory tactics on the matter of modifying the Lebanese regime.[27]

Difficulties were largely overcome, however, during the interlude from July 1912 to January 1913 when the Liberal Entente party temporarily ousted the Committee of Union and Progress from power. The party proved much less intractable to French reform suggestions. Nevertheless it took nearly six months of delicate negotiations before an agreement concerning constitutional changes in the Lebanese charter could be hammered out. On 23 December 1912 the ambassadors of the six powers and the

Ottoman foreign minister signed a protocol modifying the regime in the Lebanon. The protocol made the following provisions: (1) an Armenian Catholic, Ohannes Bey Couyoumdjian, was named governor general; (2) a wider electoral basis for the Administrative Council was outlined; (3) no duly elected Council member could be arbitrarily dismissed by the governor general without a review of his case before the entire Council; (4) the governor general was to undertake an examination of the whole tax structure and to present a report to the Sublime Porte, which would then negotiate with the European powers for a revision of the *Règlement* concerning taxes; and (5) the gendarmerie was to be increased. An important separate protocol was annexed to the total agreement calling for the opening up of the ports of Djounieh and Beni-Jounes to unrestricted steamship traffic.[28] The verdict about the importance of this reform program to France was aptly summed up in 1913 by Ludovic de Contenson, whose book on reforms in Asiatic Turkey became a standard source. He called it simply "a real success for the French Ambassador."[29]

The Lebanese response to the changes in the *Règlement organique* was gratifying so far as France was concerned. Expressions of loyalty and gratitude for France's role in initiating the reforms were delivered to French officials in Beirut and Cairo by various Lebanese groups and leaders.[30] Despite this response, however, the documents for 1912, 1913, and 1914 show numerous appeals from Lebanese organizations and individuals for French assistance in achieving the annexation of Beirut, Baalbek, and the Bekåa' to the Lebanon. Appeals such as these were dealt with in much the same way French diplomats handled the violent Syrian separatists; that is, the annexationists were counseled to observe patience, prudence, and moderation, but their aspirations were not entirely discouraged.[31] These appeals for French assistance were important since they were invariably prefaced by sincere expressions of loyalty to France and gratitude for her role in achieving a moderation of the Lebanese regime. And shortly after World War I erupted, Mgr. Hoyek, the Maronite patriarch, wrote to French Foreign Minister Gaston Doumergue on 27 August 1914 to assure him that "whatever the attitude of Turkey may be, the Maronites and the Lebanon have decided to remain faithful to the traditions of attachment . . . toward France, their generous protectress."[32]

France thus succeeded in maintaining her political influence in the Lebanon by steadfastly adhering to her determination to achieve a reform program there. And her efforts were rewarded when substantial segments of the Lebanese population welcomed the French mandate after the war. Whether France would have lost her enthusiasm for Lebanese reform if she had received her railroad concessions from Turkey and Germany before December 1912 is an unanswerable question. Certainly the fact that the majority of the people living in the Lebanon were Christian is important in evaluating the welcome extended to the concept of a French mandate in 1920. But the fact that France maintained her paramount political influence there during the prewar period cannot be overlooked. Whether the rest of Syria would have been more amenable to a French mandate after the war if France had not abandoned the Syrian reformist aspirations in early 1914 is again another unanswerable question. But the French experience in the Lebanon at least suggests that France would have been better served in the long run had she followed through with support for genuine reforms in the rest of Syria.

9 FRANCO-BRITISH RIVALRY IN PREWAR SYRIA

If the Lebanese welcomed the establishment of the French mandatory regime after World War I, Syrians rejected it decisively. Even after the downfall of Faisal's Arab kingdom, French influence was greeted with outright rebellion. French authorities tended to brush off the Syrian disaffection as the result of British jealousy and intrigue in the area. There probably was at least a grain of truth in the French allegations. But the report submitted to the Peace Conference in 1919 by the King-Crane Commission concluded that French control in Syria was genuinely unpopular among the great mass of the population. This report indicated a Syrian preference for independence or, failing that, for their country's development under the auspices of the United States. This was most likely a further manifestation of the general euphoria with President Wilson after the war. But if the United States failed to assume the mandate, Syrians preferred, by a wide margin, English tutelage to French. Indeed the commission found itself unable to recommend French control in Syria under any circumstances.[1]

In considering this phenomenon one cannot overlook the fact that it was the British army under General Edmund Allenby which had liberated Syria from the Turks. The wartime exploits of another Englishman, T. E. Lawrence, earned him considerable reknown among the Arabs of Syria. These factors certainly increased English popularity and prestige among the Syrian peoples. But what pro-English feeling there was in Syria among both Muslims and Christians, a sentiment which dovetailed neatly with the loss of France's political influence resulting from her abandonment of Syrian reform early in 1914, found its roots in the prewar era.

The years from 1903 to 1914 were years of rivalry between London and Paris for economic and political influence in Syria, a competition both overt and covert in nature. This antagonism cannot be overestimated, since the stakes were the final disposition of Syria in case the Ottoman Empire in Asia should collapse. The fact that the Mandate Commission of the League of Nations assigned Syria to French overlordship is of secondary importance in evaluating the effects of the prewar Anglo-French rivalry. The King-Crane report, after all, demonstrated French unpopularity among Syrians and recommended American or British assumption of the mandate. All this makes the Franco-British prewar competition in Syria of especial interest and importance. For England emerged from this competition with an enhanced political influence and popularity in Syria which was certainly not diminished by the circumstances of the war in the Middle East, where English soldiers participated far more extensively than French.

The first significant conflict of interest between Britain and France during the period under consideration occurred in 1903. It concerned the possibility of opening the Lebanese port city of Djounieh to steamship traffic, a promise made by Mouzaffer Pasha upon assuming the duties of governor general of the Lebanon. A Lebanese journal observed on 23 February 1903 that French officials had expressed no opinion on Mouzaffer's promise and implied that France would probably oppose the idea of a Mediterranean port for the Lebanon because it would allow competition to the French-dominated port of Beirut. France would not want to face competition from England. The author concluded by hoping France would not oppose such a development, because "France knows that her refusal would break the alliance and the good understanding which has existed between her and the Lebanese for so long."[2]

In March 1903 a Lebanese businessman told the French minister in Cairo that the English attached a great deal of importance to the creation of the port of Djounieh in order to put a check on the port of Beirut. The English adopted this attitude, according to the Lebanese businessman, because they hoped "to capture there the commerce of Lebanon to the profit of the merchant marine and English influence."[3] Basing himself upon observations such as these, the director of political affairs at the Quai d'Orsay noted late in March that there was no doubt about the lively interest taken in the matter by English and Egyptian authorities, who wanted more than ever to "compete with French enterprise at Beirut and attract Lebanese sympathy to England."[4] Several days later the same official recorded that it would indeed be unfortunate to permit a counterweight to French enterprise to develop so near Beirut.[5] It should be mentioned at this point that there is nothing in the available British documents concerning the Djounieh port question of 1903 to indicate that England considered the matter as a confrontation of French and British interests. The British attitude, expressed in early February by the consul general in Beirut, was that even if the port were opened, the amount of cargo handled there would be small. But even so, its development would be opposed by the French Port Company of Beirut, by the French-administered Imperial Ottoman Bank, and by French diplomatic officials.[6] In light of these documents it seems ironic that France received the lion's share of the credit when Djounieh was finally opened in December 1912.

Early in April 1903 Delcassé received dispatches from both the consul general in Beirut and Ambassador Constans agreeing that the establishment of port facilities at Djounieh would be detrimental to French establishments at Beirut. Both concurred, however, that France should take no initiative in opposing the port, but that if the question were raised France should not permit England to resolve it alone in her own favor.[7] Fortunately for France the Turkish authorities themselves took her off the hook by opposing out of hand the creation of the new Lebanese port. The Turks enjoyed the customs monopoly at Beirut and also feared any diminution of imports to that city, which had easy and direct links to the important Islamic center of Damascus.

There were indications throughout 1904 and 1905 that France took quite seriously the possibility of an English threat to her influence in Syria and the Lebanon. Those, of course, were the years when Italy was making important inroads in the previously sacrosanct French religious protectorate over Levantine Catholics, and France was particularly sensitive about her position there. In August 1904 the French consul general in Beirut notified Delcassé about the enthusiastic manner in which the Turkish authorities in Beirut had greeted an English fleet which had stopped there to show the flag. This attitude contrasted sharply with the cool reception accorded the French naval demonstration a few weeks before. The consul general maintained that this kind of development was damaging to French prestige among Christians, because it made the latter feel that "France has completely abandoned Syria to England in order to concentrate on West Africa."[8] Two months later the French chargé d'affaires in Constantinople complained to the Quai d'Orsay about the obsequious behavior of British Ambassador Sir Nicholas O'Conor to the sultan. Bapst reported that "this Prince George" was posing as the champion of the Ottoman cause in the Lebanon by ordering his consul general in Beirut to avoid all differences with the Turkish authorities and the governor general.[9] What must have been even more alarming, however, was the report the French official in Damascus sent to the Foreign Ministry on 27 June 1905. The dispatch recalled several conversations between leaders of the Christian communities in Damascus and the French consul. The former were upset about the increasing taxes, but were notified that the French consulate could do little about this matter. The dispatch closed by reporting a "current of sympathy which has been working here for quite some time and which is growing each day in favor of England. This sentiment is not the result . . . of the action of British agents in Syria; it comes more from Egypt, the present prosperity of which is incontestable. It is the consequence of this easy comparison [with the Syrian administrative chaos]."[10] The population of Damascus was overwhelmingly Muslim, but significantly enough, the consul's remarks embraced sentiment among Christians as well.

On 14 February 1907 the London *Daily Graphic* published an article which proved alarming to French officials. The *Daily Graphic* noted the fact that numerous Catholic missions had recently abandoned the French Tricolor to place themselves under the protection of the Quirinal. The Italian example, it was predicted, would soon be followed by Austrian and German missionaries, thus reducing French influence in Asia Minor to a mere shadow. In these circumstances it would be impossible for France to resist for any length of time a revision of the capitulations proportionate to her reduced influence. The author concluded: "In view of our close 'entente' with France, this diminution of the French 'patrimony' in the Levant cannot but be regarded by us with apprehension. It means the transfer of the hegemony of the Orient to the Triple Alliance. . . . Here is a danger which we shall do well to watch vigilantly, especially in view of the great activity of Germany in Asia Minor and the prestige which the Kaiser has conquered for himself in Constantinople." Ambassador Paul Cambon regarded the article as being of some importance and sent a copy to Paris with the observation that the *Daily Graphic* was occasionally inspired by Whitehall. He felt that the article represented "a significant symptom of the anxiety with which the English Government follows everything which tends to diminish our influence in the Orient."[11]

That the French were becoming increasingly sensitive about their position in Syria, and especially about England's interest in it, can be gauged by the reaction in Beirut to the six-day sojourn in Syria of Sir Eldon Gorst, Lord Cromer's successor as British high commissioner in Egypt. Gorst's visit to Syria in April 1909, coinciding as it did with the Hamidian attempt at counter-revolution, gave rise to rumors that Britain was preparing for an intervention of some kind to ameliorate the administrative backwardness of Syria.[12] There is no evidence to suggest that Sir Eldon's visit had any such purpose. What made this matter controversial, however, was the appearance in a Syrian newspaper of a fanciful story depicting how Sir Eldon might write his report on his Syrian experiences to Whitehall. According to this newspaper, Gorst would report to London that "all the sympathies of the Syrians are for England to the exclusion of other foreign nations" and that the Syrians "envy their brothers in Egypt for the security, the tranquility and the wealth under the shadow of the [English] occupation."[13]

What made this story significant was that a number of Syrians apparently took it at face value as coming straight from the pen of Sir Eldon Gorst. French consular dispatches referred on several occasions to examples in the Syrian and Lebanese press displaying enthusiasm for England's interest in their countries and her apparent intention to do something about their problems. The British consul general in Beirut reported that the imaginary report "represents fairly well the actual state of things and reflects the inward feeling of many people, especially of the Lebanese, on the possibility therein mooted of a British occupation in the eventuality of a breaking up of the Ottoman Empire."[14] French officials, too, were aware of this alteration of Syrian opinion in favor of England and away from France. The French minister in Cairo commented upon this phenomenon on 26 May 1909 in his analysis of the furor raised by the publication of Sir Eldon Gorst's "report." But the French diplomat also viewed Gorst's sojourn as an indication of increasing British interest in Syria. This, coupled with the recent shift in Syrian sentiment, could prove dangerous for France. He recommended that France must show herself resolutely determined to oppose English penetration in order to avoid the development of English political action tending to prepare the way for a take-over of Syria should the Ottoman Empire dissolve.[15]

In response to the warning about Syrian opinion from his minister in Cairo, Foreign Minister Pichon, on 11 June 1909, ordered Paul Cambon in London to clarify French Syrian policy to the British government. Pichon stressed France's adherence to the principle of Ottoman territorial integrity, which obliged her to refrain from all actions implying a desire to lay hands on Syria. This policy, however, did not mean that France was disinterested or that she would remain quiet while another power insinuated itself in the seat of France's traditional influence.[16] The next day Pichon notified his other ambassadors of the instructions he had sent to Cambon. He urged them to contact the governments to which they were accredited "to rectify the false interpretation which our policy in Syria seems to have been given and to define the character of French policy in this part of the Ottoman Empire."[17]

France thus served warning to London that she was determined to preserve her political influence in Syria and Lebanon and would take a dim view of any British attempts to supersede it. The British, however, were not to be distracted so easily. On 17 October 1909 the acting French consul general in Beirut informed Pichon of a recent trip made by his British counterpart throughout the Lebanon. He viewed this excursion with alarm, coming so soon after the well-publicized adventure of Sir Eldon Gorst, and reported that the Englishman was warmly received, not only by his Druze protégés, but by Maronite leaders as well. The French official proffered the opinion that "the prestige of England thus seems to me to increase perceptibly at this moment, and by the force of circumstances, it is ours which suffers."[18] One of the main purposes of the trip had been to investigate further the matter of opening up Lebanese ports to steamship commerce, a question which had been raised again in 1909 but about which nothing was done.[19] Nevertheless, Consul General Cumberbatch waxed enthusiastic about the warmth of the reception extended to him throughout the Lebanon. He interpreted these expressions of good will as more than simple flattery. They were rather the result of favorable reports on British administration in Egypt and Cyprus brought back to the Lebanon by returning Christian emigrants. He went even further to say that the pro-English feeling was prompted by a vision of possible foreign intervention in Syria in the event of Turkey's dissolution and that "it was covertly intended to make me understand that if the mandate were to fall on England's shoulders, she would be welcome."[20] Cumberbatch's report reveals the same weakness that tended to appear in French documents dealing with evidences of pro-French behavior in Syria; that is, the tendency to overgeneralize from isolated instances and to assume that liberated Ottoman territories would prefer to develop under the auspices of a European power rather than to attain complete independence. It cannot be denied, however, that English influence was on the rise in this area after 1909. France's role in securing reforms in the *Règlement organique* in 1912 saved her political position in the Lebanon. It was to be a different story in the rest of Syria.

Political influence was not Britain's only concern in Syria and Lebanon during these years. Her commercial position there, especially regarding her exports to Syrian markets, was unrivaled, and her merchants enjoyed a very favorable balance of trade. But other powers, primarily France, Germany, and Italy, were making significant gains during the first decade of the twentieth century, enough at least to encourage British officials to look to their commercial interests in Syria. On 1 June 1911 M. E. Weakley, a special commissioner of the Advisory Committee to the Board of Trade, submitted a report on the prospects of British trade in Syria to the House of Commons. This long, dreary manuscript was an exhaustive statistical study of British and foreign trade in all the principal commercial centers of the Syrian littoral and hinterland. Weakley reached the conclusion that there was indeed room for British commercial expansion in Syria. He recommended an influx of cheap manufactured goods to fit the pocketbook of the average Syrian consumer. In the area of entrepreneurial technique, Weakley urged the adoption of the French language in all communication with Syrian businessmen and consumers, since this was the European language most universally understood there. Many Syrians had complained about commercial correspondence in English and about weights and measures being incomprehensible unless quoted in the metric system. Weakley's report concluded: "Not withstanding the prominant place occupied by British trade, it is difficult not to believe that more could be done if merchants and manufacturers in England made themselves more familiar with the conditions and ways prevailing in the country. Foreign merchants have succeeded in obtaining a very good footing, and it might be worthwhile adopting some of their methods by which this success has been obtained."[21] This report would indicate to France that England intended to capitalize on the rise in her political fortunes in Syria to expand her commercial influence as well.

The years 1912 and 1913 were crucial to France's fears about expanding British influence in Syria, and the misunderstanding between the two Entente powers erupted in occasionally acrimonious diplomatic exchanges. This was especially true as France became increasingly defensive about her position there. Italy was challenging France's religious protectorate, and England was concerned lest Triple Alliance powers supersede France in that strategically important area. An indication of Britain's interest in the eventual disposition of Syria appeared in an unofficial report submitted to Parliament in 1939. George Antonius, one of the authors of the report and himself an Arab nationalist figure of some importance, wrote that by 1912 Britain had for the most part accepted the view that Syria was politically a French preserve. But, he added, "the thought began to gain ground in certain British circles that, in the event of a breakup of the Ottoman Empire, an effort should be made to detach southern Syria as far north as Haifa and Acre to form a separate entity and to fall under British influence." He noted that Lord Kitchener, British high commissioner in Egypt, had become strongly imbued with this idea and worked for its propagation in official circles before the war.[22] Although some evidence suggests that the French may have believed that Kitchener had extensive ambitions in southern Syria,[23] recent research in the British documents has produced no support for Antonius' allegations. It appears, in fact, that Kitchener accepted the French presence in that area.[24] More will be said about these matters in the pages which follow.

The year 1912 saw the emergence in Syria of two developments which have already been noted in a previous chapter, phenomena which could not help but alarm French officials and put them, rather justifiably, on the defensive regarding their nation's future in Syria. The first of these was the development by the Committee of Union and Progress of a virulently anti-French campaign in the Syrian press, the purpose of which was to encourage Muslims to look upon France as the great enemy of Islam. The Muslim Arabs were encouraged to believe that a French occupation of Syria would entail wholesale persecutions of Muslims and a determined effort to convert them to Christianity. What made the situation particularly vexatious for the French was the simultaneous development, among an influential segment of the Muslim notability, of a movement to detach Syria from the Ottoman Empire and unite it to Egypt under English auspices. The fear in Paris that this movement had developed under British sponsorship was given a fillip by the appearance, on 1 March 1912, of an article in the *Fortnightly Review*. The unsigned article hinted darkly that the Egyptian empire of the past might well be recreated, Syria and Palestine being brought under the control of Cairo.[25] This article was later called to Sir Edward Grey's attention in January 1913 in a private letter from Paul Cambon. The ambassador maintained that "the French press has naturally reproduced [this article] and has wanted to interpret the author's anonymity as a proof of official inspiration."[26] These developments in 1912 gave point and direction to French attempts to combat the growing prestige of England in Syria.

Some Syrians at least were obviously amused at the rivalry between French and British officials in their country. In March 1912 a satirical journal in Damascus printed a mock Anglo-French treaty which, although intended as ridicule and satire, conveyed the inescapable fact of the growth of British influence in Syria. The mock treaty, which created a brief stir among Syrians, many of whom did not realize it was satire, provided that France would not resist the English occupation of Palestine, Syria, and other Arab countries as far east as the Persian Gulf. As compensation England would close the Straits of Gibraltar to all powers on earth except France and would also cede to her the island of Cyprus.[27] The provisions of the "treaty" were patently ridiculous, but Syrian levity did nothing to cool the growing Franco-British tension.

The disparity between French and British views of their own popularity in Syria can be seen by comparing two documents. On 18 November 1912 a telegram from the French Havas Agency in Beirut appeared in the French press and was forwarded by the British ambassador to Sir Edward Grey in London. In discussing Syria, Havas reported that "all the Catholics and the great majority of the Muslims express their ardent sympathy for France." These people, the report continued, were genuinely apprehensive about the Muslim notables' appeal to link Syria to Egypt and about rumors that England was considering an occupation of Syria in the near future.[28] On the other hand British

Consul General Cumberbatch alerted Ambassador Lowther on 21 November, just three days after the Havas dispatch, that "everything is keeping quiet at Beirut where, however, the pro-Anglo-Egyptian and anti-French agitation is spreading."[29] The difference between these French and British assessments is obvious and was perhaps symptomatic of the increasing tensions between the two European powers. It has already been noted in a previous chapter that French officials were increasingly worried about their country's prestige in Syria vis-à-vis England. On 23 November Négib Azoury, whose visionary Arab Committee continued to operate in Cairo after abandoning its Paris operations in 1908, wrote to Foreign Minister Poincaré to underline the seriousness of France's position. He noted that "the secular prestige of France, as well as her economic interests, are in jeopardy. Many sympathies are going to England."[30]

The whole matter came to a head in late November 1912, when several members of the British diplomatic service in Cairo took their vacations in Syria. French agents observed these men and reported that their vacation concealed ulterior purposes. Poincaré thus instructed Paul Cambon to engage Sir Edward Grey in conversations with the purpose of securing some kind of guarantee from him regarding Syria. The result was a series of Grey-Cambon discussions and exchanges which lasted from 26 November to 5 December 1912. On the first day of the talks Grey assured Cambon that England had no intention of joining Syria to Egypt and that the rumors bruiting the possibility of a trip by Lord Kitchener to Syria were baseless.[31] Cambon reported this information to the Quai d'Orsay. His concluding statement clearly showed the nature of French intentions in Syria but was couched in the kind of diplomatic language designed to display France's determination in Syria without committing any open indiscretion. Cambon noted, referring to his discussions with Sir Edward Grey, that he "was careful to affirm our desire not to modify the *status quo* in Syria; but that if Asiatic Turkey fell to the same fate as European Turkey, we could not ignore the titles which confer on us the interests and traditions to which I had made allusion."[32]

Rumors still continued to fly, however, concerning plans for an

English occupation of Syria.[33] On 5 December Cambon once again pressed Sir Edward to clarify England's intentions in Syria. Grey responded quite frankly that "we were carrying on no intrigues in Syria, and we had no intentions or aspirations respecting it."[34] It was Grey's statement of political *desintérresement* that set in motion France's drive to recapture some of her waning influence there. The Quai d'Orsay was also whipped into action by Ambassador Cambon, who earlier had placed much of the blame for the loss of French prestige in Syria on the French Foreign Ministry. Cambon had castigated the government of the Republic for maintaining the principle of French rights in Syria only in its correspondence with the diplomatic posts. France, he said, had been much less rigorous, even negligent, in demonstrating this vigilance to the Syrians themselves and to foreigners.[35] Such was the state of affairs when Poincaré made his famous speech to the French Senate on 21 December 1912.

On that day the foreign minister and president of the Council of Ministers made his subsequently controversial statement from the tribune of the Senate in the following terms:

I have no need to tell the Senate that in Syria and Lebanon we have traditional interests and that we intend to see they are respected.

I am happy to be able to add that the rumors about the existence of some disaffection between the English Government and us on this point are completely baseless.

The English Government has declared to us in a very friendly manner that in these regions it has neither intentions, nor designs, nor political aspirations of any sort.

We ourselves are resolved to maintain, in Asia, the integrity of the Ottoman Empire, but we shall not abandon any of our traditions there, nor repudiate any of the sympathies we have acquired, nor leave any of our interests there in abeyance.[36]

Recalling the events which led up to his speech some fourteen years later, Poincaré remembered getting Grey's permission to make the statements he did and even submitting a copy of his speech to the British foreign secretary for prior approval. But in his memoirs Poincaré tended to dismiss the whole affair as the result of "some little excess of zeal" on the part of English agents in Egypt. By 1926 he had conveniently forgotten the prewar consular reports attesting to the reality of English popularity and implied that he made his emphatic statements of 21 December 1912 because French public opinion was becoming apprehensive at the idea that England "could covet a country where so many of its inhabitants have considered themselves as our protégés for so long."[37]

Poincaré's speech, coupled with the simultaneous realization of reform in the Lebanese *Règlement organique,* thrust the initiative into France's hands. Indeed British sources suggest that the whole French campaign of November-December 1912 against British "intrigues" in Syria had been designed to intensify interest on the part of French public opinion and to prepare the way for Poincaré's dramatic affirmation of France's special rights in that region.[38] In any case her prestige among both Lebanese and Syrians was increased virtually overnight. French consular officials reported that the plan to unite Syria to Egypt under English auspices had received a crippling blow. But Anglo-French friction concerning Syria was not to end at this point. Grey would seem to have damped down the embarrassing situation by publicly disclaiming British political aspirations in Syria. But the matter was rekindled by the reaction given Poincaré's speech in the French press, a response which may best be described as chauvinistic.

On 24 December 1912 the conservative *Gaulois* vigorously applauded the foreign minister's words and went on to hope that Poincaré's success would make him go "even farther; and that someday he will lay out the complete list of rights which France has abandoned or ceased to claim, and also the duties which these rights imply." Equally strident comments came from the journals *Correspondance d'Orient* and *Bulletin du Comité de l'Asie française,* although all of these sources continued to pay lip service to the policy of preserving Ottoman integrity. So far as England was concerned, however, the most objectionable manifestation of French journalism came from the usually responsible *Le Temps.* That newspaper claimed that as a result of Poincaré's words "French opinion will realize without any doubt that it is a great success to have obtained from Great Britain such a clear recognition of French interests in Syria and Lebanon."[39]

The British ambassador in Paris, Sir Francis Bertie, observed on 26 December that Grey's assurances to the French which Poincaré quoted in the Senate "have excited the appetite of the French newspapers. They appear to conclude that our *desintérresement* is equivalent to a free hand for France."[40] The intemperate behavior of the French press made Grey's gesture to France appear to be a diplomatic surrender or a binding Franco-British accord similar to the one on Morocco. Sir Edward protested along these lines to Paul Cambon, who pleaded an inability to control the expressions of a free press.[41] This new furor put Grey on a spot in his own country, and he hastily issued dispatches to the diplomatic corps emphasizing that his only purpose in the Grey-Cambon conferences and correspondence was to deny that Britain was carrying on the intrigues or had the designs attributed to her in Syria.[42] In a conversation with the German ambassador on the subject, Grey emphasized that his words to Cambon "did not imply a disturbance of the *status quo,* which it was our object to preserve."[43] Forced to defend his actions in the House of Commons over a year later, Grey said that he had given the French the "most unqualified denial" of rumors of British political aspirations in Syria for two reasons. First of all, to have refused to do so would have been an unfriendly act toward an ally who already had established economic interests there. And second he had denied British political pretensions because not to have done so would have been unfriendly to Turkey, whose territorial integrity England held sacrosanct.[44]

Poincaré's speech of 21 December 1912 was certainly a critical point in the rivalry between Britain and France for political influence in Syria. For one thing it put new life in France's Syrian policy, and France's serious collusion with Arab reformist and separatist groups can be dated from this period. Also of some importance, a fact which will emerge shortly, was that Sir Edward Grey had been somewhat less than absolutely candid with Cambon and Poincaré. Whitehall, too, it appears, was willing to compromise with her pious pledges of Ottoman territorial integrity. British agents, like their French counterparts, maintained close and relatively cordial contact with Syrian separatist societies. It is clear that, despite the tone of the French press, no deal was made between Britain and France concerning the fate of Syria. Nevertheless, at least one observer has viewed the verbal engagements of December 1912 as a precedent for the deals which were subsequently arranged in 1914 for the partition of Asiatic Turkey into spheres of economic influence.[45]

After the Young Turks returned to power in January 1913, the Arabs were near revolution, and various separatist societies began to seek aid from either France or England. France soon discovered that England was faking indifference in Syria merely to allow sentiment in her favor to ripen. Grey's assurances to Cambon and Poincaré caused a brief lull in the pro-Anglo-Egyptian sentiment in Syria, but unpublished sources indicate that Britain still had hopes that she could gain political influence in the country. Propaganda from Egypt made some progress along this line. Throughout 1913 and 1914 British officials kept in close touch with Muslim leaders, not only in the Nejd and the Hijaz, but in Beirut, Damascus, and Aleppo as well. The published British documents say very little about this aspect of English Middle Eastern policy. Referring vaguely to the period from November 1912 to March 1913, the editors avow that Muslim groups did contact British officials in Damascus and visited Lord Kitchener in Egypt. Their only comment about these visits, however, is intriguing. The editors say that both Kitchener and Whitehall were "aware of the importance of extending British influence in western Arabia as well as on the coast of the Persian Gulf and with Ibn Saud." This was necessary to combat German influence and to realize the project of creating railway links between Egypt and the persian Gulf. "The advances of the Syrians and of the Arab Nationalists were, therefore, tactfully received."[46] This alone suggests that Britain was not nearly so politically disinterested in Syria as Sir Edward Grey made it appear in December 1912. The unpublished British sources are decidedly more specific on the matter.

Before the Grey-Cambon conferences had ended, the British consul general in Beirut reported to Ambassador Lowther that the pro-English and anti-French agitation had sensibly increased in recent weeks and had spread from Beirut to Tripoli-in-Syria, Sidon, and other areas. The sentiment was especially strong among Muslims and Greek Orthodox Christians, who "utterly dislike the idea of a possible occupation by France whose administration of her Muslim colonies is unfavorably compared with that of England in India and Egypt." Muslims, Consul General Cumberbatch said, prefer local self-government or autonomy for Syria. But failing that they would turn toward British administration instead of French. Even many Catholics favored direct British occupation, but he admitted that the Maronites of Lebanon remained favorable to France.[47] After the Grey-Cambon talks had been concluded, however, Lowther informed the foreign minister that he had warned Cumberbatch of "the necessity of being especially prudent and circumspect in his attitude in the matter," so as to create the impression in Syrian minds that no serious rivalry existed between Britain and France.[48] Britain's influence, like that of France in regard to the Syrian separatists, would be cultivated covertly.

The role of Lord Kitchener remains somewhat ambiguous. On 7 December 1912 Sir Edward Grey telegraphed Kitchener to notify him of his conversations with the French ambassador and to order him to scotch all local rumors of British intrigue and ambition in Syria. The high commissioner responded with his compliance the next day, but his telegram is quite revealing about his own estimation of British popularity and influence in Syria. It is worth quoting at some length:

Of course rumours are without any foundation; they are based on the fact that large sections of the people of Syria, both Mohammedan and Christian, would prefer British to French administration, and consider future prosperity of their country depends largely on close connection with Egypt. Some time ago local papers here reported that deputation of Syrian Mohammedans and Christians intended to pay me a visit. I let it be known that I would not receive them, and have heard nothing more on the subject. There are no rumours here of intrigue on our part in Syria; on the contrary, our attitude of aloofness has been subjected to comment.[49]

Kitchener's estimation of Syrian sentiment vis-à-vis England and France may have been correct, but he also may have been somewhat less than candid in categorically denying any interest in annexing parts of Syria. During World War I he expressed the desirability of acquiring Alexandretta and linking it to a British protectorate in Mesopotamia.[50] Prince K. M. Lichnowsky, the German ambassador in London, wrote in his memoirs that "Kitchener's attempts to carry on from Egypt a campaign of English propaganda in Syria . . . were doubtless by no means welcome in Paris." But Lichnowsky implied that Kitchener's activities were not endorsed by the English government.[51] Négib Azoury observed in a letter to his cohort Eugène Jung on 16 March 1913 that groups of Muslim notables in the principal cities of Syria had sent requests to Lord Kitchener begging him to annex Syria to Egypt or to have it accorded an independent regime. Azoury said that, in order not to antagonize her French ally, England "welcomes this movement with subtle encouragement without favoring it on the surface."[52]

In mid-December 1912 the British consul general in Aleppo alerted Lowther to the general rise in pro-British sentiment in his circumscription and the desire to obtain a British or Egyptian protectorate over Syria. He said that a monster petition was in the offing, to be signed by thousands of local Arabs, begging Great Britain to take over the administration of the country.[53] On 29 January 1913 word came from the British consul in Jerusalem that, "aside from the comparatively insignificant Latin communities under French influence, the one desire of the population seems to be some sort of union with Egypt."[54] Similar sentiments arrived from the British vice-consul in Mosul in late March. At the same time the British representative in Aleppo notified Lowther of his French counterpart's activities in fostering Muslim and Christian desires for a French occupation of Syria. But, the Briton continued, "the very great majority of Muslims desire that England should take over the administration of the country, and the Christians, including even the Catholics, declare that they could wish for nothing better. I have studiously avoided, however, any language calculated to inspire hope, locally, of such desires being fulfilled *at the present time*"[55] [my italics]. This same official described on 21 April 1913 the warm reception he gave to several influential Arab notables of Aleppo, who paid him a visit to solicit British help in escaping Ottoman rule. They desired some form of British administration, preferably in conjunction with the Egyptian government, and assured the British consul that they could bring about a general movement in Aleppo in favor of England.[56] Lowther later reprimanded the British consul for his "somewhat injudicious" initial reaction to the Aleppo notables' overtures.[57]

These documents indicate that although the Foreign Office counseled soft-pedaling the issue, some British officials in the Middle East maintained close contact with Syrian separatist opinion. But the general publics in England and France, if they remained unaware of the intricacies of their countries' policies in Syria, were quite awake to the fact that a rivalry between them continued to exist. In February 1913 the secretary general of the *Mission laïque* declared in the French press that "it would be puerile to deny" that the great majority of Syrian Muslims were pro-British and anti-French. But he maintained that these same Muslims greatly preferred French culture and were only pro-English because of the benevolent control they observed in Egypt. He urged France to liberalize her regime over the Muslims in Algeria, "then the moral prestige of France could be without rival in the Levant."[58] In May 1913 Count Cressaty warned the *Alliance française* of the great progress England had made in Syria. Her schools and hospitals were spreading English influence and preparing the conquest of the country. He went on to describe the committees existing at Beirut and Damascus, which were working to lead the Syrian population to claim English occupation. Cressaty concluded with an exhortation to France to assert her interests and rights in Syria and not abandon them to England. "England . . . must not misunderstand our special interests in Syria; I say interests, but I ought rather to say rights, for who would dare to contest them."[59] A week earlier *Le Temps* had expressed alarm at France's "negative" policy in Syria. The newspaper accused the Constantinople Embassy of imposing on the French consuls in Syria an attitude which discouraged France's Syrian friends and left the initiative there open to the British. The paper charged that the policy of ignoring Syrian aspirations "may well be a mortal blow to our position there."[60] *Le Temps* and Cressaty were, of course, unaware of the efforts being made by French officials to nurture their contact with

Syrian separatists while on the surface encouraging legitimate reformers.

Across the Channel public comment on the continuing Anglo-French competition for influence in Syria was not so prevalent, but such examples as there were proved intriguing. In April 1913 an article appeared in the *Fortnightly Review* which took arrogant and cynical cognizance of the Anglo-French rivalry in Syria. The author, however, frivolously dismissed France as an unreliable ally, predicting that "Syrian questions may soon suffice to reproduce the sort of hysteria which sprang from the swamps of Fashoda." He considered Germany a much more severe threat to English influence in Syria, but once German aspirations were eliminated, "the old healthy rivalries between good-natured Albion and perfidious Gaul may be satisfactorily resumed. I say satisfactorily, for history has never hesitated about colonial issues between England and France. Pondicherry, the heights of Abraham, the dual control of Egypt, indicate the results of any possible rivalries in Asiatic Turkey."[61] The author displayed a healthy dose of Gaulophobia and not a little bit of irony, but the implications of his article, so far as English ambitions in Syria were concerned, could hardly have been viewed with comfort in Paris.

The Quai d'Orsay was certainly aware of and concerned about the increase in pro-English sentiment during the first half of 1913. On 30 June 1913 the Foreign Ministry received a report in which the author concluded that England presented the most serious threat to French influence in Syria. The author, a certain M. Duborg, pointed out that the Muslims were suspicious of France's position as protectress of Christians in Asiatic Turkey and were therefore tending more and more to seek sympathy with England. English consuls in Syria were cultivating the Muslim citizens. Duborg urged the Quai d'Orsay to be more energetic in wooing Muslims away from English influence, perhaps by subsidizing Muslim newspapers in Beirut and Damascus.[62] The Quai d'Orsay, however, never took these warnings seriously. It continued naïvely to suppose that the Muslims and Christians of Syria would fall into line once France decided to assert her claims there.

In any case the British purpose in continuing contact with Syrian separatist groups was not to encourage the dissolution of the Ottoman Empire, but merely to maintain British influence there in order to provide a bargaining point with France in case the Turkish regime should collapse. Sir Edward Grey notified his ambassadors in Berlin and Constantinople in late June and early July 1913 that England must work to avoid the collapse and partition of Asiatic Turkey. The foreign minister felt that the effect of an Ottoman dissolution would be disastrous on British administration over the Muslims of India.[63] But British officials nevertheless kept a close watch upon the pulse of Syrian sentiment. Admiral A. B. Milne, cruising in Syrian waters on a flag-showing expedition, reported to the Admiralty on 16 July 1913 that there was a strong desire for administration by some European power—"preferably British." Milne emphasized that this attitude was especially prevalent among Muslim Syrians. But he continued, in perhaps a slightly overexuberant manner, to say that "the native Christian is naturally swayed largely by the influence of the church to which he belongs, but there is no doubt that native Christians as a whole prefer British rule to any other."[64] On 15 November 1913 the British consul general in Beirut described how French agents seized every possible pretext to attempt to augment the influence of France in Syria. France's purpose was to condition the public to the idea of a future annexation, "a contingency which is not as generally popular in Syria as is made out in French and Catholic quarters, and particularly not among Moslems . . . and most decidedly not among the Druzes of the Lebanon and the Hauran."[65]

The documents show conclusively that, although Grey had denied any British aspirations in Syria in December 1912, Britain's interest in the area continued unabated. And despite the British foreign secretary's assertions of June and July 1913 that Britain must work to avoid any dissolution of Asiatic Turkey, there is no indication in any of the documents that British officials in Syria sought to disabuse their Arab petitioners of the possibility of future British annexation or attachment to Egypt. The feeling in both England and France of an Anglo-French rivalry for political influence in Syria remained very real.

During the latter stages of 1913 this rivalry became enmeshed in the problem of Syrian oil concessions, a share of which Great Britain, despite Grey's expressions of *desintérresement* in 1912, was determined to obtain. The ground was prepared in August 1913 when a British delegate to the post-Balkan War London Conference told the Turkish ambassador that Britain would "probably ask for petroleum concessions in Syria and Farsam."[66] Anticipating difficulties with the French on this matter, Sir Edward Grey, on 22 August 1913, requested his ambassador in Constantinople to forward all the information he had about oil at Farsam "and in what parts of Syria it is believed to exist, whether any *'permis de recherche'* have been issued, and, if so, to whom, and whether the French have any prior claims there."[67] The British ambassador reported that a certain E. T. Boxall, a British subject and director of the Syrian Exploration Co., Ltd., had secured some short-term concessions to prospect for oil in Syria. The Foreign Office contacted Boxall and hinted that it could possibly secure an extension of these rights, but only on the condition that Boxall gave assurances that the concessions would be worked entirely as a British undertaking and that his company would not transfer such concessions or enter into any arrangement respecting them except with the consent of the British government. Boxall complied with Whitehall's terms.[68]

The first indication that France was aware of British petroleum activity in Syria came only on 3 December 1913, when Cambon notified the Quai d'Orsay that England was negotiating with Turkey for concessions to all petroleum mine sources in Mesopotamia, Arabia, and Syria. Cambon's announcement caused considerable alarm at the Foreign Ministry. Foreign Minister Pichon wrote to Cambon on 9 December bitterly recalling Grey's statements of a year before concerning England's disinterestedness in Syria. He linked the matter of petroleum to the Anglo-French political rivalry in the following manner: "If Syria, as well as Mesopotamia and Arabia, were included in the zone which the London Cabinet claims for her petroleum concessions, this concession could appear as an indication that England does not intend to disinterest herself politically in this province. It would add to the success of all the propaganda undertaken in Syria and the Hauran in favor of England, the increased activity of which has recently been reported by the French consul at Damascus." He ordered Cambon to take the matter up most urgently with Sir Edward Grey.[69] Conversations were engaged, and on 22 December 1913 Sir Edward handed a note to the French representatives assuring them that Britain was only seeking one oil concession in Syria and that "there was no question of any attempt to obtain a monopoly of such enterprise."[70] The fact remains, however, that it was Whitehall which had taken the initiative in extending the concession of the Boxall concerns. Grey's assurance apparently satisfied the French, for their document collections contain nothing more on the matter. This conclusion can be substantiated by the fact that Sir Edward on 30 April 1914 assured his ambassador in Constantinople that "the French Government have never raised any objection" to the British government's supporting certain oil claims in Syria. What they did protest against was the establishment of a British oil monopoly over the whole of Asiatic Turkey, "which we have assured them was never in contemplation."[71] Whether the oil concession would have led to a further intensification of Anglo-French rivalry and distrust in Syria is a moot question, since the outbreak of the First World War intervened to put an end to the matter.

Before World War I, therefore, both France and Great Britain had publicly disavowed any intentions of fomenting rebellion in Syria. The documents show, however, that both powers maintained close and cordial contact with Syrian separatist societies. But the events which more than anything else helped to swing the majority of Syrian opinion irrevocably toward the British were created by the policies of the Committee of Union and Progress during 1913 and 1914. After the decree of August 1913, which nullified most of the reform agreement reached between the C.U.P. and the Syrian delegates to the Paris Syrian Congress, the Young Turks began to make wholesale arrests of suspected Arab nationalists. One of their victims was Major Aziz Ali al-Masri, an Egyptian Arab who had been an original member of the C.U.P. and had taken part in the revolution of 1908 and the march on Constantinople in April 1909. He later had become disenchanted with the centralizing and antireformist tendencies of the Young

Turks and had joined several underground Arab movements. He was extremely popular among Muslims, and his sentence of death for treason raised an uproar against the C.U.P. throughout the whole Muslim community of Asiatic Turkey and Egypt.[72] The outcry was so loud and so insistent that the popular Arab figure's sentence was eventually squashed completely and al-Masri was freed. He received a hero's welcome on his return to Cairo.

British documents show that English officials intervened forcefully with Turkish authorities on the matter of al-Masri, and it is evident that this intervention played an important role in securing his pardon.[73] The result was a tremendous coup for British prestige among all the Muslims of Asiatic Turkey, Syria included. French officials merely observed and reported on the events but made no attempt to intervene, even when it became evident that their own prestige might be at stake.[74] The contrast between British and French attitudes could not have been sharper. One example will suffice. During the height of the furor raised by the al-Masri affair, the London *Times* published four leading editorials over a period of six weeks pleading in his behalf. On 9 April 1914 the *Times* editorialized in the following manner: "should the injustice which has already been done to the gallant Arab officer be followed by what would be neither more nor less than a judicial murder, the relations between the Ottoman Government and Egypt would be seriously affected, and probably not only the relations between Turkey and Egypt."[75] This editorial appeared, it must be emphasized, on the same day that France concluded her loan negotiations with the Turkish government, negotiations in which France completely abandoned her efforts to secure reform and decentralization in Syria.

The contrast was telling and it was out in the open for Syrians, especially Syrian Muslims, to see. It is no wonder that after the war, when Asiatic Turkey was being divided up among the powers in the form of mandates, Syrians should express a preference for British over French tutelage. During the prewar period British consular officials in Syria were just as mistaken as their French colleagues in underestimating the strength of the Syrian national consciousness. Like the French, they could not view Syria in any other position except dependent upon outside administration and control. But if the British officials erred in undervaluing Syrian desires for independence, they were certainly correct in placing British popularity above French among the majority of Syrians. It can be assumed therefore that the extensive anti-French attitude of the Syrians during the mandatory period after the war was genuine and not, as Frenchmen accused, the result solely of British intrigue.

The prewar political rivalry with England in Syria was obviously of vital concern to France. At the same time Italy was making a serious attempt to supersede France in the religious protectorate. German railroads in Anatolia had increased the Kaiser's influence tremendously in areas immediately to the north of Syria. All of these developments coalesced to convince France that her historical "moral traditions" in Syria were simply not enough during the heyday of imperialism to assure that that country would fall into France's lap in the likely event of an Ottoman collapse. An economic basis in Syria, laid down and explicitly recognized by the Great Powers, was fast becoming a necessity for France.

10 THE RAILROAD QUESTION: CREATION OF AN ECONOMIC SPHERE OF INFLUENCE

On the eve of the First World War the French financial investment in the Turkish Empire was enormous. French financiers controlled 62.9 percent of the Ottoman public debt. The Imperial Ottoman Bank, which acted as a state bank, was owned entirely by French and British capital. This bank controlled the tobacco monopoly, several utilities, railway and industrial issues, and other business ramifications. Although its head office was in Constantinople and there were alternate French and British directors-general, its loan and other fiscal operations were determined from Paris. The bank often acted as an agent of the Quai d'Orsay. French financial enterprise constructed and operated docks and warehouses in the Mediterranean, Black, and Red seas. Its role was preponderant in the operation of the waterworks, the electricity board, and telephones in Constantinople. The part played by French capital was hardly less prominent in other major Ottoman cities, including the important Syrian entrepôt of Beirut, while throughout several Asiatic provinces it held contracts for road construction and other transport enterprises. French capital was also heavily engaged in land and mortgage companies, in coal, silver, manganese, and copper mines. By 1914 French entrepreneurs also held concessions for port construction in Haiffa, Jaffa, Tripoli-in-Syria, Beirut, Zonguldak, Bandirma, and Inebolu.[1]

138

From the financial point of view, therefore, French capitalists had a tremendous investment in Turkish securities and a large stake in the continued good health of the always precarious Ottoman economy. French investment was more than twice that of Germany, which held second place, with Britain coming in a poor third. Trade statistics, however, tell another story. Here Great Britain was far in the lead, although Germany was making strong gains. Turkish exports to Germany increased more than 50 percent between 1900 and 1911, while German imports to the Ottoman Empire tripled. Exports to England dropped slightly during this period, but imports made some increase, although not nearly so spectacularly as those of Germany. French commerce with the Ottoman Empire slipped from second place in 1900 to a position inferior to England, Germany, Austria, and Italy in 1914.[2] These figures show that French commercial influence was on the wane at the same time that her financiers were growing more and more predominant.

One aspect of the French economic position in the Ottoman Empire has yet to be mentioned, an aspect which proved in the long run to be the most important of all—railroads. This facet was decisive, because it was through railroads that France succeeded in hammering out an economic sphere of influence in the Syrian provinces. This must, therefore, be considered in some detail and in close conjunction with previously mentioned developments—the Franco-Italian competition for religious influence in Asiatic Turkey (the protectorate), the French participation in Arab reform programs, and the French suspicion of British activities in Syria. In the end France's interest in establishing an extensive railway network in Syria and thereby creating a recognized sphere of influence superseded her involvement in these other aspects of the whole Syrian question. France succeeded in creating an economic sphere, a development which assured her eventual acquisition of Syria in the form of mandated territory, but in order to do so she deemphasized much of the religious and political prestige which she had spent the last prewar decade attempting to advance. In 1902 French firms were operating five different railroad lines in Asia Minor. These were the Mudanya-Bursa, the Mersin-Adana, the Beirut-Damascus-Muzeirib, the

Jaffa-Jerusalem, and the Izmir-Kasaba. The total French investment in these railroads by 1902 amounted to some 202 million
francs.[3] But any one of these lines, or all of them put together for
that matter, could not equal in potential influence the concession
German financiers achieved to build the Anatolian railway, with
future extensions to Baghdad.

Turkey granted the original concession to German developers
in October 1888. At that time the concession could be regarded as
a victory over French finance, since the Turks scrapped a French
plan to construct a line crossing Asia-Minor from the Mediterranean to the Persian Gulf in favor of the German Baghdad
scheme. The French project was abandoned for several reasons
even though the cost of construction would have been less and the
prospects of making money immediately much greater. In the
first place such a railroad would have developed the southern
provinces of the empire without connecting them to the Anatolian
homeland of the Turks. Second it might have promoted the
rapidly spreading Arab separatist movement. And third its
termini on the Mediterranean and Persian Gulf could have been
controlled by a foreign fleet.[4] The German-financed Anatolian
railway reached Ankara in 1893, but there it ran into financial
snags. Foreign opposition also developed, particularly from
French groups which feared that the railway would lead to an
overwhelming degree of German influence in the area to be
traversed. The French ambassador at the Porte, Paul Cambon,
expressed dismay in a private letter dated 27 Febuary 1893 that
"the Sultan is giving everything to the Germans." He threatened
to leave Constantinople in his frustration over the railroad issue.[5]

The deadlock was breached finally in May 1899, when German
interests (the Deutsche Bank and the Anatolian Railway Company) and French interests (the Imperial Ottoman Bank and the
Izmir-Kasaba Railway Company) reached an agreement. The two
main groups were to have equal participation in ownership and
control of a new company to be formed to build from Konya to
the Persian Gulf. Forty percent of the capital was to be German,
40 percent French, while Turkish investors would be offered the
remaining 20 percent. This accord between French and German
financiers was generally applauded in France. Ambassador

Constans' role in fostering it was regarded appreciatively, and many felt that the agreement of 1899 represented an important commercial success, furnishing France with a powerful instrument of economic expansion and political influence.[6] A final clause in the accord of 1899, however, stipulated that both the French and the German banking groups would work to secure the support of their governments, without which no securities could be listed on the national markets. This final provision was of prime importance, because it transformed an initially financial issue into a political and diplomatic question involving the extent of French influence in the administration of the proposed line.

The debate was joined on 24 March 1902 when Felix Faure rose in the Chamber of Deputies to denounce the merger of French and German capital and to move that the Paris Bourse not be opened to subscriptions from the new Baghdad Company. Faure cited three arguments to support his motion. First of all, although French and German capitalization were technically equal, Germany would retain political and administrative control over the company by manipulating the 20 percent share reserved for Turkish investors. Second, such a development would lead to the decline of French influence in Asia Minor, leaving it a veritable German colony. And finally, the most important argument so far as Faure was concerned, he viewed the railroad as an anti-Russian device *par excellence.* He pointed out the importance of the Russian alliance for France and argued that in case of a general conflagration, the strategic significance of the railway would assure Turkey's entrance against Russia. Faure went on to quote several pieces from the Russian press protesting against French participation in the enterprise.[7]

Foreign Minister Delcassé's response to Faure's speech is important, because within eighteen months he was to change his position completely on the Baghdad question. Delcassé responded that the French government had not as yet entered into the affair diplomatically at all. He felt that the agreement of 1899 offered a splendid opportunity for French capital and averred that it would be detrimental for French influence in Asia Minor if French financiers did not participate in the Baghdad project. The Chamber upheld the foreign minister by defeating Faure's motion to squash French involvement in the Baghdad project by a vote of 398 to 72.[8] Delcassé had not, however, committed himself irrevocably to French participation in the project. He emphasized that French financiers must have an equal role with the Germans in the administration of the new line. It was this loophole which Delcassé eventually used to block the use of the Paris Bourse to the Baghdad titles.

Early in 1903 the matter of French equality in the construction and exploitation of the Baghdad line was complicated by German agitation in Constantinople to unify the whole Ottoman debt. Such a development would tend to stabilize the Ottoman treasury and thus facilitate Turkey's payment of the kilometric guarantees to the Baghdad Company. Unification, however, could not take place without the consent of all the Great Powers. Delcassé informed Ambassador Constans on 21 January 1903 that France could not possibly agree to such a development until the "absolute equality" of the French and German elements in the Baghdad consortium had been established "in terms that left no room for doubt."[9] Constans, however, was of the opinion that the unification of the public debt was absolutely necessary to Turkey, whose credit was all but ruined. In a dispatch of 16 June 1903 the ambassador admitted that French financiers very probably were not going to secure equality with their German partners in the administration and exploitation of the Baghdad project. But he urged the desirability of achieving debt unification, if only as a favor to Turkey, even though the ultimate effect would be to help Germany build a German-dominated railroad.[10] Constans' conclusions about French inferiority to Germans in the Baghdad project were based upon a preliminary agreement reached on 13 June 1903 between the Deutsche Bank and the Imperial Ottoman Bank. According to this agreement, not yet finalized, both French and German financiers were to get 30 percent of the financial participation in the new Baghdad Company, with 10 percent reserved for the German-dominated Anatolian Railway Company. Additional 10 percent blocks were conceded to the Swiss and the Turks, both of whom were German-represented, and 10 percent was put up for subscription. If the agreement stood, Germany might well control 60 percent of the finances, with a corresponding influence in the administration of the railroad.[11] The French pipe dreams of parity with Germany in this great enterprise were becoming ever more remote.

The dichotomy between the French participation in the Baghdad Railway and the unification of the Ottoman debt erupted, in the summer of 1903, in an acrimonious exchange between Delcassé and Maurice Rouvier, the minister of finance. On 13 July Delcassé informed Rouvier of Constans' opinions on the Baghdad and unification matters, with particular reference to the preponderant influence of Germany as a result of the preliminary accord of 13 June. He also drew the finance minister's attention to some agreements of 1901 which would permit the Baghdad society to build branch lines to the Mediterranean Sea. These latter agreements hit the foreign minister in a particularly sensitive spot: "These agreements," he told Rouvier, "which I knew nothing about, would involve, if they exist, the most serious prejudice to French lines in Syria." For this reason Delcassé reversed his position of 24 March 1902 and told Rouvier that it was not in France's interest to join in the Baghdad enterprise. The Quai d'Orsay would also reserve judgment on the unification matter until it had been completely informed by the Imperial Ottoman Bank on all agreements with the German financiers.[12]

Rouvier responded to Delcassé with two letters on 20 and 23 July 1903, saying it would be the greatest disaster for Frenchmen not to participate in the Baghdad project, since not to do so would make it a completely German-dominated venture. The finance minister also saw no connection between the matter of unification of the Ottoman public debt and the Baghdad enterprise.[13] Both Constans and Delcassé had previously sketched in the connection between the two problems. But Rouvier had to defend the idea of unifying the Ottoman debt, since French documents show that it was originally his own proposal. It was later picked up and enthusiastically endorsed by the German ambassador and German financiers in Constantinople. This explains why the Germans did not give Frenchmen equality with them in the Baghdad project. They felt that since unification of the debt was originally Rouvier's proposal, France would eventually agree to it even if she were not going the participate in the Baghdad railway.[14]

French and German financiers signed the preliminary agreement on 1 October 1903. In addition to the arrangements which
assured the German group 60 percent of the financial control of
the Baghdad project, the final accord set up a twenty-nine
member Council of Administration. The German group was able
to control eighteen of these members.[15] In light of the Brussels
accord, which did not meet with the French government's
demands for complete equality with the Germans, Delcassé persuaded the French Council of Ministers on 23 October 1903 that
the government could not sanction the participation of French
money in the project.[16] French financiers were already committed
and in effect actually did subscribe 30 percent of the capital of the
Baghdad Railway Company. But the effect of the government's
decision of 23 October was to deny the use of the Paris Bourse as
a market for floating Baghdad securities. The bonds languished
in the hands of the Imperial Ottoman Bank until 1914. Delcassé
had come full circle; he was transformed from an advocate to an
opponent of French participation in the Baghdad scheme, and he
succeeded in pulling the French government along with him. As a
result of the decision of October 1903, France lost the opportunity
to have at least some voice in the construction, administration,
and exploitation of potentially one of the most important
economic and political instruments in Asia Minor. What were the
factors which motivated France's seemingly frivolous decision?
The question is an important one, for its answer involved the
whole future of her economic position in Syria.

The answer most often cited to explain Delcassé's refusal to
sanction French involvement in the Baghdad scheme is that
Russia opposed it out of hand. And Delcassé did not want to
prejudice the Franco-Russian alliance, so vital to the future of
French security. Sir Francis Bertie, the British ambassador in
Paris, cited the Russian opposition as the principal motive in
1906.[17] Professor John B. Wolf maintained that Russian pressure
on the Quai d'Orsay was the deciding factor in France's refusal to
allow Baghdad securities on the Bourse.[18] The great French
historian Pierre Renouvin came to similar conclusions. He maintained that one of Delcassé's primary aims was the strengthening
of the Franco-Russian alliance. He therefore opposed Rouvier on

the Baghdad matter in the belief that his action was a service France was rendering to Russia.[19] Documentary evidence does indeed exist to support this conclusion. In March 1903 Maurice Bompard, at that time ambassador to St. Petersburg, notified Delcassé that everybody in Russia, including Foreign Minister Count U. N. Lamsdorff and Finance Minister Sergei Witte, viewed the construction of a railroad between the Bosporus and the Persian Gulf as prejudical to Russian interests and favorable only to Germany. Throughout the spring and summer of 1903 Bompard reported massive Russian press campaigns against the Baghdad project and particularly against her ally France's participation in the enterprise.[20]

It can be granted that pressure from Russia was an important factor in France's decision. But it most decidedly was not the only factor. None of the sources cited above mentioned the important railway commitments France already had in Syria and the threat presented to these commitments by French participation in a German-dominated Baghdad railway. Unpublished sources at the Quai d'Orsay show that French diplomats were vitally concerned with the preservation and prosperity of the Syrian network, a concern which grew increasingly more pressing in 1903 when the Arab national movement was beginning to assume momentum and it became clear that Italy was determined to capitalize on French anticlerical sentiment at home in order to try to supersede France in the Catholic protectorate in the Middle East. It has already been pointed out that Ambassador Constans felt that France must consent to the unification of the Ottoman debt, even though the main beneficiary would be the Baghdad project, simply because Turkey's economic life depended upon it. He reiterated this contention on 16 June 1903 but maintained that certain guarantees must be exacted in return for consenting to unification. "We must preoccupy ourselves first of all with the health of our railroad lines in Syria: Beirut-Damascus, Damascus-Muzeirub and Rayak-Hama." Constans maintained that a German-dominated (but French-financed) Baghdad railway in the north with its projected junctions to Aleppo and the Gulf of Alexandretta, coupled with the Ottoman-administered Hijaz railway in the south, "would mean a quick ruin for our Syrian railways." He urged Delcassé to insist upon concessions guaranteeing France against the danger of being squeezed out of Syria.[21] What Constans feared (and Delcassé shared his concern) was that French money would be used to finance the line to Baghdad and its junctions to the Mediterranean, which eventually would ruin the French economic basis in Syria. As early as 13 October 1901 Delcassé had stated, in a letter to the president of the Administrative Council of the Imperial Ottoman Bank, that the proposed junctions to Aleppo and Alexandretta would conflict with the interests of the French network in Syria. "I must not conceal from you," Delcassé maintained, "that if the concession of these two branches were maintained in the definitive contract, it would be necessary for me to refuse to the Baghdad enterprise the support which my Department is in a position to lend to it and also to refuse the facilities of the Paris market to the financial operations which the construction of this railroad will need."[22]

This document shows that Delcassé's mind was made up as early as 1901. The fact that French financiers were denied equality with their German counterparts in the administration of the Baghdad line in 1903 only served to harden his determination not to permit the French market to float Baghdad bonds. The Russian pressure certainly was an important factor in Delcassé's decision of October 1903, but the threat posed by the German enterprise to French economic interests in Syria was equally vital and must not be neglected or undervalued. Despite the government's decision, French financiers continued to subscribe 30 percent of the Baghdad securities, but the fact that they could not float these bonds on the Paris Bourse caused considerable recrimination between them and their German colleagues. The decision of October 1903 created this condition, but it also set in motion the chain of events which ultimately led to the Franco-German agreement of February 1914, which set Syria aside as a French economic sphere of influence. In the long run it was this development which paved the way for France's assumption of the Syrian mandate after the First World War.

It was the matter of the Baghdad railway which served to draw the Quai d'Orsay into the fray. Thereafter, the Foreign Ministry was to cooperate extensively with French railroad enterprises in Syria in an attempt to expand and solidify their influence in that area. A notable example, one worth examining in some detail, is the case of the most important French-owned line operating in Syria—the *Société de Damas-Hamah et Prolongements.* One of the main problems this line faced after the turn of the century involved its junction from Damascus south to the city of Muzeirib. Shortly after 1900 the Hijaz Railway Company, an Ottoman-owned line financed by subscription among the Muslim faithful, undertook to build a link from Damascus to Deraa, which was exactly parallel to the French Damascus-Muzeirib line. Officials of the latter maintained that this parallelism was contrary to the guarantees given the *Damas-Hamah et Prolongements* in 1890. The Porte had offered to repurchase this section of the D.H.P. in 1902 for 5.5 million francs. This offer was, however, unsatisfactory to French directors, who maintained that there was already 11.5 million francs invested in that section. The D.H.P. requested the intervention of the Quai d'Orsay to help prevent the construction of the parallel line.[23]

The Foreign Ministry was unable to exercise that much influence in Constantinople, but Delcassé was nonetheless very concerned about the future of the D.H.P. in Syria. In January 1904 he was notified that the D.H.P. administration had decided to undertake negotiations with the Porte with a view toward ceding the Damascus-Muzeirib section for 7.2 million francs. Delcassé wrote to Ambassador Constans in the following manner: "Since this solution is considered . . . by my Department as unfavorable to our influence in Syria, I have let the Society know . . . that it was impossible for me to support this request, but that I remained disposed to support the principle of an indemnity."[24] Delcassé was not willing to sell out in Syria. After all, he had sacrificed French participation in the Baghdad scheme in order to protect her investment there. But the foreign minister would put pressure on the Porte to indemnify the D.H.P. for financial losses due to the Damascus-Deraa parallelism.

The method by which pressure was to be applied emerged in a Foreign Ministry note of 11 June 1904. It suggested that Delcassé prevent the floating of a loan of 2.5 million Turkish pounds "until the Ottoman Government has disinterested herself in the

Damascus-Hama Society either by granting a kilometric guarantee to the Damascus-Muzeirib line or, a preferable solution, by authorizing the construction of a junction from Hama to Aleppo, the natural terminal point for our Syrian network."[25] The loan negotiations dragged on for nearly a year, with France attaching very stiff conditions concerning the Syrian railways. The debate waxed acrimonious, and France even broke off negotiations, threatening a recall of her ambassador and calling to mind a repeat performance of the Lorando-Tubini rupture of 1901. The tactic worked, for in April 1905 Turkey granted the concession for an extension of the Damascus-Hama line to Aleppo with a kilometric guarantee of 13,667 francs. The Porte also agreed to an indemnity of 3.5 million francs to the Damascus-Muzeirub line for losses it had suffered as a result of the Hijaz parallelism.[26] The tactic of attaching unpleasant concessions to the granting of a loan was nothing new in international relations. But in this case the Quai d'Orsay had intervened and applied this strategy to the Syrian railroads with very satisfactory results. The Foreign Ministry was to use this method again in 1913 and 1914 with even more spectacular consequences.

But governmental intervention in the matter of the Syrian railway network was not merely a one-way street. The Quai d'Orsay often applied pressure on the railway companies, occasionally against the latter's wishes, to improve their services and undertake new enterprise. For example, in 1907 the Quai d'Orsay urged the D.H.P. to rebuild a workable line from Rayak to the sea at Beirut, since the existing one was narrow gauge and resulted in delays in the transshipment of Syrian crops. The resulting dissatisfaction, if not corrected, could result in the Syrians' transferring their shipping business to the Baghdad line, once its connections to the Mediterranean were in operation. The D.H.P. was reluctant to cooperate, preferring to devote its capital to the improvement of existing lines in the form of more and better rolling stock.[27] The company, however, eventually capitulated. Similarly, in 1909 the Quai d'Orsay persuaded the D.H.P. to seek a concession to build a line from Homs to Tripoli-in-Syria even though the company could not secure a kilometric guarantee from the Ottoman government. The project was described as "perhaps not too advantageous from the financial point of view but of capital importance for the maintenance of France's position in Syria."[28] The examples show clearly that the Quai d'Orsay was vitally concerned with promoting the Syrian railway network.

As far as the *Damas-Hamah et Prolongements* was concerned, the years 1911-1914 witnessed a recrudescence of the problem of competition with the Hijaz railway in the matter of the parallelism of the Damascus-Muzeirib link. The settlement of 1905 had called for a rate agreement to be established for these parallel lines. This had never occurred, and despite the indemnity accorded to the D.H.P. in 1905, the gross receipts for the Damascus-Muzeirib line showed that the competition from the Hijaz line was ruining it. The figures recorded a decline in gross receipts from 788,000 francs in 1904 to 386,000 francs in 1912.[29] The D.H.P. again sought the intervention of the Quai d'Orsay. The latter responded by undertaking negotiations with the Porte to secure a rate agreement between the D.H.P. and the Hijaz lines, and also to seek another concession to build a junction from Rayak to Lydda, which eventually would be used to connect Syria with Egypt. Poincaré wrote to Ambassador Bompard on 24 December 1912 that if these two matters were settled to French satisfaction, "our Syrian network would present a character of homogeneity and unity which will put a large enterprise into French hands, capable of erasing past misfortunes and destined in the future to render the most valuable services to French influence in the vast region extending from Aleppo to Jerusalem."[30] Poincaré's grandiose dreams about a French sphere were undoubtedly influenced by his recent successes in securing a British *desintérresement* in Syria and in achieving some important alterations in the Lebanese *Règlement organique*. But the concessions he spoke so glibly about in 1912 were not to be achieved easily. In the end they were to involve long and difficult negotiations with both Turkey and Germany.

France had set the precedent for using the penury of the Turkish treasury as a means for exacting concessions from that country in 1905 in the matter of the Damascus-Muzeirib parallelism. She attempted the same technique again in 1910, but with much less satisfactory results. In the early autumn of 1910 Javid Bey, the Turkish finance minister, arrived in Paris to begin negotiations with French financiers for a 150-million-franc loan to Turkey. Javid indeed succeeded in signing a contract with a French banking syndicate, but at this point the Quai d'Orsay intervened, and Foreign Minister Stéphen Pichon told the bankers that official sanction for the loan, including the use of market facilities, would be withheld unless the Ottoman government would consent to having its budget administered by a resident French adviser. Such a condition seemed excessive to the Turks, who took the position that it was incompatible with Turkey's national integrity.[31] French officials, however, saw the matter from a strictly entrepreneurial point of view. The deficit in the Turkish budget for 1909 was 5,460,583 Turkish pounds. The budget for 1910 foresaw a deficit of 6,800,000 Turkish pounds. Under these conditions it was quite natural that the French government, before approving a new Turkish loan, would demand certain conditions which would give France a degree of control over Turkish finances.[32]

The whole situation was complicated by the fact that Javid was greeted in Paris by a virulently anti-Turkish press campaign, led by André Tardieu of *Le Temps*. Tardieu himself was involved in a scheme, under the joint sponsorship of French and British promoters, to secure a concession from the Ottoman government to build a trans-Arabian railroad from Homs to Baghdad. The road was obviously designed to compete with the German Baghdad project, and Tardieu was engaged, for a rather substantial fee, to use his influence with Foreign Minister Pichon to persuade the latter to intervene on behalf of the Anglo-French promoters. Pichon at first showed signs of interest and even was willing to consider making the concession of the Homs-Baghdad line a condition for the granting of the Ottoman loan in 1910. But the foreign minister backed away upon hearing from Ambassador Bompard that the Turks were unalterably opposed to such a railroad. Their opposition was based upon the same criteria which had led them to refuse to sanction a similar scheme in the 1880s. Strategic reasons governed this decision. The Quai d'Orsay, therefore, ignored the Homs-Baghdad scheme, and Tardieu led a violent press campaign against Pichon, Bompard, and the Turkish government which lasted from June 1910 to February 1911.[33] Such virulence poisoned the atmosphere for the loan negotiations between Javid and the French government.

With Tardieu in the background making unpleasant noises about Turkey, the Turkish finance minister could not make financial concessions which would lower his country's prestige vis-à-vis France any further. In September 1910 he refused absolutely to bend to France's demands for virtual financial control over the budget in Constantinople. The loan negotiations fell through. England, unwilling to go against her French ally, also refused to sanction Javid's appeals for money. The latter turned to Germany and on 7 November 1910 achieved a loan agreement with that power.

The result was a political victory for the Triple Alliance. Germany gained substantial prestige at Constantinople. It appeared that France had made a mistake by demanding so much from Turkey in exchange for a loan that the latter was forced to have recourse to Berlin. Such, as least, was the analysis of Gerard Lowther, the British ambassador at Constantinople. He wrote to Sir Arthur Nicolson on 2 November 1910 that France had erred in losing the monopoly of lending money to the Turks. "Once they get it from the Germans, which evidently they will do . . . [the loan] it seems to me will give a great handle to the Germans."[34] But the fact of the matter was that German financiers had no end of trouble scraping up the money to lend to Turkey. In the end it took a great consortium of German and Austrian banks to underwrite the loan. And with a Turkish budgetary deficit forecast for the following year, it was clear that the Young Turks would need still further recourse to the French money market. Financial relations between the two powers were not yet irreparable. France indeed would get another chance to exact concessions from the Porte in return for a loan. This was to occur in 1913-1914 and involve France's whole position and future in Syria.

The failure of the Homs-Baghdad scheme, coupled with Germany's momentary success in lending money to the Ottoman regime in 1910, served the purpose of making French officials painfully aware of the need to consolidate their position economically in Syria. This need was forcefully underlined early in 1911 when the Syrian Carmelites, long considered protégés of France, transferred their allegiance to the Italian government. The situation acquired further complexity in 1910 when Germany began to exert pressure on the powers to agree to a 4 percent increase in Turkish customs duties, so that Turkey could devote the increased receipts to paying off the kilometric guarantee on the Baghdad Railway. Both France and England demurred on this point, demanding railway networks in Asiatic Turkey approximately equal to Germany's 4,000 kilometers before they would agree to a customs increase. France was especially insistent on this matter, and Bompard told Javid in December 1910 that if Turkey could not countenance additional railroads for France "at present," she could at least "reserve them to us for the day when they would become desirable to you."[35] Turkey indeed did notify Bompard in January 1911 that she was prepared to give French investors concessions for 2,000 kilometers of railroads in Albania and in the Black Sea region in order to get an agreement on the customs increase.[36] But Bompard pointed out that this offer ignored the Syrian system, which was of primary importance to France. One alternative, which Bompard suggested to Pichon on 23 January 1911, was to request future guarantees for railroads in Syria, railroads which would eventually link that area to Mesopotamia and Egypt. Another choice would be to attempt to persuade the Porte to permit the *Société de Damas-Hamah et Prolongements* to exploit the Damascus-Deraa section of the Hijaz railway. Bompard admitted, however, that the latter alternative would meet stiff Ottoman resistance.[37]

Two events, profoundly disturbing to France, occurred in the early months of 1911 and served to galvanize French determination to do something to assure her future position in Syria. The first of these was the revelation of the fact that on 4-5 November 1910 Germany and Russia had reached agreement on the Baghdad question. Tsar Nicholas had met the Kaiser at Potsdam, and the two had tentatively agreed that Germany would give Russia a free hand for her policies in northern Persia. In exchange St. Petersburg promised no longer to oppose the Baghdad railway and even to arrange for a connection of the latter with the Persian railway network.[38] The revelation of this accord produced disappointment and anger in Paris, since one of the reasons for France's refusal to sanction her financiers' involvement in the Baghdad project in 1903 was Russia's overt opposition to it.

The second development which served to catalyze French determination in Asiatic Turkey was the signature of a railroad agreement between the Baghdad Railway Company and the Ottoman government on 27 March 1911. By this agreement the Baghdad Company was definitively granted the right to prolong its line from El Helif to Baghdad. But what really wounded French *amour propre* was Turkey's agreement to permit the Baghdad Company to build a junction from the Aleppo section of the line to Alexandretta in northern Syria. Along with this concession went Turkey's permission for the German company to construct port facilities at Alexandretta.[39] The French reacted to these developments immediately. Paul Cambon wrote a letter to his brother Henri on 31 May 1911 in which he maintained that "everywhere . . . we are our own worst enemies. . . . I have just received a dispatch from Bompard confirming what I already know to be true, that we, and we alone, by our continued weakness, have permitted the Germans to pursue the Baghdad project alone for the last ten years."[40] Nor was this anger and self-criticism peculiar to diplomats. French citizens spoke out as well. In a speech to the *Alliance française* in May 1913, Count R. J. M. Cressaty referred in the following manner to the Alexandretta junction and Turkey's concession to the Baghdad Company to develop a port in that city: "When these projected works will be achieved Germany will become mistress of the best natural port in Syria, will rival the French lines and will complete its economic and political stranglehold on this region."[41]

This critical attitude toward French diplomacy and anxiety at the recent agreements concluded by Germany with both Turkey and Russia dovetailed in the years from 1909 through 1913 with an increasingly bitter and critical appraisal of the conduct of French enterprise in Asiatic Turkey, especially in Syria. In 1909 Alfred Durand, the French Conseiller du Commerce Extérieure, published a book which was little more than an exhortation to

French businessmen and traders to get busy in Asiatic Turkey before France was completely outstripped by other powers. He urged them to capitalize on the historical influence France had held in Turkey. Alone among the six Great Powers, this French official noted, France had witnessed a decline in her total business with the Ottoman Empire in the years from 1901 to 1905. He was particularly alarmed by the tremendous increases in commercial activity made by Italy and Germany.[42] Durand's accusations can be amply documented by examining some of the available statistical material on commercial exchange. This material shows clearly that between 1900 and 1912 the rate of French growth in commercial exchange with the Ottoman Empire was alarmingly slow, while that of Italy, Germany, and Great Britain was increasing steadily. This generalization holds true even for the major exchange entrepôts in Syria—Beirut, Alexandretta, and Damascus. Another important feature of the commercial picture for France in Syria was the strikingly unfavorable balance of trade she endured there. What she bought in that country far outweighed the products she was able to sell to it. Ironically France was paying for the tremendous gains made by other powers in the area of commercial importation into the Ottoman Empire.[43]

French diplomatic officials were not unaware of these statistics and of the dangerous possibilities portended therein. On 13 January 1913 Paul Cambon wrote to Poincaré and deplored the lethargy of French industrial enterprises and economic interests in Syria. Something had to be done, he said, to inject vitality into this aspect of the French presence there. Cambon spoke of "historic memories, traditional links between our country and the native populations, an unhappily dented religious protectorate . . . all that risks not being considered as sufficient title to justify eventual pretentions on Syria, if, from the economic point of view, other powers can claim interests equal or superior to ours."[44] Cambon's pregnant reference to "eventual pretentions on Syria" is illustrative of just how sincere were France's continued pious pronouncements on the territorial integrity of the Ottoman Empire. Cambon was not alone in his anxiety about France's economic position in Syria. French agents in Haiffa and

Beirut both alerted the Quai d'Orsay in strong language about the deficiencies in the French-operated port facilities at Beirut, the D.H.P. railway, the gas company at Beirut, and the *Tramways libanais*. All of these operations, the notes maintained, were lethargically and inefficiently run, without any initiative or ambition. As a result the Syrian people were becoming more and more dissatisfied with French influence.[45] Between 1911 and 1913 even British diplomats in Beirut and Paris were aware of the inadequacies of French business in Syria and the increasing concern of the Quai d'Orsay with this problem.[46]

On 1 June 1913 M. Boppe, chargé d'affaires at Constantinople, wrote an important and revealing Foreign Ministry note. He contended that France was spending too much time worrying about her moral and political action in Syria. More attention, he maintained, must be paid to the deplorable condition of French business enterprise there. The diplomat wrote: "If we are not careful, in spite of the genuine moral influence which we possess in Syria, we shall find our place taken when the time arrives for the liquidation of Asiatic Turkey. . . . Our whole future in Syria depends on our economic and industrial activity. If we do not modify our methods, our position will be lost and in several years Syria will be English, German and Italian. . . ."[47] This note, coupled with Cambon's dispatch of 13 January, makes the thinking of official France quite clear on the matter of Syria. Between 1909 and 1913 a change had been effected in French attitude. Both Cambon and Boppe foresaw the imminent collapse of Ottoman authority in Asiatic Turkey. And they firmly believed that if France were to have her share of the spoils in Syria, this area would have to be clearly nailed down by means of an economic preponderance. Ambassador Bompard wrote in 1921 that France embarked on a "new course" in the years from 1911 to 1914. In an article for the *Revue de Paris* Bompard said that during those years he and the officials at the Quai d'Orsay became increasingly preoccupied with the lagging material interests of France in Syria. He even affirmed that it was his own idea to seek an economic sphere of influence in Syria, indeed to work toward the economic partition of all of the Sick Man's Asian domains.[48]

The Potsdam Agreement of 1910 between Germany and Russia and the Turko-German railway accord of 1911 frightened France. These events forced her to appraise her own economic position in Syria, which she found wanting. The result was an alteration in the emphasis of France's Syrian policy—a shift from a stress upon her religious and political influence to a concentration upon her economic stature. It remains to describe exactly how France achieved her economic sphere of influence in Syria before the eruption of the First World War.

In February and March 1912 the Quai d'Orsay circulated two Foreign Ministry notes, which proved to be seminal documents in France's future negotiations with the Ottoman Porte. The notes speculated that, due to the exigencies of the Italo-Turk War, Turkey would soon be trying to persuade France, as Germany already had, to agree to a 4 percent increase in customs barriers. The notes agreed that France could probably assent to this, but in exchange some compensations would have to come from Turkey. Among the claims France would make were: railway concessions equal to Germany's, with emphasis upon southern extensions to the Syrian network; a number of port concessions to French developers in Tripoli-in-Syria and Jaffa; and satisfaction of the claims of the *Société de Damas-Hamah et Prolongements* on the Hijaz railway.[49] While this aspect of France's foreign policy was in its formative period, the matter of French financiers' participation in the Baghdad railway was forcibly called to the attention of the Quai d'Orsay. On 29 February 1912 Arthur von Gwinner, head of the Baghdad Railway Company, presented a *démarche* to Arsène Henry, president of the Imperial Ottoman Bank, requesting the latter to choose between the two following solutions concerning its 30 percent participation in financing the railway: (1) either abandon its 30 percent participation, leave the project completely, and be reimbursed; or (2) no longer to base its involvement on a simple guarantee that it would finance the amount; that is, to float its bonds on the French market and not on the German market as it had done since 1903.[50] These two developments—the formulation of demands to be made on Turkey and the formal *démarche* issued by von Gwinner—

coalesced to form the bases of France's new thrust to achieve an economic partition of Asiatic Turkey. Negotiations toward this end with both the Turks and the Germans were carried on simultaneously.

French financiers were naturally eager to continue their involvement in the Baghdad project, and a scheme was propounded whereby an unofficial French market could be created by forming a grand consortium of French banks. (The Quai d'Orsay still opposed opening the Paris Bourse to Baghdad securities.) This consortium would divide the responsibilities and advantages of participation in the Baghdad project.[51] Ambassador Bompard, however, was horrified at this suggestion, seeing it as just another example of how French finance was helping Germany to establish a tremendous arm of influence in Asiatic Turkey. Bompard, supported by Paul and Jules Cambon, urged that the Quai d'Orsay "must not let our banking houses make this last outlay, even in an indirect manner, to an enterprise which supports the position of our rivals in the Ottoman Empire."[52] Bompard was to convince the Quai d'Orsay that France's best interests would be served by selling out her participation in the Baghdad project to the Germans. But in exchange Germany would have to recognize Syria as a French sphere of influence. The "new course" in France's Syrian policy had taken definite form during 1912.

In May 1913 representatives of the Great Powers met in Paris to attempt to regulate Ottoman affairs, thrown out of kilter by the Balkan wars. On 8 May the French Embassy in Constantinople notified the Foreign Ministry that the conference would certainly try to restore the deficits which the war losses had caused in the revenues of the Ottoman public debt. The real beneficiary of this measure, the embassy advised, would be the Baghdad railway, which was constructed to a large extent on the surplus revenue conceded to the public debt. In these circumstances the embassy suggested that France could use her adhesion to the matter of regularizing the public debt as a lever to exact certain concessions from the Germans, notably to secure a German agreement that railway networks in Turkey be limited by a common agreement.[53] Three weeks later Bompard linked the matter of the public debt to that of France's 30 percent participation in financing the

Baghdad line. Bompard told Pichon on 31 May 1913 that France's agreement to restore the deficits to the public debt could be made conditional upon the withdrawal of French money from the Baghdad project and the demand for German concessions to French railway interests in Syria. According to Bompard all the railroads should exist on the principle "to each his own. . . . The object of the arrangement will thus consist in limiting our respective networks, fixing their points of contact and regulating their relations."[54]

Late in May France succeeded in persuading her English ally not to conclude an agreement with Germany on the Baghdad affair until after some understanding had been reached between Paris and Berlin.[55] With this preliminary out of the way conversations began on 1 July 1913 between Karl Helfferich, director of the Deutsche Bank, and the French financial representative, Sallandrouze de Lamornaix. These initial negotiations proved unfruitful. On 23 July Pichon notified his ambassadors that Germany refused further discussion of France's Syrian network until after the Baghdad question had been liquidated and the reconstitution of the Ottoman debt had been accomplished. Pichon maintained, therefore, that negotiations for railroad concessions must be pushed directly with Turkey. France must get concessions for an important network in Armenia with provisions for connecting it to an expanded Syrian system. Also some regulation must be made concerning that part of the Hijaz railway which ran parallel to the Damascus-Muzeirib line. The solution to these problems, he maintained, would not affect the Franco-German railroad rivalry in Asiatic Turkey, but it would strengthen France's bargaining position when conversations with Germany were reinitiated.[56] France's campaign for an economic sphere of influence in Syria thus focused momentarily upon the Turkish government.

Negotiations with the Turks had begun before *pourparlers* with the Germans were curtailed. In January 1913 the Porte applied anew for a French loan. During the early months of 1913 Turkey also applied to Paris for permission to tax the personal property of French protégés in Asiatic Turkey and for France's concession to a 4 percent increase in Turkish customs rates. The Turkish petitions set in motion the French plan to secure a definitive recognition of her preponderance in Syria. Between 24 February and 13 March 1913 France submitted to the Porte a list of demands to which Turkey must agree before Paris would underwrite the requested loan, acquiesce in the raising of the Turkish customs, and submit to the taxing of the personal property of French protégés. The French demands were lengthy and can be summarized in the following manner. First of all France wanted Turkish recognition of certain rights and immunities in reference to her missionary schools and religious establishments in the Levant. Second, France submitted a series of requests for railway concessions in Asiatic Turkey including: an Armenian (Black Sea) railway network; the concession to the Damascus-Hama Company to build a branch line from Rayak to Lydda for a future link-up between the D.H.P. and a line to Egypt; the leasing of the parallel section of the Hijaz railway from Damascus to Deraa to the D.H.P.; and the permission to construct port facilities in the Syrian cities of Tripoli, Haiffa, and Jaffa.[57] It is particularly important to notice that none of the concessions demanded by France pertained to the matter of Syrian reforms, an issue which French diplomats had championed ceaselessly up to this time. Turkish authorities considered the French demands extravagant,[58] but France remained intransigent, and negotiations were begun in Paris and in Constantinople. Railroads were discussed in the French capital, while officials at the Porte concerned themselves with the matter of the ecclesiastical establishments.

On 11 September 1913 a preliminary agreement was signed in Paris between Pichon and Javid by which the latter submitted to all of the French demands concerning the railways in Asiatic Turkey. In return Pichon agreed to a 4 percent increase in Turkish customs and to favor, as soon as the market permitted, the conclusion of a liquidation loan to the Ottoman government.[59] An annex to this general accord stipulated, however, that final negotiations could begin only after Turkey had submitted to all the French demands concerning her schools and charitable establishments in Asiatic Turkey, a matter still in negotiation in Constantinople. This issue was finally settled to French satisfaction on 18 December 1913.

The negotiations were therefore an unqualified success for France. Turkey's need for money had acted as a sword of Damocles and forced her to concede virtually every one of the French demands. Sir Louis Mallet, the British ambassador to the Porte, wrote to Sir Edward Grey on 26 December 1913 to inform him that the two agreements were "so favorable to the French that nothing but urgent need of money could have induced the Turkish Government to sign. . . ."[60] But the accords of 11 September and 18 December were not definitive. Indeed France had to tread lightly. She had to avoid blackmailing Turkey to such an outrageous extent that Germany would become unwilling to recognize the French sphere of influence in Syria. Negotiations with the Germans had been recommenced in November 1913, and Berlin had made it absolutely clear that France would be unwise to finalize matters with Turkey before Germany was satisfied on the Baghdad question. This is precisely why the loan to Turkey (and all that hinged upon it in the way of Turkish concessions to France in Asia Minor) was delayed until after an agreement had been hammered out between French and German financiers. After 18 December, therefore, the focus of French diplomacy in the Syrian matter shifted once again to Berlin.

French and German financiers had reconvened negotiations on 15 November 1913. The Germans wanted to settle the matter of French participation in financing the Baghdad project. They also claimed the right to build a railroad link from Aleppo to Meskene and to construct a junction to the Syrian port city of Alexandretta. Poincaré noted later that the German negotiator added that "if the French did not accept this combination, Germany might well obstruct their intellectual and moral expansion in Syria and elsewhere."[61] The well-known series of *pourparlers* which took place in Berlin between French and German financiers reached fruition on 15 February 1914. The net result was the first official step in the economic partition of Asiatic Turkey. The agreement accorded to France a section of northern Anatolia and Syria as spheres of influence for railway development. In return for this recognition, French financiers agreed to the German terms in the matter of railway links to Aleppo and Alexandretta. The areas traversed by the Anatolian and Baghdad railways were recognized as a German sphere of influence. In addition the Imperial Ottoman Bank agreed to sell to the German group all of the shares and debentures it held in the Baghdad railway, thus insuring that the project would be completely German. In return the Imperial Ottoman Bank received German approval to underwrite a loan to the Turkish government amounting to some 800 million francs. [62] The agreement of 15 February was, superficially, a convention between bankers. But the presence of French and German diplomatic officials lent the negotiations a political importance which was recognized by both the Quai d'Orsay and the Wilhelmstrasse.

The news that an agreement recognizing French preponderance in Syria had been reached with the Germans received a mixed reception in Paris. Poincaré himself believed that France had made a considerable sacrifice. Her large concessions to Germany "justified our concern for peace, but . . . in fact limited our economic and moral action in Asiatic Turkey to a very narrow zone."[63] Qualified approval for the accord came from the popular *Petit Parisien,* but the prestigious *Le Temps* and the conservative *Gaulois* took a dim view of the French concessions, lamenting the fact that France had been evicted from the Baghdad project, potentially the most influential in Asiatic Turkey.[64]

But the importance of this agreement could not yet be fully assessed, because its definitive ratification was further linked to two factors: (1) the conclusion of the accord between the French group and the Imperial Ottoman government on the subject of the Syrian and Black Sea railroad networks; and (2) the conclusion of a Turko-German accord on the matter of a German sphere of influence around the Anatolian and Baghdad networks. By 15 February 1914, then, France had secured German recognition of a French sphere of influence in Syria. This accomplished, her financiers were free once again to continue the loan negotiations with the Turkish government, a process temporarily interrupted in December 1913 because France feared that Germany might not recognize the concessions previously exacted from the Turks unless provisions were made for German ambitions as well.

Putting off the matter of granting Turkey a loan until after an agreement with the Germans had been accomplished proved particularly difficult for the French. Several dispatches arrived at the Quai d'Orsay in January 1914 from men such as Jules Cambon in Berlin and Boppe, the chargé in Constantinople, urging France to hasten the conclusion of loan negotiations with the Turks. These men argued that unless the loan were granted quickly Turkey might well withdraw all the economic and political concessions made as a result of the preliminary accords of 11 September and 18 December 1913. The wishes of the Francophile finance minister, Javid Bey, might be overridden and financial aid sought in Berlin instead of Paris.[65]

Despite the pleading of key diplomats for quick action, France used several dilatory tactics to keep the Turks at bay while prior agreement was reached with the Germans. French officials informed the Ottoman government that a loan could be arranged as soon as Liman von Sanders, a German general the Turks had invited in May 1913 to reorganize the Turkish army and assume command of the garrison at Constantinople, was removed from that command, thereby calming French fears about German control of the Turkish army. The Turks responded in January 1914 by giving Sanders the rank of field marshal, which excluded him from the Constantinople command. Later France hesitated to grant a loan for fear that the money would be used to finance an attack upon Greece in an attempt to regain the Aegean Islands, lost in the Balkan wars.[66] Once the Franco-German agreement of 15 February emerged, however, serious negotiations between French diplomats and Turkish officials began in earnest.

France and Turkey finally signed a general accord on 9 April 1914. France granted an 800-million-franc loan to the Ottoman government, to be floated by the Imperial Ottoman Bank and administered by the Public Debt Administration. Turkey also received France's consent to raise customs rates 4 percent and to establish government monopolies on several key luxury articles such as alcohol, tobacco, and gasoline. In a perfectly innocuous article France also declared herself "ready . . . to determine in what areas the present capitulatory regime is susceptible to amelioration, as soon as the other interested powers will have accepted the principle of such a revision." In return France received the definitive Turkish signature to all the concessions previously granted in the two preliminary accords of September and December 1913.[67] French businessmen thus acquired the right to build 1790 kilometers of new railways in the Black Sea region and in Syria, as well as to construct new port facilities in the latter area and to administer the long-disputed parallel sector of the Hijaz railway. The privileges and immunities of all the French religious and charitable establishments, concentrated for the most part in Syria and the Lebanon, were reasserted in the manner of the Mitylene exactions of 1901. As a result of the Franco-Turk accord of 9 April 1914, an economic sphere of influence had been delineated for France in Syria. And both Germany and Turkey recognized this fact.

The British reaction to French economic success in Syria is interesting in light of the intense competition that had taken place between the two powers for influence there since 1911. Sir Louis Mallet remarked in a private letter to Sir Edward Grey that "Turkey's independence is a vanishing quanitity before the advance of the French financiers."[68] Mark Sykes, the consul general in Beirut, spoke to the House of Commons on 18 March 1914. His speech was a denunciation of French activities in Syria, and he fulminated against the concessions demanded by France in return for a loan. "These concessions," he said, "which have been extracted from Turkey in return for this loan . . . mean a monopoly of all Syrian transit. . . . One knows what the defence of this sort of thing is—that all nations have to do it, that they have to protect their interests. But in practice, loans, kilometric guarantees, monopolies . . . must, whether the financiers desire it or not, pave the way to annexation."[69] But Sykes' words could be applied equally well to Britain's own position. In June 1914 she concluded an agreement with Germany which recognized English economic preponderance in the area of the Persian Gulf.

The revelation of the Potsdam Agreement of 1910 thus had opened the final period of furious diplomatic activity which led to the partition of Asiatic Turkey. This and the rapid progress of the German-dominated Baghdad railway served to convince French diplomats that France's long tradition of religious influence in Syria simply would not be enough to assure her title to Syria should the Ottoman Empire collapse in Asia as it had done in Europe. Commercial statistics proved that Germany and England were making rapid economic progress in Syria, while France was losing ground or, at best, standing still. French officials came to believe, therefore, that France must insure her traditional heritage in Syria by creating an economic sphere of influence there, one which would be clearly recognized by the powers. Turkey's need for French money provided the opportunity, and the grand design reached fruition in the Franco-German and Franco-Turk agreements of 15 February and 9 April 1914. Mark Sykes' speech to the British House of Commons provides an indication that, after 9 April 1914, a French claim to Syria in the event of Ottoman collapse would be honored, as it was by the Mandate Commission of the League of Nations after the First World War.

It is curious, however, that not one word about a reform program for Syria can be found in all the negotiations leading up to the granting of a loan to Turkey in 1914. Surely the Porte's need for money was a lever by which France could have helped the Syrians achieve their desired reforms. But the fact that this issue was not even broached in the Franco-Turk negotiations buttresses the view that France was interested in Syrian reform only insofar as this interest bolstered French prestige and influence in Syria vis-à-vis the other Great Powers. As soon as France saw an opportunity to insinuate herself economically in Syria in the form of a clearly recognized sphere of influence, she pushed the matter of reform aside as an issue which would only have blurred and perhaps confused and delayed the conclusion of agreements with Germany and the Porte. It is not any wonder then that substantial numbers of the politically aware in Syria tended to view the accords of 1914 as a betrayal of their cause by France. Nor is it any wonder that they were somewhat less than enthusiastic about their country's being assigned to France as mandated territory after World War I.

11 CONCLUSION

The foregoing chapters explain why France was eventually given the mandate for Syria after the First World War. Clearly, France's military contribution to the war effort in Syria and Lebanon was negligible. Military aid played no role in France's assumption of the Syrian and Lebanese mandates, although it can perhaps be cited as partial explanation for the fact that Palestine was separated from the French preserve.[1] The negotiations with Turkey and with Germany in 1913 and 1914 concerning the Ottoman loan and the Baghdad railway formed the keystone to the whole prewar edifice. These negotiations cemented the French presence in Syria and Lebanon both economically and religiously. Not only was this area set aside as a French economic sphere of influence in the form of a zone of exploitation for railroads and port facilities, but the traditional religious protectorate was also reasserted in a grand manner. These two developments assured the Third Republic that when the Ottoman Empire in Asia collapsed, Syria and Lebanon would go to France.

But these same negotiations of 1913 and 1914 also contributed to the growing hatred and suspicion of France among substantial segments of the Syrian population and illustrate why France remained genuinely unpopular in Syria after the war was over. In the postwar period French officials tended to blame their mandatory troubles on two factors—the confusion created by the wartime agreements and British intrigue. There can be no doubt that the McMahon-Hussein correspondence of 1915 and the Sykes-Picot Agreement of the following year contributed to the conditions of chaos and uncertainty in Syria. But chapter 9, on the Anglo-French competition for predominance in this area, shows quite clearly that Syrians favored English to French tutelage if they could not have independence. The King-Crane report after the war reflected such a preference.

This extensive and often acrimonious competition between France and England in the prewar period was largely responsible for the enduring suspicion of England which France harbored in the postwar era. And indeed it may be suspected that British officials did very little to ease the French problems in Syria after 1920. But the point is that the Syrian disenchantment with France had its roots deep in the prewar period. Syrians could and did compare the order and stability of English administration in Egypt with the chaos and suppression of the French administration in Algeria, and they found French colonialism wanting. The British championship of Aziz Ali al-Masri, which occurred at the same time that France was attempting to assert her imperialistic position in Syria and the Lebanon, further increased the prestige of the English among the Muslim populations of Syria.

Closely linked to the problem of French unpopularity was her complete abandonment of all projects for Syrian reform. The period 1901-1913 was an era in which French diplomats sought to increase French prestige among Syrians of all religious persuasions by championing efforts to achieve some form of decentralization and administrative autonomy vis-à-vis the regime of the Ottoman Turks. The documents show that French officials led Syrians to believe that the Quai d'Orsay was taking the initiative at Constantinople to achieve an amelioration of conditions in Syria. Yet when the critical loan negotiations began in 1913 and France had a real lever with which to pry reforms from the Turks, no proposals were made in this direction. Instead the French concentrated solely upon realizing an economic and religious sphere of influence. It is no wonder that Syrians, Christian and Muslim alike, regarded these negotiations as a betrayal of their interests by the French. And the documents show conclusively that in the period after the publication of the Franco-Turk accord in April 1914, Syrian opinion turned radically and decisively against French influence in Syria. The Franco-Turk and Franco-German negotiations of 1913 and 1914 made some form of French protectorate in Syria virtually inevitable. Ironically enough these same negotiations made it equally certain that France would have considerable difficulty with the Syrian peoples when she would attempt to assume her stewardship.

Once again it is instructive to point to the contrast between the welcome extended to French troops in 1920 by the Lebanese with the hostility which greeted French mandatory assertions in Syria. The fact that the Lebanese were predominantly Christian while the Syrians were largely Muslim is an important factor and should not be overlooked in assessing this difference in attitude. But also significant is the fact that in Lebanon France did not abandon her reform initiatives in the prewar period. The Lebanese remembered France's role in securing favorable alterations in the *Règlement organique* in December 1912. And these people consequently trusted France and welcomed her in 1920. The opposite was true in Syria, where France was opposed not only by Muslims, but by native Christians as well. It is undeniably true that a great many Syrians would have preferred an independent Syria after the war to any kind of foreign tutelage. But the King-Crane report demonstrated that Syrians would have been much more receptive to an American- or English-assumed mandate. Both of these were Christian powers, although neither the United States nor Great Britain had supported missionary efforts on the same scale as France.

One final point calls for summary and evaluation. That is the apparent contradiction between France's often repeated policy of maintaining Ottoman integrity in Asia and her practice, especially in the years from 1911 to 1914, of encouraging some of the Syrian separatists. The documents on this subject show that French officials in the Levant did urge moderation among the more volatile separatist societies, but these counsels were quite clearly not made in the interests of Ottoman integrity. They were undertaken simply to prevent any sudden outbreak of rebellion which would have occasioned an international intervention in

Syria, a development which would have imperiled the exclusive action of France in that area.

The policy of Ottoman integrity, then, was really only a lip-service doctrine, a condition obvious to many diplomats. Moukhtar Pasha, the Turkish ambassador to Berlin, wrote in 1921 that "since the beginning of the nineteenth century, France followed two different paths concerning her relations with the Ottoman Empire: one concerning the African and Syrian possessions of Turkey and the other concerning the rest of the Empire. The first was always directed against Turkish domination."[2] In a rather refreshing piece of straight talk, Sir Louis Mallet wrote to Sir Edward Grey from Constantinople on 17 December 1913: "All the Powers, including ourselves, are trying hard to get what they can out of Turkey. They all profess to wish the maintenance of Turkey's integrity but no one ever thinks of this in practice."[3] That France actually subscribed to such principles must be clear from the documents already cited in the text. Further proof can be supplied by examining a dispatch from Ambassador Bompard to the Quai d'Orsay in May 1913. Bompard said: "I believe, as do many others, that the Turkish Empire is finished, as much in Asia as in Europe; but is it not in our interest to prolong its agony, so that its territory is not now divided to our disadvantage? . . . The important thing is to supply resources to the [Turkish] Government which ought, as compensation for our support and sacrifices, to accord us legitimate satisfactions."[4]

Where France erred, however, and erred seriously, was in misjudging and undervaluing the strength of Syrian national sentiment. French and British documents for the period after April 1914 underline this mistake. Yet France appeared to hold tenaciously to outmoded ideas about Syria. The evaluation of the Syrian national movement made by the French consul general in Beirut in 1905 was tacitly accepted by French officials even in 1913 and 1914. He had said at that early date that "in effect, an Arab national sentiment does not exist among the people of this country, who are completely divided on questions of religion, rite and clan and who, by nature, are destined to live, for a long time if not forever, under the domination of a foreign element."[5]

Eugène Jung, the indefatigable advocate of a huge Arab empire in which Syria was also to be included, was equally out of touch with Syrian national opinion. Even after the First World War he continued to advocate his scheme, which the Syrian delegates to the Syrian Congress in Paris had rejected in June 1913. But at the same time Jung seemed to understand the French attitude and the French blindness in regard to Syria. He wrote in 1924: "Unfortunately no one in France understood the evolution of these peoples, of this proud race. One always thought in terms of the Syria of Chateaubriand, of the expedition of 1860, of old memories of the Crusades; one spoke constantly of our rights in these regions, moral rights certainly, but not territorial. . . . The Arabs . . . love France, but they want freedom."[6] The Syrian attitude was expressed perhaps most eloquently in an anonymous pamphlet which appeared in Beirut as early as 1908. The pamphlet, titled "La question sociale et scolaire en Syrie," said:

> We love France, but our affection cannot go so far as to forget our-
> selves. It is essential in the interests alike of Syria and of France that our
> countrymen should preserve their national character and their own
> individuality, whilst deriving inspiration from French ideas. We give
> preference to French culture, for it harmonizes better than any other
> with our own mentality and our aspirations. But we will never allow our
> own national culture to die. We will toil and slave, we will exhaust every
> atom of our strength and energy, our youth and our spirit, we will sacri-
> fice our very lifeblood if necessary, but our own culture will not die, and
> the sun's fair and burning rays will never shine upon the mighty ruins of
> our Syrian fatherland.[7]

This kind of cultural nationalism was translated into political terms as early as 1913 in the Syrian Arab Congress held in that year in Paris. It was further galvanized by the French abandon-ment of Syrian reform in 1913 and 1914, when France asserted her imperialistic claims to Syria and Lebanon in economic and religious terms. France reaped the fruits of her undervaluation of the strength of this national sentiment during the mandatory period after 1920.

REFERENCE MATTER

APPENDIXES

Appendix A. Population According to Religion in Syria and Lebanon, November 1912

Muslims	
Sunnites and Shiites	1,500,000
Metawlis	150,000
Cherkess	50,000
Kurds	50,000
Turkumans	50,000
Persians	8,000
	1,808,000
Various Non-Christians	
Druzes	200,000
Nossairieh	170,000
Ismailieh	25,000
Jahidieh and Haramieh	15,000
	410,000
Catholic Christians	
Maronites	500,000
Greek Catholics	120,000
Syrian Catholics	15,000
Armenian Catholics	15,000
Chaldean Catholics	7,000
Latins	50,000
	707,000
Non-Catholic Christians	
Greek Orthodox	250,000
Syrian Orthodox	15,000
Armenian Orthodox	15,000
Chaldean Orthodox	8,000
Protestants	30,000
Israelites	20,000
	338,000
General population total	3,263,000

Source: M.A.E., Turquie, N.S. 117, p. 147. These figures come very close to those cited in K. T. Khairallah, *La Syrie* (Paris, 1912), and in *La Grande Encyclopedie,* vol. 30 (Paris, n.d.), p. 795.

Appendix B. French Religious Protectorate (statistics showing the number and nationality of the personnel of all religious establishments protected by the French government in the circumscription of the consulate general of Beirut, 27 September 1904)

	French	English	German	Austrian	Italian	Swiss	Belgian	Spanish	Ottoman	Miscellaneous	Total
Beirut and Lebanon	491	11	9	2	19	5	8	1	147	4	697
Tripoli	33	1		2	10	1		1	18	1	67
Saida	17				2				12	3	34
Lattakia	6				2			2	1	1	12
Haiffa	92	10	7	8	15		2	26	46	9	215
Total	639	22	16	12	48	6	10	30	224	18	1025

Source: M.A.E., Saint-Siège, N.S. 42, pp. 242-244.

ABBREVIATIONS

B.D. Great Britain, Foreign Office, *British Documents on the Origins of the War, 1898-1914,* ed. G. P. Gooch and Harold Temperly, vols. X¹, X² (London, 1926-1938).

D.D.F. France, Commission de Publication des Documents relatifs aux Origines de la Guerre de 1914-1918, *Documents diplomatiques français, 1871-1914,* 41 vols. (Paris, 1929-1959).

F.O. Unpublished British Foreign Office documents located in the Public Record Office, London.

M.A.E. Unpublished French documents located in the Archives du Ministère des Affaires étrangères, Paris. All citations also bear a volume number prefaced by the letters "N.S." This refers to documents classified in the Nouvelle Série.

NOTES

CHAPTER 1: INTRODUCTION

1 Herbert I. Priestley, *France Overseas, A Study of Modern Imperialism* (New York, 1938), p. 369.

2 For particulars see Great Britain, "Report of a Committee set up to Consider Certain Correspondence between Sir Henry McMahon and the Sharif of Mecca in 1915 and 1916," in *Reports from Commissioners, Inspectors, and Others,* vol. 14 (London, 1938-1939), cmd. 5974.

3 Recent scholarship in British archives, however, rejects the notion of inconsistencies between the McMahon-Hussein correspondence and the Sykes-Picot Agreement, although the secrecy surrounding these matters may have fostered uncertainty and recrimination. See Isaiah Friedman, "The McMahon-Hussein Correspondence and the Question of Palestine," *Journal of Contemporary History* 5, no. 2 (1970): 83-122, and *The Question of Palestine, 1914-1918: British, Jewish, Arab Relations* (New York, 1973).

4 C. and Paul Roederer, *La Syrie et la France* (Paris, 1917), pp. 45, 113, 117-118.

5 For example see *L'Echo de Paris,* 20 October 1919; Maurice Barrès, *Une Enquête aux pays du Levant en 1914,* 2 vols. (Paris, 1923).

6 *Comité central syrien, L'Opinion syrienne à l'étranger pendant la guerre* (Paris, 1918), p. 1.

7 *Comité central syrien, La Question syrienne exposée par les Syriens* (Paris, 1919), p. 27.

177

8 Sir Harold George Nicolson, *Peacemaking 1919* (Boston, 1933), p. 143. See also Zeine N. Zeine, *The Struggle for Arab Independence: Western Diplomacy and the Rise of Faisal's Kingdom in Syria* (Beirut, 1960), p. 73.

9 John Presland, *Deedes Bey, A Study of Sir Wyndham Deedes, 1883-1923* (London, 1942), p. 244.

10 Zeine, *Struggle for Arab Independence,* p. 101; George Antonius, *The Arab Awakening, The Story of the Arab National Movement* (New York, 1946), pp. 296-297.

11 Antonius, *Arab Awakening,* p. 296.

12 Elie Kedourie, *England and the Middle East* (London, 1956), p. 147.

13 Stephen H. Longrigg, *Syria and Lebanon Under French Mandate* (London, 1958), pp. 106-107.

CHAPTER 2: BACKGROUND

1 Baron de Testa, *Recueil des traités de l'Empire ottoman,* vols. 1-3 (Paris, 1864-1898), 3: 140.

2 Ibid., 1: 17.

3 A. Schopoff, *Les Réformes et la protection des Chrétiens en Turquie, 1673-1904* (Paris, 1904), no. 1. This source contains only those treaty clauses relating to the protection of Christians. For complete texts of the capitulatory agreements see Gabriel Effendi Noradounghian, ed., *Recueil d'actes internationaux de l'Empire ottoman,* 4 vols. (Paris, 1897-1903), vol. 1.

4 Noradounghian, ed., *Recueil d'actes,* vol. 1, no. 32.

5 Testa, *Recueil des traités,* 3: 140-141.

6 Ibid., 2: 252.

7 Great Britain, Foreign Office, *France and the Levant,* Handbook 95 (London, March 1919), p. 10; René Ristelhueber, *Traditions françaises au Liban* (Paris, 1918), p. 116.

8 For example see Schopoff, *Les Réformes,* nos. 2, 3, 4.

9 For a discussion of the Tanzimat period, see the excellent book by Roderic H. Davison, *Reform in the Ottoman Empire, 1856-1876* (Princeton, N.J., 1963).

10 Philip M. Brown, *Foreigners in Turkey: Their Juridical Status* (Princeton, N.J.: 1914), pp. 42-47.

11 Georges Samné, *La Syrie* (Paris, 1921), p. 45; K. S. Salibi, *The Modern History of Lebanon* (New York, 1965), pp. 55-56, 77; A. H. Hourani, *Syria and Lebanon, A Political Essay* (London, 1946), pp. 148-149.

12 Alyce Edythe Mange, "The Near Eastern Policy of Emperor Napoleon III," in *Illinois Studies in the Social Sciences,* vol. 25 (Urbana, Ill., 1940), pp. 85, 91-92.

13 Schopoff, *Les Réformes,* nos. 92, 94.

14 Samné, *La Syrie,* pp. 187-190; Noël Verney and George Dambmann, *Les Puissances étrangères dans le Levant en Syrie et en Palestine* (Paris, 1900), p. 82.

15 Joseph Burnichon, *La Campagnie de Jésus en France, 1814-1914,* vol. 4 (Paris, 1922), p. 589. See also Eliot Grinnell Mears, *Modern Turkey, 1908-1923* (New York, 1924), p. 173.

16 *Correspondance d'Orient,* vol. for January-June 1914 (16 February 1914), p. 177; Samné, *La Syrie,* p. 186n; Mears, *Modern Turkey,* pp. 130-131.

17 Négib Azoury, *Le Réveil de la nation arabe dans l'Asie Turque* (Paris, 1905), pp. 104-114; Eugène Jung, *Les Puissances devant la révolte arabe* (Paris, 1906), pp. 188-189.

18 Jung, *Les Puissances,* p. 190.

19 Verney and Dambmann, *Les Puissances étrangères,* pp. 38-43.

20 Sir Edward Hertslet, ed., *The Map of Europe by Treaty,* 4 vols. (London, 1875-1891), 4: 2796.

21 France, Ministère des Affaires étrangères, *Documents diplomatiques: Affaires arméniennes, projets de réformes dans l'Empire ottoman, 1893-1897* (Paris, 1897), no. 12.

22 Ibid., no. 43.

23 Ibid., no. 65.

24 Ibid., nos. 269, 287.

25 Ibid., no. 271.

26 Ibid., no. 324.

27 William L. Langer, *The Diplomacy of Imperialism, 1890-1902* (New York, 1956), p. 164.

28 Paul Cambon, *Correspondance, 1870-1924,* 3 vols. (Paris, 1940-1946), 1: 343-346.

29 Ibid., pp. 397-398.

30 Frantz Despagnet, *La Diplomatie de la Troisième République et le droit des gens* (Paris, 1904), p. 659.

CHAPTER 3: THE LORANDO-TUBINI AFFAIR

1 M.A.E., Turquie, N.S. 169, p. 45.

2 France, Ministère des Affaires étrangères, *Documents diplomatiques: Turquie, 1900-1901* (Paris, 1902), no. 4; hereafter cited as *Livre Jaune.*

3 M.A.E., Turquie, N.S. 169, pp. 15-16.
4 *Livre Jaune*, no. 18; *D.D.F.*, ser. 2, vol. 1, no. 368.
5 For example see *Le Temps*, 2 September 1901; *Le Petit Parisien*, 1 November 1901; *Le Gaulois*, 23 August 1901.
6 Paul Leroy-Beaulieu, "Neuf pour cent," *L'Economiste français* 29 (12 October 1901): 497-499.
7 *D.D.F.*, ser. 2, vol. 1, no. 461.
8 M.A.E., Turquie, N.S. 170, p. 80.
9 Ibid., p. 31.
10 *Le Temps*, 31 August 1901.
11 *Le Gaulois*, 1 September 1901.
12 M.A.E., Turquie, N.S. 170, pp. 170-171.
13 Ibid., N.S. 171, pp. 40-41.
14 *D.D.F.*, ser. 2, vol. 1, no. 455; *Livre Jaune*, no. 52. Emile Thomas the Chaldean patriarch, had been elected by his sect, an election unsanctioned by the sultan. This sect, an offshoot of the Nestorians, claimed protection under the traditional French protectorate of Catholic institutions in the Orient. This Uniate group was located in Persia and the Turkish provinces of Baghdad, Armenia, Kurdistan, and Syria (*Le Temps*, 7 November 1901).
15 Cambon, *Correspondance*, 2: 62.
16 M.A.E., Turquie, N.S. 172, p. 51.
17 Hardinge mss, vol. 3, cited in Christopher Andrew, *Théophile Delcassé and the Making of the Entente Cordiale* (New York, 1968), p. 234.
18 *D.D.F.*, ser. 2, vol. 1, nos. 474, 475.
19 Ibid., nos. 471, 481, 482, 499 (cited in Andrew, *Delcassé*, p. 234).
20 Sembat's Order of the Day was jointly sponsored by the following deputies: Zévaès, Vaillant, Bouveri, Bénézech, Allard, Dufour, Létang, Groussier, Dejeante, Sauvanet, Coutant, Chauvière, and Walter. The depth of concern for the Armenians on the part of the Chamber was revealed by the fact that Sembat's Order of the Day was originally adopted. It was turned back only after the government's refusal to accept it and after the president of the Council of Ministers, Waldeck-Rousseau, appealed for a vote of confidence.
21 France, *Journal Officiel. Annales de la Chambre: Débats parlementaires*, vol. 2 (Paris, 1901), pp. 2018-2027.
22 *La Petite République*, 7 November 1901.
23 *Livre Jaune*, no. 65 (annex).
24 M.A.E., Turquie, N.S. 173, p. 106.
25 Ibid., p. 138.
26 Ibid., pp. 51-53.

27 *D.D.F.,* ser. 2, vol. 2, no. 419.
28 *Le Petit Parisien,* 9 November 1901; *Le Gaulois,* 10 November 1901; *Le Temps,* 11 November 1901.
29 *Le Temps,* 13 November 1901.
30 Cambon, *Correspondance,* 2: 62-63.
31 France, *Annales de la Chambre: Débats,* vol. 2 (Paris, 1901), p. 2023.

CHAPTER 4: THE PROTECTORATE: PART 1

1 Ernest Lavisse, "Notre politique orientale," *Revue de Paris* 2 (15 May 1897): 277.
2 Jules Cambon, *The Diplomat* (London, 1931), pp. 90-91.
3 Delcassé mss, cited in Andrew, *Delcassé,* p. 84.
4 Cited in René Pinon, *L'Europe et l'Empire ottoman* (Paris, 1908), p. 556.
5 M.A.E., Saint-Siège, N.S. 53, p. 290; Verney and Dambmann, *Les Puissances étrangères,* pp. 38-43; Jung, *Les Puissances,* p. 216.
6 "La Politique allemande et le protectorat des missions catholiques," *Revue des deux mondes* 149 (1 September 1898): 8-9.
7 Pinon, *L'Europe et l'Empire ottoman,* pp. 558-559; Andrew, *Delcassé,* pp. 85-86.
8 *D.D.F.,* ser. 2, vol. 2, no. 419.
9 This sweeping controversy, trivial though it may seem, had precedents. In 1864 a fight erupted between Greek and Armenian monks over sweeping out the Cathedral of the Nativity. And in 1870 Latin monks infringed upon Armenian sweeping privileges in the Grotto of the Nativity. See Avedis K. Sanjian, *The Armenian Communities in Syria Under Ottoman Domination* (Cambridge, Mass., 1965), p. 198.
10 *D.D.F.,* ser. 2, vol. 1, no. 479.
11 Ibid., vol. 2, no. 122.
12 Ibid., no. 224.
13 Ibid., nos. 123, 155.
14 Hertslet, ed., *Map of Europe,* 4: 2797.
15 *D.D.F.,* ser. 2, vol. 2, no. 204.
16 Ibid., nos. 205, 233.
17 M.A.E., Saint-Siège, N.S. 30, pp. 126-127.
18 Delcassé mss, cited in Andrew, *Delcassé,* pp. 84-85.
19 M.A.E., Saint-Siège, N.S. 30, p. 228.
20 M.A.E., Turquie, N.S. 176, p. 101.
21 *D.D.F.,* ser. 2, vol. 2, no. 477.
22 M.A.E., Saint-Siège, N.S. 30, p. 209.

23 *D.D.F.,* ser. 2, vol. 3, no. 335; M.A.E., Saint-Siège, N.S. 53, pp. 320-321, N.S. 30, pp. 394-395. This question will be examined more thoroughly in the next chapter.

24 *D.D.F.,* ser. 2, vol. 5, no. 287; Pierre Renouvin, *La Politique extérieure de la IIIe République* (Paris, 1953), p. 231.

25 *Le Gaulois,* 30 July 1904.

26 M.A.E., Saint-Siège, N.S. 31, p. 159.

27 Ibid., N.S. 30, p. 145, N.S. 32, p. 381.

28 Ibid., N.S. 31, pp. 63-64.

29 *D.D.F.,* ser. 2, vol. 5, no. 30 and annex.

30 Jung, *Les Puissances,* pp. 186-191; Azoury, *Le Réveil,* pp. 115-130.

31 M.A.E., Saint-Siège, N.S. 32, pp. 150, 157.

32 Ibid., pp. 9-10.

33 Ibid., pp. 102-103.

34 *D.D.F.,* ser. 2, vol. 6, no. 290; M.A.E., Saint-Siège, N.S. 44, pp. 171-176.

35 The texts appear in M.A.E., Saint-Siège, N.S. 32, pp. 190-194.

36 M.A.E., Saint-Siège, N.S. 36, pp. 238-239; Maurice Pernot, *Rapport sur un voyage d'étude à Constantinople, en Egypt et en Turquie d'Asie* (Paris, n.d.), pp. 304-305.

37 M.A.E., Turquie, N.S. 109, pp. 105-107.

38 M.A.E., Saint-Siège, N.S. 33, pp. 48-49, 200-203.

39 Ibid., N.S. 44, pp. 38-39.

40 M.A.E., Turquie, N.S. 110, p. 51.

41 Ibid., pp. 284-285.

42 M.A.E., Saint-Siège, N.S. 33, pp. 104-105.

43 Ibid., N.S. 41, pp. 5-9.

44 Ibid., N.S. 31, pp. 275-276.

45 Ibid., N.S. 41, p. 266.

46 France, *Annales de la Chambre: Débats,* vol. 74 (Paris, 1904), p. 753ff.

47 M.A.E., Saint-Siège, N.S. 41, pp. 5-9.

48 *D.D.F.,* ser. 2, vol. 2, no. 419, vol. 4, no. 148.

49 M.A.E., Saint-Siège, N.S. 33, pp. 8-13, N.S. 44, pp. 171-176.

CHAPTER 5: THE PROTECTORATE: PART 2

1 Charlot's report was published in the *Journal Officiel* on 26 October 1906 and was reproduced in full in the *Revue de l'enseignement coloniale* 2 (December 1906): 132-137.

2 M.A.E., Saint-Siège, N.S. 31, pp. 20-21. By 1906 the number of establishments falling officially under French protection in the Ottoman Empire was 537. Included in this figure were a "certain number" of native establishments belonging to oriental rites. The total number of students in these native schools was 14,742 out of a general total of 74,276 French protégés (M.A.E., Turquie, N.S. 298, p. 98, N.S. 177, p. 195; Saint-Siège, N.S. 33, p. 121).

3 M.A.E., Turquie, N.S. 123, pp. 173-174.

4 F.O. 226/229.

5 *Revue de l'enseignement coloniale,* 2 (September 1905): 101-109; *Bulletin de la Mission laïque française* 8 (June 1911): 130-131; Henry Hauser, "L'Influence française en Orient et les écoles laïques," *Revue politique et parlementaire* 48 (April 1906): 55-68.

6 Louis Bertrand, "Les écoles d'orient," *Revue des deux mondes* 79 (15 August 1909): 786.

7 For example see Gaston Bordat, "L'Influence française en Orient et les écoles laïques," *Revue politique et parlementaire* 52 (May 1907): 332-341; André Malzac, "L'Evolution de l'action française en Orient," *Revue politique et parlementaire* 53 (September 1907): 469-482; René Pinon, *L'Europe et l'Empire ottoman,* p. 536.

8 M.A.E., Saint-Siège, N.S. 44, pp. 165-166.

9 M.A.E., Turquie, N.S. 110, pp. 196-207.

10 M.A.E., Saint-Siège, N.S. 44, pp. 208-218.

11 Ibid., N.S. 33, pp. 358-359.

12 France, *Annales de la Chambre: Débats,* vol. 80 (Paris, 1906), pp. 978-983.

13 *L'Asie française* 8 (March 1908): 109-110; France, *Annales de la Chambre: Débats,* vol. 89 (Paris, 1909), pp. 1931-1934.

14 Jules Harmand, *Domination et colonisation* (Paris, 1910), pp. 256-284. Harmand was a spokesman for the theory of colonial "association" as opposed to "assimilation." His book is a treatise on the theory of French colonialism in general and does not deal specifically with any one area.

15 M.A.E., Saint-Siège, N.S. 33, pp. 313-314.

16 Paul Cambon, *Correspondance,* 2: 215-216 (7 May 1906), 227-228 (1 January 1907), 3: 30 (6 December 1912).

17 *Le Temps,* 24 January 1907.

18 *D.D.F.,* ser. 2, vol. 12, no. 185.

19 M.A.E., Saint-Siège, N.S. 35, pp. 153-154, N.S. 54, p. 199.

20 Ibid., N.S. 54, pp. 142-143.

21 Ibid., p. 217.

22 Ibid., pp. 238-239. See also *D.D.F.*, ser. 2, vol. 13, no. 337.
23 M.A.E., Saint-Siège, N.S. 35, pp. 221-223.
24 Ibid., N.S. 55, p. 18.
25 Ibid., N.S. 35, pp. 171-172.
26 *D.D.F.*, ser. 2, vol. 13, no. 337.
27 M.A.E., Saint-Siège, N.S. 54, p. 220.
28 Ibid., N.S. 55, pp. 55-59.
29 Ibid., p. 97.
30 Ibid., p. 118.
31 Ibid., p. 186.
32 Ibid., N.S. 56, p. 60.
33 Ibid., p. 130.
34 Ibid., N.S. 36, pp. 268-270.
35 *D.D.F.*, ser. 3, vol. 1, p. 276n.
36 Ibid., ser. 2, vol. 14, no. 384.
37 Ibid., ser. 3, vol. 1, no. 292; M.A.E., Saint-Siège, N.S. 35, p. 262,
    N.S. 36, pp. 118-125.
38 M.A.E., Saint-Siège, N.S. 35, pp. 276-281.
39 Ibid., N.S. 36, pp. 108-111, 238-239.
40 Pernot, *Rapport sur un voyage d'étude à Constantinople,* introd.
41 Ibid., pp. 289-308.
42 *D.D.F.*, ser. 3, vol. 10, nos. 172, 319.
43 M.A.E., Saint-Siège, N.S. 47, pp. 8-10.
44 Ibid., N.S. 38, pp. 75-76.
45 Ibid., N.S. 47, pp. 34-35.
46 Ibid., p. 77.
47 Ibid., N.S. 48, pp. 215-218.
48 France, *Annales de la Chambre: Débats,* vol. 102, pt. 2 (Paris, 1914),
    p. 1685ff.
49 Ibid., pt. 1, pp. 1476-1479.
50 Both of these problems will be examined in chapters 8 and 9.
51 The railroad question will be considered in chapter 10.

CHAPTER 6: FRANCE AND THE ORIGINS OF THE SYRIAN
NATIONAL MOVEMENT TO 1912

1 J. A. S. Grenville, *Lord Salisbury and Foreign Policy, the Close of the
   Nineteenth Century* (London, 1964), pp. 24-53.
2 A. L. Tibawi, "Syria in Wartime Agreements and Disagreements:
   Fresh Evidence from the British Foreign Office Records," *Middle
   East Forum* 43, nos. 2-3 (1967): 97-98.

3 Patrick Seale, *The Struggle for Syria, A Study of Post-War Arab Politics, 1945-1958* (London, 1965), pp. 1-2.

4 Gabriel Hanotaux, *Etudes diplomatiques, la politique de l'équilibre, 1907-1911* (Paris, 1912), pp. 135-136. From an article written originally in 1908.

5 Salibi, *Modern History of Lebanon,* pp. 156-158; Zeine N. Zeine, *Arab-Turkish Relations and the Emergence of Arab Nationalism* (Beirut, 1958), p. 124.

6 Bernard Lewis has pointed out that the Young Turks have often been judged with undue harshness, especially in regard to their policies toward the nationalities. Their main concern was for the survival of the empire, and they sincerely felt that certain radical measures were necessary to save it from inner decay and foreign attack. "Though their work was often ill-conceived, incomplete, and frustrated by events, they did nevertheless help prepare the way . . . for the new Turkey that was to emerge after their disappearance" (Bernard Lewis, *The Emergence of Modern Turkey* [London, 1961], p. 223).

7 Hourani, *Syria and Lebanon,* pp. 103-104.

8 "Les Courants politiques dans la Turquie," *Revue du monde musulman* 21 (December 1912): 170.

9 Jung, *Les Puissances,* p. 18.

10 Turquie, IVème Armée, *La Vérité sur la question syrienne* (Istanbul, 1916), pp. 136-137.

11 Zeine, *Arab-Turkish Relations,* pp. 43-45.

12 Antonius, *Arab Awakening,* pp. 92-95.

13 Ibid., pp. 79-86.

14 Gabriel Charmes, *Voyage en Syrie* (Paris, 1882), pp. 171-172. See also Denis de Rivoyre, *Les Vrais Arabes et leur pays* (Paris, 1884), pp. 294-295.

15 M.A.E., Turquie, N.S. 108, pp. 46-53.

16 *Bulletin du Comité de l'Asie française* 3 (January 1903): 12-21.

17 Azoury, *Le Réveil,* pref.

18 Ibid., pp. 129-130.

19 M.A.E., Turquie, N.S. 177, pp. 139-140, 149-151.

20 Ibid., pp. 27-28.

21 Ibid., pp. 76-77.

22 Dispatch from British consul general in Beirut to Ambassador Gerard Lowther in Constantinople, 3 February 1911, F.O. 195/2370.

23 Pinon, *L'Europe et l'Empire ottoman,* p. 382.

24 *Bulletin du Comité de l'Asie française* 5 (August 1905): 331.

25 M.A.E., Turquie, N.S. 177, pp. 27-28.

26 *L'Indépendence arabe,* June 1908.

27 For example see Antonius, *Arab Awakening,* pp. 98-99; Syliva G. Haim, ed., *Arab Nationalism, An Anthology* (Berkeley, Calif., 1962), p. 30. One exception is Herbert I. Priestley, who reports that Jung and Azoury had a great deal of influence on the Quai d'Orsay, even as late as 1912 and 1913 (*France Overseas,* p. 373). The presently available documents tend to prove the contrary.

28 M.A.E., Turquie, N.S. 111, pp. 106, 110, 112.

29 F.O. 195/2277, 1 August 1908.

30 *D.D.F.,* ser. 2, vol. 11, no. 419.

31 Cited in Wade Dewood David, "European Diplomacy in the Near Eastern Question, 1906-1909, in *Illinois Studies in the Social Sciences,* vol. 25 (Urbana, Ill., 1940), p. 65n.

32 Moutran sent this proclamation to the Quai d'Orsay on 25 December 1908. M.A.E., Turquie, N.S. 111, pp. 256-258. This group is not to be confused with the *Comité* of the same name founded by Chekri Ganem in 1917.

33 M.A.E., Turquie, N.S. 112, pp. 30-32.

34 F.O. 195/2311, 21 January 1909.

35 F.O. 195/2342, 16 June 1910.

36 M.A.E., Turquie, N.S. 114, pp. 13-14.

37 Ibid., N.S. 113-115. These three volumes contain numerous documents on the anti-French activity in Syria during 1910 and 1911.

38 Mahmud Moukhtar Pasha, *La Turquie, l'Allemagne et l'Europe* (Paris, 1921), p. 141.

39 F.O. 195/2371, 10 October 1911.

40 César Vidal, "Le Duel diplomatique Poincaré-Tittoni, 1912-1914," *Rassegna Storica del Risorgimento* 3-4 (1951): 691-699.

41 M.A.E., Turquie, N.S. 117, pp. 65-68. See also N.S. 116, p. 7.

42 For example, M.A.E., Turquie, N.S. 116, pp. 32, 43, N.S. 117, pp. 37-38, 125-129, N.S. 118, pp. 19-20. See also Eugène Jung, *La Révolte arabe,* 2 vols. (Paris, 1924), 1: 56-57.

43 M.A.E., Turquie, N.S. 116, pp. 167-168. See also N.S. 117, pp. 47-48.

44 Ibid., N.S. 117, p. 74.

45 Ibid., N.S. 118, pp. 70-72.

46 Ibid., N.S. 117, pp. 171-173.

47 Ibid., pp. 101-104.

48 Raymond Poincaré, *Au service de la France,* 10 vols. (Paris, 1926-1933), 1: 42.

49 Turquie, *La Vérité,* pp. 139-140. See the following chapter for a discussion of this book and how Turkish authorities came into possession of French documents.

CHAPTER 7: FRANCE AND THE SYRIAN NATIONAL
MOVEMENT, 1912-1914

1 France, *Journal Officiel. Annales du Sénat: Débats parlementaires,* vol. 82 (Paris, 1912), p. 340.
2 M.A.E., Turquie, N.S. 118, p. 153.
3 M.A.E., Saint-Siège, N.S. 36, pp. 181-182.
4 M.A.E., Turquie, N.S. 118, pp. 166-167.
5 Ibid., N.S. 119, p. 34.
6 Cited in K. T. Khairallah, *Le Problème du Levant, les régions arabes libérées* (Paris, 1919), p. 39.
7 *Bulletin du Comité de l'Asie française* 13 (April 1913): 164-176.
8 M.A.E., Turquie, N.S. 9, pp. 193-195.
9 F.O. 195/2451, no. 340.
10 M.A.E., Turquie, N.S. 119, p. 123.
11 *Correspondance d'Orient,* 16 January 1913, pp. 49-52.
12 M.A.E., Turquie, N.S. 120, pp. 59-62. See also Djemal Pasha, *Memories of a Turkish Statesman, 1913-1919* (London, n.d.), pp. 229-231.
13 M.A.E., Turquie, N.S. 120, pp. 123-131.
14 Ibid., N.S. 119, pp. 191-194, N.S. 121, pp. 80-84; Turquie, *La Vérité,* pp. 69-71; Jung, *La Révolte arabe,* 1: 162-164.
15 M.A.E., Turquie, N.S. 120, pp. 4-5, 114.
16 Ibid., pp. 166-168, 219, 220-221, 222-225.
17 Ibid., pp. 166-168; F.O. 195/2451, no. 484.
18 M.A.E., Turquie, N.S. 120, pp. 244-253.
19 T. E. Lawrence, *Seven Pillars of Wisdom* (London, 1935), p. 47; André Mandelstam, *Le Sort de l'Empire ottoman* (Paris, 1917), pp. 342-344. The documents cited in *La Vérité sur la question syrienne* are genuine. The originals can be found in the archives of the Quai d'Orsay in Paris.
20 Djemal Pasha, *Memories,* p. 197.
21 Turquie, *La Vérité,* pp. 41-43.
22 Ibid., pp. 72-73.
23 Ibid., pp. 75-78.
24 Recent scholarship supports this contention. See Tibawi, "Syria in Wartime Agreements," pp. 97-98.
25 Antonius, *Arab Awakening,* p. 111.
26 Count R. J. M. Cressaty, *Les Intérêts français en Syrie* (Paris, 1913), pp. 1, 35.
27 Turquie, *La Vérité,* p. 125.

28 *Bulletin du Comité de l'Asie française* 13 (June 1913): 257-259. The prime mover in initiating the congress, however, was the secret society of *al-Fatat,* which moved its headquarters to Syria shortly afterward. See George E. Kirk, *A Short History of the Middle East from the Rise of Islam to Modern Times* (New York, 1963), p. 121; Anthony Nutting, *The Arabs, A Narrative History from Mohammed to the Present* (London, 1964), p. 277.

29 Cumberbatch to Lowther, 30 May 1913, *B.D.,* vol. X², pp. 825-826; L. D. Carnegie in Paris to Grey, 26 June 1913, F.O. 424/238, no. 478.

30 M.A.E., Turquie, N.S. 121, pp. 94-95.

31 *Le Temps,* 29 June 1913.

32 They were publicized so well that the French chargé d'affaires in Constantinople suggested that the similarity of language indicated that the protests were in fact inspired by the Turks (Turquie, *La Vérité,* pp. 87-89).

33 M.A.E., Turquie, N.S. 122, p. 45.

34 The entire program of the Syrian Congress can be found in Samné, *La Syrie,* pp. 90-91.

35 Antonius, *Arab Awakening,* p. 115.

36 Djemal Pasha, *Memories,* p. 264. See also Turquie, *La Vérité,* p. 82.

37 M.A.E., Turquie, N.S. 122, pp. 87-88.

38 Ibid., N.S. 186, p. 88.

39 Ibid., N.S. 123, p. 57.

40 F.O. 195/2451, no. 484.

41 F.O. 424/239, no. 292; *Correspondence d'Orient* (1 October 1913), pp. 330-332; *L'Echo de Paris,* 26 August 1913 (cited in Jung, *La Révolte arabe,* 1: 70-73).

42 Haim, *Arab Nationalism,* pp. 32-33.

43 *Le Temps,* 11 September 1913.

44 M.A.E., Turquie, N.S. 123, pp. 114-115.

45 Kedourie, *England and the Middle East,* pp. 60-61.

46 M.A.E., Turquie, N.S. 9, pp. 245-247.

47 Ibid., N.S. 123, pp. 87-96.

48 Ibid., pp. 154-156.

49 Ibid., N.S. 124, pp. 31A-33.

50 Jung, *La Révolte arabe,* 1: 89-90.

51 For example see M.A.E., Turquie, N.S. 124, pp. 58-61, 62-67, 98-101.

52 F.O. 371/2136, no. 42807.

53 A. L. Tibawi, "Syria in the McMahon Correspondence: Fresh Evidence from the British Foreign Office Records," *Middle East Forum* 42, no. 4 (1966): 8.

54 F.O. 195/2460, nos. 3421, 3546, 4242, 4475, 4721.
55 A typical example occurred in J. Aulneau, "La Question syrienne," *Revue politique et parlementaire* 81 (10 July 1914): 93-95. Aulneau maintained that "the Syrian, avid for instruction, admiring our literature, our ideas, our civilization, prefers French schools to all the others. . . . The love of the Syrians for France is always deep-rooted. . . . Syria remains as always harmonious in relation, ideas and brotherhood with us."

CHAPTER 8: FRENCH POLITICAL INFLUENCE IN LEBANON, 1901-1914

1 M.A.E., Turquie, N.S. 108, pp. 117-119.
2 Ibid., pp. 139-140.
3 Ibid., pp. 143-157.
4 Ibid., pp. 169-170.
5 Ibid., pp. 177-182.
6 Noradounghian, ed., *Recueil d'actes,* vol. 4, no. 1000.
7 M.A.E., Turquie, N.S. 109, pp. 72-88, 159-160.
8 Ibid., pp. 198-199.
9 *L'Indépendence arabe,* no. 3 (June 1907), pp. 43-45.
10 F.O. 195/2217, 5 February 1906.
11 M.A.E., Turquie, N.S. 109, pp. 27-37.
12 Ibid., N.S. 111, p. 34.
13 Mgr. Emmanuel Pharès, *Les Maronites, leur vie et leurs moeurs, leurs rapports avec la France, leur situation actuelle* (Lille, 1908), pp. 20-32.
14 Cited ibid., p. 17.
15 M. Jouplain, *La Question du Liban, Etude d'histoire diplomatique & le droit international* (Paris, 1908), pp. 597-598.
16 *Comité libanais de Paris, Memoire sur la question du Liban* (Paris, 1912). A copy of this pamphlet can be located in M.A.E., Turquie, N.S. 116, pp. 127-138.
17 F.O. 195/2277.
18 M.A.E., Turquie, N.S. 112, pp. 159-164.
19 Ibid., pp. 235-237. In mentioning "Syria," Pichon was not referring to the area known today by that name but to geographical Syria, which, before the First World War, included the Lebanon.
20 A further illustration of this attitude can be observed in the rather extensive negotiations that took place between the Quai d'Orsay and a man named Farid el-Khazen, a representative from the Maronite

archbishop. Discussions took place sporadically from June through November 1911 and ranged over numerous basic questions of reform as well as Irredentist issues. The Foreign Office made no attempt to discourage Farid until he requested permission in November to purchase French military equipment to protect Lebanese Christians against "Muslim fanaticism." The request was refused. The whole incident demonstrates that France, although anxious to consider rather substantial reform measures, was not inclined to support potentially imprudent behavior, which might well have provoked an international intervention by the Great Powers (M.A.E., Turquie, N.S. 115, pp. 130-132, 186-187, 193-195, 213-214, 215).

21 Ibid., N.S. 114, pp. 79-81, 96-98.
22 Ibid., N.S. 113, p. 113.
23 Ibid., N.S. 112, pp. 96-102. This document is chronologically out of place in this volume.
24 Ibid., N.S. 115, pp. 130-160.
25 Ibid., N.S. 116, pp. 53-67. The *Règlement organique* of 1864 prohibited Lebanese ports from being opened to steamships. The Turkish authorities at Beirut operated all customs bureaus, and the receipts went to the Ottoman treasury.
26 F.O. 424/231, no. 75.
27 M.A.E., Turquie, N.S. 117, pp. 6-7, 43, 49-58.
28 *Correspondance d'Orient* (1 January 1913), p. 46; Samné, *La Syrie,* p. 224.
29 Ludovic de Contenson, *Les Réformes en Turquie d'Asie: la question arménienne, la question syrienne* (Paris, 1913), p. 85.
30 M.A.E., Turquie, N.S. 118, p. 153, N.S. 119, pp. 218-220.
31 Ibid., N.S. 117, pp. 27-30, N.S. 119, pp. 47-48, 218-220, N.S. 122, pp. 55-70, 79-81, N.S. 124, pp. 198-202.
32 Ibid., N.S. 124, pp. 210-211.

CHAPTER 9: FRANCO-BRITISH RIVALRY IN PREWAR SYRIA

1 Walter Laqueur, ed., *The Israel-Arab Reader* (New York, 1969), doc. 9.
2 The consul general in Beirut translated and submitted the article to the Quai d'Orsay. M.A.E., Turquie, N.S. 109, p. 24.
3 Ibid., pp. 38-41.
4 Ibid., N.S. 320, p. 58.
5 Ibid., p. 66.

6　F.O. 195/2140, 5 February 1903.

7　M.A.E., Turquie, N.S. 109, pp. 51-57, 58.

8　Ibid., pp. 183-185.

9　Ibid., N.S. 176, pp. 218-219.

10　Ibid., N.S. 109, pp. 231-233.

11　M.A.E., Saint-Siège, N.S. 34, pp. 49-50.

12　M.A.E., Turquie, N.S. 112, pp. 48-52.

13　F.O. 195/2311, 12 April 1909; M.A.E., Turquie, N.S. 112, p. 67.

14　F.O. 195/2311, 12 April 1909.

15　M.A.E., Turquie, N.S. 112, pp. 81-82.

16　Ibid., pp. 102p-102q.

17　Ibid., p. 102s.

18　Ibid., pp. 201-204.

19　F.O. 195/2312, 16 August 1909; F.O. 195/2342, 3 February 1910.

20　F.O. 195/2312, 5 November 1909.

21　M. E. Weakley, "Conditions and Prospects of British Trade in Syria," in Great Britain, *House of Commons Accounts and Papers,* vol. 87 (London, 1911), cmd. 5707.

22　Great Britain, *Reports from Commissioners,* vol. 14, cmd. 5974, p. 51.

23　Poincaré, *Au service,* 7: 362-363.

24　Isaiah Friedman, "The McMahon-Hussein Correspondence and the Question of Palestine," *Journal of Contemporary History* 5, no. 2 (1970): 111-112. Friedman has discussed the same problem in greater detail in *The Question of Palestine,* pp. 16-17, 87.

25　"Lord Kitchener in Egypt," *Fortnightly Review* 91 (1 March 1912): 515-516.

26　F.O. 800/54, January 1913.

27　M.A.E., Turquie, N.S. 116, pp. 48-50.

28　F.O. 371/1521, no. 49191.

29　F.O. 424/233, no. 127.

30　Cited in Jung, *La Révolte arabe,* 1: 47-48. This warning prefaced an appeal for French money and arms to aid Azoury in his drive to create the great Arab empire of his dreams. Needless to say his appeal was refused.

31　F.O. 371/1522, no. 51018.

32　M.A.E., Turquie, N.S. 117, pp. 154-161.

33　Jung, *La Révolte arabe,* 1: 52-55; Nagib Sadaka, *La Question syrienne pendant la guerre de 1914* (Paris, 1940), p. 18.

34　*B.D.,* vol. IX², no. 336.

35　M.A.E., Turquie, N.S. 117, pp. 154-161.

36　France, *Annales du Sénat: Débats,* vol. 82 (Paris, 1912), p. 340.

37 Poincaré, *Au service,* 2: 400.
38 Sir Francis Bertie to Sir Edward Grey, 24 December 1912; Consul General Cumberbatch to Gerard Lowther, 25 January 1913, F.O. 195/2451, no. 153.
39 *Le Gaulois,* 24 December 1912; *Correspondance d'Orient,* 1 January 1913, 1-3; *Bulletin du Comité de l'Asie française* 12 (December 1912): 515-518; *Le Temps,* 24 December 1912.
40 F.O. 800/174, ME/12/15.
41 M.A.E., Turquie, N.S. 119, pp. 42-45; F.O. 371/1775, no. 253.
42 *B.D.,* vol. IX², no. 426, vol. X¹, no. 476.
43 Tibawi, "Syria in the McMahon Correspondence," p. 9.
44 Great Britain, Hansard, *The Parliamentary Debates* (House of Commons), vol. 59 (London, 1914), col. 2188 (18 March 1914).
45 Sadaka, *La Question syrienne,* p. 19.
46 *B.D.,* vol. X², pp. 824-825 (ed. note).
47 F.O. 371/1522, no. 52330.
48 Ibid.
49 F.O. 424/233, no. 135.
50 Friedman, "McMahon-Hussein Correspondence," p. 111.
51 Prince Karl Max Lichnowski, *Heading for the Abyss* (London, 1928), pp. 318-319, cited in Leonard Stein, *The Balfour Declaration* (New York, 1961), p. 46n.
52 Jung, *La Révolte arabe,* 1: 60-61.
53 F.O. 424/237, no. 10.
54 F.O. 195/2452, no. 621.
55 F.O. 424/238, no. 40.
56 Ibid., no. 151.
57 F.O. 195/2453, no. 1966.
58 *Le Temps,* 13 February 1913.
59 Cressaty, *Les Intérêts français,* pp. 16-17.
60 *Le Temps,* 14 May 1913.
61 Herbert Vivian, "Turkey's Asiatic Problems," *The Fortnightly Review* 93 (April 1913): 675.
62 M.A.E., Turquie, N.S. 122, pp. 139-170.
63 *B.D.,* vol. X¹, nos. 525, 541.
64 F.O. 371/1775, no. 253.
65 F.O. 371/1848, no. 52892.
66 *B.D.,* vol. X², no. 139.
67 F.O. 424/239, no. 287.
68 Ibid., nos. 348, 354.
69 M.A.E., Turquie, N.S. 186, pp. 124-125.

70 Ibid., p. 131.
71 F.O. 800/80, 30 April 1914.
72 Nutting, *The Arabs,* pp. 278-279.
73 *B.D.,* vol. X², pp. 828-838.
74 M.A.E., Turquie, N.S. 186, pp. 187-188, 205-206, 212, 213.
75 London *Times,* 9 April 1914.

CHAPTER 10: THE RAILROAD QUESTION: CREATION OF AN
ECONOMIC SPHERE OF INFLUENCE

1 Herbert Feis, *Europe, the World's Banker, 1870-1914* (New York, 1961), p. 53; Harry N. Howard, *The Partition of Turkey, 1913-1923* (Norman, Okla., 1931), pp. 49-50; W. W. Gottlieb, *Studies in Secret Diplomacy During the First World War* (London, 1957), pp. 20-21, 80. Recent scholarship has demonstrated that silk merchants in Lyon and the Lyon Chamber of Commerce had invested heavily in Syria in the years before 1914 and consequently placed considerable pressure on the government of the Republic to seek permanent political influence in that area. See Dominique Chevallier, "Lyon et la Syrie en 1919: les bases d'une intervention," *Revue historique* 224 (October-December 1960): 275-320; John Laffey, "Les Racines de l'impérialisme français en extrême-orient," *Revue d'histoire moderne et contemporaine* 16 (April-June 1969): 282-299.
2 Howard, *Partition of Turkey,* pp. 49-50.
3 *Bulletin du Comité de l'Asie française* 2 (December 1902): 549-550; M.A.E., Turquie, N.S. 321, pp. 120-128.
4 Edward M. Earle, *Turkey, the Great Powers and the Bagdad Railway* (New York, 1923), pp. 62-63.
5 Cambon, *Correspondance,* 1: 357-358.
6 For example, see *Bulletin du Comité de l'Asie française* 1 (April 1901): 23-28; *Le Petit Parisien,* 19 August 1901. (The latter was a rather sensational newspaper but politically moderate, with the largest daily circulation in Paris at the time.)
7 France, *Annales de la Chambre: Débats,* vol. 66, pt. 2 (Paris, 1902), pp. 1856-1857.
8 Ibid., p. 1857.
9 *D.D.F.,* ser. 2, vol. 3, no. 36. See also Sir Nicholas O'Conor in Constantinople to the Marquess of Lansdowne, 10 March 1903, *B.D.,* vol. 2, no. 210.
10 *D.D.F.,* ser. 2, vol. 3, no. 303.

11 Ibid., no. 302.
12 Ibid., no. 347. The agreements Delcassé mentioned indeed did exist. They had been signed by the Deutsche Bank and the Imperial Ottoman Bank on 13 and 21 May 1901 and accorded to the German group the exploitation of all junction and branch lines between the Baghdad railway and the main French Syrian network of the Damascus-Hama line. These arrangements, however, were not revealed officially until 1903. See M.A.E., Turquie, N.S. 337, pp. 74-82.
13 *D.D.F.,* ser. 2, vol. 3, nos. 361, 367.
14 M.A.E., Turquie, N.S. 174, pp. 226-227. Germany was correct in this respect. France eventually did consent to the unification of the Ottoman public debt, but not until 1908.
15 M.A.E., Turquie, N.S. 337, pp. 24-25.
16 *D.D.F.,* ser. 2, vol. 4, nos. 34, 106.
17 Unpublished papers of Sir Francis Bertie, in F.O. 800/174, ME/06/6.
18 John B. Wolf, "The Diplomatic History of the Bagdad Railroad," in *The University of Missouri Studies,* vol. 11, no. 2 (Columbia, Mo., 1936), pp. 45-46.
19 Pierre Renouvin, *La Politique extérieure de Théophile Delcassé* (Paris, 1954), pp. 16-17.
20 *D.D.F.,* ser. 2, vol. 3, nos. 135, 199, 260.
21 M.A.E., Turquie, N.S. 336, pp. 131-133.
22 M.A.E., Papiers Delcassé, "Constantinople-Moyen-Orient, 1903-1904," vol. 15, pp. 4-6.
23 M.A.E., Turquie, N.S. 319, pp. 8-9.
24 Ibid., N.S. 321, p. 141.
25 Ibid., N.S. 322, pp. 63-64. Delcassé relayed this suggestion to the Ministry of Finance on 30 June 1904. Rouvier added his approval to that of the foreign minister. See Turquie, Situation économique et financière (1871-1915), série F³⁰ 356, in Ministère des Finances, Archives Nationales, Paris.
26 *D.D.F.,* ser. 2, vol. 6, no. 180. One reason the D.H.P. was losing so much money on the Damascus-Muzeirib connection, according to the British consul general in Beirut, was that it was "making prohibitive charges for the conveyance of goods." Hence, shippers were turning to the Hijaz line, whose charges were more reasonable. F.O. 195/2165, 28 January 1904.
27 M.A.E., Turquie, N.S. 324, pp. 189-190.
28 Ibid., N.S. 325, pp. 204-206, 235-237, N.S. 326, p. 33.
29 Ibid., N.S. 329, p. 174.
30 Ibid., N.S. 328, pp. 294-295.

31 Moukhtar, *La Turquie,* pp. 104-110.

32 Mandelstam, *Le Sort de l'Empire ottoman,* pp. 64-65.

33 For more details on this incident see Félicien Challaye, "Politique international et journalisme d'affaires," *La Revue du mois* 11 (10 June 1911): 749-757; and Charles Paix-Séailles, *La Diplomatie sécrète sous la troisième République, 1910-1911; Homs-Bagdad; du Quai d'Orsay à la correctionnelle; Recueil documentaire* (Paris, n.d.). The best account in English appears in Rudolph Binion, *Defeated Leaders: The Political Fate of Caillaux, Jouvenel and Tardieu* (Morningside Heights, N.Y., 1960), pp. 214-239.

34 Sir Gerard Lowther papers, F.O. 800/193B, pt. 4, pp. 126-127.

35 *D.D.F.,* ser. 2, vol. 12, no. 479, vol. 13, no. 109.

36 Paul Cambon also referred to Turkish offers of railroad concessions in Albania and the Black Sea region. He feared that such a development might meet with Russian objections but observed that a Black Sea network would be extremely valuable in countering German influence, especially if it could be linked to the French lines in Syria (Cambon, *Correspondance,* 2: 309-310).

37 *D.D.F.,* ser. 2, vol. 13, no. 128.

38 Great Britain, *British and Foreign State Papers, 1912,* vol. 105 (London, 1915), pp. 657-658.

39 Wolf, "Diplomatic History," pp. 62-63.

40 *D.D.F.,* ser. 2, vol. 13, no. 329.

41 Cressaty, *Les Intérêts français,* p. 13.

42 Alfred Durand, *Jeune Turquie vieille France* (Paris, 1909).

43 For example, see Mears, *Modern Turkey,* p. 349; *Annuaire du commerce extérieure français, 1908* (Paris, 1908); Earle, *Turkey,* pp. 104-105; Great Britain, *House of Commons Accounts and Papers,* vol. 87 (1911), cmd. 5707, pp. 616-619.

44 M.A.E., Turquie, N.S. 119, pp. 42-45.

45 Ibid., N.S. 120, pp. 238-242, N.S. 121, pp. 50-52.

46 F.O. 195/2370, 20 April 1911; *B.D.,* vol. X², no. 73.

47 M.A.E., Turquie, N.S. 122, pp. 2-6.

48 Maurice Bompard, "L'Entrée en guerre de la Turquie," *La Revue de Paris* (1 July 1921): 64-65.

49 M.A.E., Turquie, N.S. 403, pp. 151-168, 181-184.

50 *D.D.F.,* ser. 3, vol. 2, no. 128.

51 Ibid., vol. 3, no. 23.

52 Ibid., vol. 4, no. 38. See also no. 359.

53 Ibid., vol. 6, no. 518.

54 Ibid., vol. 7, no. 5.

55 Ibid., vol. 6, no. 646.
56 Ibid., vol. 7, no. 448.
57 M.A.E., Turquie, N.S. 186, pp. 26-28; *D.D.F.*, ser. 3, vol. 6, no. 144.
58 Djemal, *Memories,* pp. 73-76.
59 M.A.E., Turquie, N.S. 299, pp. 176-182.
60 F.O. 424/240, no. 287.
61 Poincaré, *Au service,* 4: 14.
62 The text of the accord of 15 February 1914 can be found in *D.D.F.,* ser. 3, vol. 9, no. 313. Accounts of the negotiations leading up to the accord can be located in a number of sources, among them Earle, *Turkey,* and Wolf, "Diplomatic History."
63 Poincaré, *Au service,* 4: 18.
64 *Le Petit Parisien, Le Temps, Le Gaulois,* all for 17 February 1914.
65 *D.D.F.,* ser. 3, vol. 9, nos. 152, 201.
66 M.A.E., Turquie, N.S. 186, pp. 133-136, 144-146; *D.D.F.,* ser. 3, vol. 9, nos. 79, 119; Poincaré, *Au service,* 4: 43-47.
67 *D.D.F.,* ser. 3, vol. 10, no. 90.
68 F.O. 800/80, 23 March 1914.
69 Great Britain, Hansard, *Parliamentary Debates,* vol. 59 (London, 1914), cols. 2169-2170.

CHAPTER 11: CONCLUSION

1 Prewar and wartime French documents show that France expected Palestine to form a part of the whole Syrian mandate. For example see M.A.E., Turquie, N.S. 120, p. 3 (3 March 1913); Maurice Paléologue, *An Ambassador's Memoirs,* vol. 1 (London, 1923), pp. 191-193; Pierre-Etienne Flandin, "Nos Droits en Syrie et en Palestine," *La Revue hébdomadaire* (6 June 1915): 17-32.
2 Moukhtar, *La Turquie,* p. 10.
3 *B.D.,* vol. X^1, no. 174.
4 *D.D.F.,* ser. 3, vol. 7, no. 6.
5 M.A.E., Turquie, N.S. 177, p. 27.
6 Jung, *La Révolte arabe,* 1: 112.
7 Cited in Hans Kohn, *A History of Nationalism in the East* (London, 1929), p. 271.

BIBLIOGRAPHY

DOCUMENTARY SOURCES

Unpublished Material

A. France. Ministère des Affaires' étrangères, Paris. Correspondance commerciale.
   1. Alep, 1897-1901. Vol. 39.
   2. Alexandrette, 1898-1901. Tome unique.
   3. Beyrouth, 1897-1901. Vol. 12.
B. France. Ministère des Affaires étrangères. Papiers Delcassé.
   1. Vol. 4. Lettres de diplomats.
   2. Vol. 15. Constantinople-Moyen-Orient, 1903-1904.
C. France. Ministère des Affaires étrangères. Saint-Siège. Protectorate catholique de la France.
   1. Dossier général (1897-1918). N.S. 28-N.S. 38.
   2. Ecoles et missions étrangères (1897-1914). N.S. 52-N.S. 57.
   3. Ecoles et missions françaises (1897-1918). N.S. 39-N.S. 50.
D. France. Ministère des Affaires étrangères. Turquie.
   1. Affaires commerciales (1902-1917). N.S. 400-N.S. 404.
   2. Chemins de fer, Chemin de fer de Bagdad (1897-1914). N.S. 334-N.S. 351.
   3. Chemins de fer, Reseau asiatique (1898-1917). N.S. 318-N.S. 333.
   4. Politique étrangère. Dossier général, Relations avec les puissances (1901-1914). N.S. 169-N.S. 186.

5. Politique étrangère. Relations avec la France, Affaires particulières contentieuses (1897-1907). N.S. 296-N.S. 300bis.
6. Politique intérieure. Dossier général, Jeunes Turcs, etc. . . . (1897-1914). N.S. 1-N.S. 9.
7. Politique intérieure. Dossier général, Syrie-Liban (1897-1914). N.S. 104-N.S. 124.

E. France. Ministère des finances, Archives Nationales, Paris.
1. Turquie. Chemins de fer: Dossier général; dossiers particuliers (1879-1915). Série F^{30} 362-363.
2. Turquie. Situation économique et financière (1871-1915). Série F^{30} 356.

F. Great Britain. Foreign Office, Public Record Office, London.
1. Confidential Print. Further Correspondence Respecting the Affairs of Asiatic Turkey and Arabia (1903-1913). F.O. 424/ 205-206, 231-233, 237-240.
2. Embassy and Consular Archives, Beirut (1903-1911). F.O. 195/ 2140, 2165, 2451, 2452, 2453, 2458, 2460. F.O. 226/229. Damascus, F.O. 618/3.
3. Foreign Office: Consular (1906-1914). F.O. 369/43-45, 105- 107, 173-176, 247-251, 328-332, 414-417, 513-518, 626-630, 770-778.
4. General Correspondence—Political (1907-1914). F.O. 371/345, 549, 561, 770, 781, 1495, 1521, 1522, 1523, 1775, 1781, 1789, 1794, 1800, 1811, 1827, 1843, 1848, 2136, 2146.
5. Private papers
   a. Sir Edward Grey correspondence (1905-1916). F.O. 800/53, 54, 79, 80.
   b. Sir Francis Bertie papers (Middle East). F.O. 800/174.
   c. Sir Francis Bertie papers (1898-1916). F.O. 800/180-181.
   d. Sir Gerard Lowther papers (1908-1913). F.O. 800/193.

Published Contemporary Sources

Annuaire du commerce extérieur français. Paris, 1908. The volume for 1908 is the only one available at the Bibliothèque Nationale.
Azoury, Négib. *Le Réveil de la nation arabe dans l'Asie Turque.* Paris, 1905.
Chekri Ganem (*Comité central syrien*). *L'Opinion syrienne à l'étranger pendant la guerre.* Paris, 1918.
Comité central syrien. La Question syrienne exposée par les Syriens. Paris, 1919.

Comité libanais de Paris. Memoire sur la question du Liban. Paris, 1912.

Dugdale, E. T. S. *German Diplomatic Documents, 1871-1914.* 4 vols. London, 1928-1931.

France. Commission de Publication des Documents relatifs aux Origines de la Guerre de 1914-1918. *Documents diplomatiques français, 1871-1914.* 41 vols. Paris, 1929-1959.

———. *Journal Officiel. Annales de la Chambre: Débats parlementaires.* Paris, 1901-1914.

———. *Journal Officiel. Annales du Sénat: Débats parlementaires.* Vol. 82. Paris, 1912.

———. Ministère des Affaires étrangères. *Documents diplomatiques: Affaires arméniennes, projets de réformes dans l'Empire ottoman, 1893-1897.* Paris, 1897. Published as *Livre Jaune.*

———. Ministère des Affaires étrangères. *Documents diplomatiques: Turquie, 1900-1901.* Paris, 1902. Published as *Livre Jaune.*

Great Britain. *British and Foreign State Papers, 1912.* Vol. 105. London, 1915.

———. Foreign Office. *British Documents on the Origins of the War, 1898-1914.* Edited by G. P. Gooch and Harold Temperly. Vols. X¹ and X². London, 1926-1938.

———. Foreign Office, Historical Section. *France and the Levant.* Handbook no. 95. London, March 1919.

———. *Syria and Palestine.* Handbook no. 93. London, April 1919.

———. Hansard. *The Parliamentary Debates* (House of Commons). London, 1901-1914.

———. *House of Commons Accounts and Papers.* London, 1900-1916. Especially vol. 87 (1911), cmd. 5707, and vol. 84 (1914-1916), cmd. 7628.

———. "Report of a Committee set up to Consider Certain Correspondence between Sir Henry McMahon and the Sharif of Mecca in 1915 and 1916." *Reports from Commissioners, Inspectors, and Others.* Vol. 14, cmd. 5974. London, 1938-1939.

Haim, Sylvia G., ed. *Arab Nationalism, An Anthology.* Berkeley, Calif., 1962.

Hertslet, Sir Edward, ed. *The Map of Europe by Treaty.* 4 vols. London, 1875-1891.

Jung, Eugène. *Les Puissances devant la révolte arabe.* Paris, 1906.

———. *La Révolte arabe.* 2 vols. Paris, 1924.

Laqueur, Walter, ed. *The Israel-Arab Reader.* New York, 1969.

Noradounghian, Gabriel Effendi, ed. *Recueil d'actes internationaux de l'Empire ottoman.* 4 vols. Paris, 1897-1903.

Paix-Séailles, Charles. *La Diplomatie sécrète sous la troisième République, 1910-1911; Homs-Bagdad: du Quai d'Orsay à la correctionnelle; Recueil documentaire.* Paris, n.d.

Schopoff, A. *Les Réformes et la protection des Chrétiens en Turquie, 1673-1904.* Paris, 1904.

Testa, Baron de. *Recueil des traités de l'Empire ottoman.* Vols. 1-3. Paris, 1864-1898.

Turquie. IVème Armée. *La Vérité sur la question syrienne.* Istanbul, 1916.

Young, George. *Corps de droit ottoman; recueil des codes, lois, règlements, ordonnances, et actes les plus importants du droit intérieur, et d'études sur le droit coutumier de l'Empire ottoman.* 7 vols. Oxford, 1905-1906.

MEMOIRS, SPEECHES, RECOLLECTIONS

Bompard, Ambassador Maurice. "L'Entrée en guerre de la Turquie." *La Revue de Paris* (1 July 1921): 61-85, (15 July 1921): 261-288.

_____. *Mon ambassade en Russie, 1903-1908.* Paris, 1937.

Buchanan, Sir George William. *My Mission to Russia.* London, 1923.

Cambon, Jules. *The Diplomat.* London, 1931.

Cambon, Paul. *Correspondance, 1870-1924.* 3 vols. Paris, 1940-1946.

Churchill, Winston S. *The World Crisis, 1911-1914.* London, 1923.

Djemal Pasha. *Memories of a Turkish Statesman, 1913-1919.* London, n.d.

Grey, Sir Edward. *Speeches on Foreign Affairs, 1904-1914.* London, 1931.

_____. *Twenty-five Years, 1892-1916.* London, 1925.

Hanotaux, Gabriel. *Mon temps.* 4 vols. Paris, 1933-1947.

Hardinge, Sir Arthur H. *A Diplomatist in the East.* London, 1928.

Jessup, Henry Harris. *Fifty-Three Years in Syria.* 2 vols. New York, 1910.

Lawrence, T. E. *Seven Pillars of Wisdom.* London, 1935.

Liman von Sanders, General. *Cinq ans de Turquie.* Paris, 1923.

Morgenthau, Henry. *Ambassador Morgenthau's Story.* Garden City, N.Y., 1918.

_____. *Secrets of the Bosphorus, Constantinople, 1913-1916.* London, 1918.

Moukhtar Pasha, General Mahmud. *La Turquie, l'Allemagne et l'Europe.* Paris, 1921.

Nicolson, Sir Harold George. *Peacemaking 1919.* Boston, 1933.

Paléologue, Maurice. *An Ambassador's Memoirs.* Vol. 1. London, 1923.
Pears, Sir Edwin. *Forty Years in Constantinople.* New York, 1916.
Poincaré, Raymond, *Au service de la France.* 10 vols. Paris, 1926-1933.
_____. *The Origins of the War.* London, 1922.
Rambert, Louis. *Notes et impressions de Turquie.* Paris, 1926.
Rivoyre, Denis de. *Les Vrais Arabes et leur pays.* Paris, 1884.
Sazonov, Sergiei. *Fateful Years, 1909-1916.* London, 1928.
Storrs, Ronald. *Orientations.* London, 1937.
Viviani, René. *Réponse au kaiser.* Paris, 1923.

NEWSPAPERS AND PERIODICALS*

L'Aurore (radical).
Bulletin du Comité de l'Asie française.
Correspondance d'Orient, 1908-1914. Edited by Dr. Georges Samné and
   Chekri Ganem.
L'Echo de Paris (conservative).
Le Gaulois (conservative-Catholic).
L'Humanité (Socialist).
L'Indépendence arabe, April 1907-June 1908. (These dates encompass
   the entire life of the journal, directed by Négib Azouri and edited by
   Eugène Jung.)
Le Matin (moderate-conservative).
La Petite République (Socialist).
Le Petit Parisien (sensational but politically moderate).
Revue de l'enseignement colonial, 1904-1906. Retitled *Bulletin de la
   Mission laïque française,* 1906-1914.
Le Temps (moderate).

SELECTED BOOKS AND ARTICLES

Andrew, Christopher. *Théophile Delcassé and the Making of the
   Entente Cordiale.* New York, 1968.
Antonius, George. *The Arab Awakening, The Story of the Arab Na-
   tional Movement.* New York, 1946.

---

*Unless otherwise noted, these newspapers and periodicals were consulted for
the period 1901-1914.

Arthur, Sir George Compton Archibald. *Life of Lord Kitchener.* London, 1920.

Aubès, Joseph. *Le Protectorat religieux de la France en Orient.* Toulouse, 1904.

Aulneau, J. "La Question syrienne." *Revue politique et parlementaire* 81 (10 July 1914): 81-99.

Barrès, Maurice. *Une Enquête aux pays du Levant en 1914.* 2 vols. Paris, 1923.

Baster, A. S. J. *The Imperial Banks.* London, 1935.

Bertrand, Louis. "Les écoles d'orient." *Revue des deux mondes* 79 (15 August 1909): 755-794.

Binion, Rudolph. *Defeated Leaders: The Political Fate of Caillaux, Jouvenel and Tardieu.* Morningside Heights, N.Y., 1960.

Blaisdell, Donald C. *European Financial Control in the Ottoman Empire.* New York, 1929.

Bordat, Gaston. "L'Influence française en Orient et le Protectorat catholique." *Revue politique et parlementaire* 47 (February 1906): 321-335.

————. "L'Influence française en Orient et les écoles laïques." *Revue politique et parlementaire* 52 (May 1907): 332-341.

Brogan, D. W. *France Under the Republic.* New York, 1940.

Brown, Philip M. *Foreigners in Turkey: Their Juridical Status.* Princeton, N.J., 1914.

Bruneau, André. *Traditions et politique de la France au Levant.* Paris, 1932.

Bullard, Sir Reader William. *Britain and the Middle East.* London, 1951.

Burnichon, Joseph. *La Compagnie de Jésus en France, 1814-1914.* Vol. 4. Paris, 1922.

Butterfield, Paul R. *The Diplomacy of the Bagdad Railway, 1890-1914.* Göttingen, 1932.

Cambon, Henri. *Paul Cambon, ambassadeur de France, 1843-1924, par un diplomate.* Paris, 1937.

Carroll, E. Malcolm. *French Public Opinion and Foreign Affairs.* New York, 1931.

Challaye, Félicien. "Politique internationale et journalisme d'affaires." *La Revue du mois* 11 (10 June 1911): 749-757.

Charles-Roux, François. *France et Chrétiens d'Orient.* Paris, 1939.

————. *Trois ambassades françaises à la veille de la guerre.* Paris, 1928.

Charmes, Gabriel. *Voyage en Syrie.* Paris, 1882.

Chastenet, Jacques. *Raymond Poincaré.* Paris, 1948.

Chevallier, Dominique. "Lyon et la Syrie en 1919: les bases d'une intervention." *Revue historique* 224 (October-December 1960): 275-320.

Contenson, Ludovic de. *Les Réformes en Turquie d'Asie: la question arménienne, la question syrienne.* Paris, 1913.

Courant, Maurice. *L'Education et la colonisation.* Paris, 1904.

"Les Courants politiques dans la Turquie." *Revue du monde musulman* 21 (December 1912): 159-221.

Courcel, Alphonse Chodron de. *Les Questions actuelles de politique en Asie.* N.p., 1910.

Cressaty, Count R. J. M. *Les Intérêts français en Syrie.* Paris, 1913.

Cumming, Henry H. *Franco-British Rivalry in the Post-War Near East.* London, 1938.

David, Wade Dewood. "European Diplomacy in the Near Eastern Question, 1906-1909." In *Illinois Studies in the Social Sciences.* Vol. 25. Urbana, Ill., 1940.

Davison, Roderic H. *Reform in the Ottoman Empire, 1856-1876.* Princeton, N.J., 1963.

Despagnet, Frantz. *La Diplomatie de la Troisième République et le droit des gens.* Paris, 1904.

Dimitroff, Deltcho. *Le Régime des capitulations en Turquie.* Sofia, 1934.

Ducruet, Jean. *Les Capitaux européens au Proche-Orient.* Paris, 1964.

Durand, Alfred. *Jeune Turquie vieille France.* Paris, 1909.

Earle, Edward M. *Turkey, the Great Powers and the Bagdad Railway.* New York, 1923.

Edib, Halidé. *Turkey Faces West, A Turkish View of Recent Changes and Their Origin.* New Haven. Conn., 1930.

Eubank, Keith. *Paul Cambon, Master Diplomatist.* Norman, Okla., 1960.

Farman, T. F. "French Claims on Syria." *Contemporary Review* 58 (September 1915): 343-353.

Feis, Herbert. *Europe, the World's Banker, 1870-1914.* New York, 1961.

Flandin, Pierre-Etienne. "Nos Droits en Syrie et en Palestine." *La Revue hébdomadaire* (6 June 1915): 17-32.

Friedman, Isaiah. "The McMahon-Hussein Correspondence and the Question of Palestine." *Journal of Contemporary History* 5, no. 2 (1970): 83-122.

_____. *The Question of Palestine, 1914-1918: British, Jewish, Arab Relations.* New York, 1973.

Georges-Gaulis, Berthe. *La Question arabe.* Paris, 1930.

_____. *La Ruine d'un Empire: Abdul Hamid, ses amis et ses peuples.* Paris, 1913.

Ghalib, Pierre. *Le Protectorat religieux de la France en Orient.* Avignon, 1920.

Gontaut-Biron, Comte R. de. *Comment la France s'est installée en Syrie, 1918-1919.* Paris, 1922.

Gottlieb, W. W. *Studies in Secret Diplomacy During the First World War.* London, 1957.

Grenville, J. A. S. *Lord Salisbury and Foreign Policy, the Close of the Nineteenth Century.* London, 1964.

Grousset, René. *L'Empire du Levant, Histoire de la question d'Orient.* Paris, 1949.

Haddad, Robert M. *Syrian Christians in Muslim Society: An Interpretation.* Princeton, N.J., 1970.

Hamilton, Angus. *Problems of the Middle East.* London, 1909.

Hanotaux, Gabriel. *Etudes diplomatiques, la politique de l'équilibre, 1907-1911.* Paris, 1912.

_____, and Martineau, Alfred. *Histoire des colonies françaises et de l'expansion de la France dans le monde.* 6 vols. Paris, 1929-1934.

Harmand, Jules. *Domination et colonisation.* Paris, 1910.

_____. *Une Necessite de l'expansion française: l'autonomie coloniale.* Paris, 1909.

Hauser, Henry. "L'Influence française en Orient et les écoles laïques." *Revue politique et parlementaire* 48 (April 1906): 55-68.

Hilaire de Barenton, Père. *La France catholique en Orient durant les trois derniers siècles.* Paris, 1902.

Hitti, Philip K. *History of the Arabs, From the Earliest Times to the Present.* London, 1937.

_____. *History of Syria, Including Lebanon and Palestine.* London, 1951.

_____. *Lebanon in History, From the Earliest Times to the Present.* New York, 1957.

_____. *A Short History of Lebanon.* New York, 1965.

Hopwood, Derek, *The Russian Presence in Syria and Palestine, 1843-1914.* Oxford, 1969.

Hottinger, Arnold. *The Arabs, Their History, Culture and Place in the Modern World.* Berkeley, Calif., 1963.

Hourani, Albert. *Arabic Thought in the Liberal Age, 1798-1939.* London, 1962.

_____. *Syria and Lebanon, A Political Essay.* London, 1946.

Howard, Harry N. *The King-Crane Commission.* Beirut, 1963.

_____. *The Partition of Turkey, 1913-1923.* Norman, Okla., 1931.

Iiams, Thomas M. *Dreyfus, Diplomatists and the Dual Alliance: Gabriel Hanotaux at the Quay d'Orsay.* Geneva, 1962.

Iskandar, Abkariyus. *The Lebanon in Turmoil.* New Haven, Conn., 1920.

Jouplain, M. *La Question du Liban, Etude d'histoire diplomatique & le droit international.* Paris, 1908.

Kedourie, Elie. *England and the Middle East.* London, 1956.

Khairallah, K. T. *Le Problème du Levant, les régions arabes libérées.* Paris, 1919.

_____. *La question du Liban.* Paris, 1915.

_____. *La Syrie.* Paris, 1912.

Kirk, George E. *A Short History of the Middle East from the Rise of Islam to Modern Times.* New York, 1963.

Kohn, Hans. *A History of Nationalism in the East.* London, 1929.

Laffey, John. "Les Racines de l'impérialisme français en extrême-orient." *Revue d'histoire moderne et contemporaine* 16 (April-June 1969): 282-299.

Lamy, Etienne Marie Victor. *La France du Levant.* Paris, 1900.

Langer, William L. *The Diplomacy of Imperialism, 1890-1902.* New York, 1956.

Lavisse, Ernest. "Notre politique orientale." *Revue de Paris* 2 (15 May 1897): 274-311, 3 (15 June 1897): 872-914.

Leroy-Beaulieu, Paul. "Neuf pour cent." *L'Economiste français* 29 (12 October 1901): 497-499.

Lewis, Bernard. *The Emergence of Modern Turkey.* London, 1961.

Longrigg, Stephen H. *Syria and Lebanon Under French Mandate.* London, 1958.

"Lord Kitchener in Egypt." *Fortnightly Review* 91 (1 March 1912): 507-520.

Lyautey, Pierre. *Le Drame oriental et le rôle de la France.* Paris, 1924.

Malzac, André. "L'Evolution de l'action française en Orient." *Revue politique et parlementaire* 53 (September 1907): 469-482.

Mandelstam, André. *Le Sort de l'Empire ottoman.* Paris, 1917.

Mange, Alyce Edythe. "The Near Eastern Policy of Emperor Napoleon III." In *Illinois Studies in the Social Sciences.* Vol. 25. Urbana, Ill., 1940.

Mears, Eliot Grinnell. *Modern Turkey, 1908-1923.* New York, 1924.

Melia, Jean. *Chez les Chrétiens d'Orient.* Paris, 1929.

Moncharville, M. "Le Conflit franco-turc de 1901." *Revue général du droit international public* 9 (1902): 677-700.

Montbel, Max. "Les Puissances coloniales devant l'Islam." *Questions diplomatiques et coloniales* 37 (16 March 1914): 348-362.

Neton, Albeni. *Delcassé.* Paris, 1952.

Nevakivi, Jukka. *Britain, France and the Arab Middle East, 1914-1920.* New York, 1969.

Nutting, Anthony. *The Arabs, A Narrative History from Mohammed to the Present.* London, 1964.

Ostrorog, Comte Léon. *Pour la réforme de la justice ottomane.* Paris, 1912.

———. *The Turkish Problem.* London, 1919.

Pelissie de Rausas, G. *Le Régime des capitulations dans l'Empire ottoman.* 2 vols. Paris, 1902-1905.

Pernot, Maurice. *Rapport sur un voyage d'étude à Constantinople, en Egypte et en Turquie d'Asie.* Paris, n.d.

Pharès, Mgr. Emmanuel. *Les Maronites, leur vie et leurs moeurs, leurs rapports avec la France, leur situation actuelle.* Lille, 1908.

Pinon, René. *L'Europe et l'Empire ottoman.* Paris, 1908.

———. *L'Europe et la Jeune Turquie.* Paris, 1911.

———. "La Réorganisation de la Turquie d'Asie." *Revue des deux mondes* 16 (August 1913): 884-918.

———. "La Rivalité des grandes puissances dans l'Empire ottoman." *Revue des deux mondes* 42 (15 November 1907): 338-375.

Poignant, Georges. "Les Intérêts français en Syrie." *Questions diplomatiques et coloniales* 35 (16 March 1913): 321-344.

"La Politique allemande et le protectorat des missions catholiques." *Revue des deux mondes* 149 (1 September 1898): 5-41.

Porter, Charles Wesley. *The Career of Théophile Delcassé.* Philadelphia, Pa., 1936.

Presland, John (pseud. for Gladys Skelton). *Deedes Bey, A Study of Sir Wyndham Deedes, 1883-1923.* London, 1942.

Priestley, Herbert I. *France Overseas, A Study of Modern Imperialism.* New York, 1938.

Ramsaur, E. E. *The Young Turks—Prelude to the Revolution of 1908.* Princeton, N.J., 1957.

Renouvin, Pierre. *La Crise européenne et la première guerre mondiale.* Paris, 1948.

———. *La Politique extérieure de la IIIe République.* Paris, 1953.

———. *La Politique extérieure de Théophile Delcassé.* Paris, 1954.

Ristelhueber, René. *Traditions françaises au Liban.* Paris, 1918.

Roberts, Stephen H. *History of French Colonial Policy (1870-1925).* 2 vols. London, 1929.

Roederer, C. and Paul. *La Syrie et la France.* Paris, 1917.

Sachar, Howard M. *The Emergence of the Middle East, 1914-1924.* New York, 1969.

Sadaka, Nagib. *La Question syrienne pendant la guerre de 1914.* Paris, 1940.

Saint-Yves, G. *Les Chemins de fer françaises dans la Turquie d'Asie.* Paris, 1914.

Salibi, K. S. *The Modern History of Lebanon.* New York, 1965.

Samné, Georges. *L'Effort syrien pendant la guerre.* Paris, 1919.

———. *La Syrie.* Paris, 1921.

Sanjian, Avedis K. *The Armenian Communities in Syria Under Ottoman Domination.* Cambridge, Mass., 1965.

Schuman, Frederick L. *War and Diplomacy in the French Republic.* New York, 1931.

Seale, Patrick. *The Struggle for Syria, A Study of Post-War Arab Politics, 1945-1958.* London, 1965.

Sousa, Nasim. *The Capitulatory Regime of Turkey: Its History, Origin and Nature.* Baltimore, Md., 1933.

Spagnolo, J. P. "French Influence in Syria Prior to World War I: The Functional Weakness of Imperialism." *The Middle East Journal* 23 (Winter 1969): 45-62.

Stein, Leonard. *The Balfour Declaration.* New York, 1961.

———. *Syria.* London, 1926.

Sykes, Mark. *The Future of the Near East.* London, 1916.

"Syrie." *La Grande Encyclopédie.* Vol. 30. Paris, n.d. Pp. 793-799.

Tabouis, Geneviève R. *The Life of Jules Cambon.* London, 1938.

Tibawi, A. L. *A Modern History of Syria Including Lebanon and Palestine.* London, 1969.

———. "Syria in the McMahon Correspondence: Fresh Evidence from the British Foreign Office Records." *Middle East Forum* 42, no. 4 (1966): 5-31.

———. "Syria in Wartime Agreements and Disagreements: Fresh Evidence from the British Foreign Office Records." *Middle East Forum* 43, nos. 2-3 (1967): 77-109.

Tyan, Ferdinand. *The Entente Cordiale in Lebanon.* London, 1917.

———. *France et Liban, Défense des intérêts français en Syrie.* Paris, 1917.

Tyler, Mason Withing. *The European Powers and the Near East, 1875-

1908. Minneapolis, Minn., 1925.

Verney, Nöel, and Dambmann, George. *Les Puissances étrangères dans le Levant en Syrie et en Palestine.* Paris, 1900.

Vidal, César. "Le Duel diplomatique Poincaré-Tittoni, 1912-1914." *Rassegna Storica del Risorgimento* 3-4 (1951): 691-699.

Vivian, Herbert. "Turkey's Asiatic Problems." *The Fortnightly Review* 93 (April 1913): 669-680.

Wolf, John B. "The Diplomatic History of the Bagdad Railroad." In *The University of Missouri Studies.* Vol. 11, no. 2. Columbia, Mo., 1936.

Wright, Gordon, *Raymond Poincaré and the French Presidency.* Stanford, Calif., 1942.

Zeine, Zeine N. *Arab-Turkish Relations and the Emergence of Arab Nationalism.* Beirut, 1958.

_____. *The Struggle for Arab Indepedence: Western Diplomacy and the Rise of Faisal's Kingdom in Syria.* Beirut, 1960.

Ziadeh, Nicola A. *Syria and Lebanon.* New York, 1957.

INDEX